I0901404

MOVING THE WORLD

HOW THE SUPPLY CHAIN'S EVOLUTION AFFECTS US ALL

CRAIG FULLER

FIRECROWN

Firecrown Media
405 Cherry St.,
Chattanooga, TN 37402

Firecrown.com

Published in 2025

29 28 27 26 25 1 2 3 4 5

Manufactured in the United States of America

ISBN: 979-8-89491-067-3
EISBN: 979-8-89491-068-0

Research Assistant: JP Hampstead
Design: Lisa Schroeder
Illustration: Theo Cobb
Charts: Scott Krall

CONTENTS

FOREWORD

TRANSFORMING THE FREIGHT INDUSTRY THROUGH DATA AND TRANSPARENCY

Although not recognized by many, the freight industry is the backbone of our economy, moving goods across the nation and around the world. Yet for decades, this $800 billion industry operated under the cloud of outdated information and opacity.

Growing up in Chattanooga, Tennessee, I was immersed in the world of trucking from an early age. After all, it was the family business; the rhythm of diesel engines and the challenge of moving freight were woven into the fabric of my life. Watching and learning from my father and grandfather ignited my own desire to leave a mark on this vital industry. My ambition eventually led to the creation of FreightWaves and SONAR, platforms designed to bring real-time news and data to the supply chain industry.

FOUNDING OF FREIGHTWAVES

Family Legacy in Trucking

As stated above, trucking runs in my blood. My grandfather, Clyde Fuller, established Southwest Motor Freight, which became one of the industry giants in the 1980s. My father, Max Fuller, continued this legacy by founding U.S. Xpress, building it into one of America's largest trucking companies. These strong foundations gave me both insight into the industry's operations and an understanding of its challenges and opportunities.

JOURNEY TO CREATING FREIGHTWAVES

My path to FreightWaves wasn't a direct one, but each step proved essential. After college, I joined U.S. Xpress and launched Xpress Direct, an innovative service connecting shippers with truckers for on-demand deliveries. The service grew to become the largest of its kind in North America, teaching me the industry's potential for rapid innovation when the right tools are available.

Later, I founded TransCard, a payment platform for truckers, which I eventually sold to U.S. Bank in 2012. Through these ventures, I identified a critical gap in the industry – the lack of timely, actionable data. Trucking companies, drivers, freight brokers and logistics providers were relying on outdated government reports that were weeks behind what was occurring when crucial decisions were being made. While watching financial updates flow in real-time across CNBC and Bloomberg screens, I wondered why the $800 billion freight industry didn't have similar tools.

I envisioned a platform that would give everyone in the industry – from owner-operators of single trucks to giants like J.B. Hunt—access to fresh, actionable data that would help them make decisions that could help them be successful. This vision, rooted in my trucking heritage and passion for problem-solving, led to the birth of FreightWaves.

LAUNCHING FREIGHTWAVES

In 2016, and in my hometown of Chattanooga, I launched FreightWaves. My goal was to make the company the freight industry's go-to source for news and data, aiming to blend the rigor of Bloomberg with the tech-savvy edge of TechCrunch. What began as a blog with just one writer quickly gained momentum, reaching 1.1 million monthly page views by 2018 and surpassing other established trucking news sites.

FreightWaves covered everything from storms delaying deliveries to trade deals reshaping freight patterns. But providing news wasn't enough – I wanted to create tools that would drive efficiency throughout the industry. This drive led to the development of SONAR, a real-time data platform, and industry events that showcase new technology and address critical issues. FreightWaves evolved into a hub for innovation, fueled by my belief that better information strengthens supply chains.

DEVELOPMENT OF SONAR

Concept and Purpose

SONAR, launched in May 2018 at FreightWaves' Transparency18 conference, represents the heart of my vision for the freight industry. Inspired by platforms like Bloomberg, my late friend Ben Murphy and I designed SONAR as a comprehensive dashboard for trucking, showing what is happening in the industry right now, not weeks ago.

Features and Capabilities

SONAR tracks truck availability, freight demand, and pricing in real time. Its "Tender Indices" function as predictive tools, forecasting price shifts days ahead of when they occur – essentially serving as a freight market weather forecast. Since its initial launch in 2018, we've continuously expanded and updated SONAR's capabilities, adding features like weather maps, dock wait times, and data on air and ocean shipping.

Impact on the Industry

SONAR brings unprecedented transparency to all participants in the freight market, providing actionable intelligence that was previously unavailable. By democratizing access to crucial market data, SONAR has transformed how companies plan routes, negotiate rates and make critical decisions. It has become an essential tool for navigating the inherent volatility of freight markets.

MISSION AND VALUES OF FREIGHTWAVES

Commitment to Transparency

FreightWaves isn't just about news or data – it's about making the freight industry transparent and equitable. When I started the company, I saw a very fragmented industry in which participants operated with vastly different levels of market understanding. Too often, the smallest players were at a severe disadvantage. I wanted to level the playing field, ensuring carriers, freight brokers, shippers and logistics companies had access to the same view of market conditions.

Methods of Achieving Transparency

At FreightWaves, transparency means openly sharing insights on pricing, market capacity, and trends. We achieve this through multiple channels – our website, podcasts, streaming TV, live events, and through SONAR's real-time data platform. By providing information and analysis through diverse media, we ensure that industry participants of all sizes can access the insights they need to make informed decisions about their businesses.

Influence on Industry Practices

FreightWaves' influence stems from clarifying the freight industry's inner workings. Before FreightWaves, the market operated much more slowly and with far greater opacity. We changed that paradigm by providing clear, accessible analysis. SONAR's dashboards, which publish 3.5 million daily data points, allow users to see the movement of the global and national economies in near real-time across every major transportation mode.

NAVIGATING THE FREIGHT MARKET

Market Volatility

The freight market is notoriously volatile, with prices and demand shifting rapidly and often unpredictably. Growing up in the trucking industry, I witnessed this unpredictability first-hand – one month might bring high demand and excellent pay, while the next could see oversupply driving rates downward and hurting profitability. The rollercoaster nature of freight makes real-time data not just valuable, but essential.

Importance of Real-Time Data

Without current data, drivers risk accepting low-paying loads, and shippers might overpay or, worse, miss the opportunity to ship their goods entirely – potentially shutting down their supply chain operations. Real-time data allows all participants to make informed decisions based on actual market conditions rather than outdated information or guesswork.

HOW I GOT HERE AND THE PURPOSE OF THE BOOK

The evolution of FreightWaves from a simple freight-focused blog to an industry-transforming news and data platform reflects the freight industry's growing recognition that transparency and real-time information are not luxuries – they are necessities to help make decisions about their business on a daily basis. By providing tools like SONAR and creating platforms for industry dialogue and innovation, FreightWaves has fundamentally changed the understanding of how freight moves across America and beyond.

The volatile nature of freight markets – with their boom-and-bust cycles – will continue to challenge the industry – from independent drivers to multinational corporations. But with access to real-time data and insights, industry participants are better equipped than ever to navigate these challenges successfully.

My journey from growing up in a trucking family to founding FreightWaves has been driven by a simple belief: better information leads to better decisions, stronger businesses, and ultimately, a more efficient and equitable freight industry.

I wrote this book to offer an overview of the past, present, and future challenges and opportunities in the logistics industry. I hope you find it informative.

INTRODUCTION

It's a story of disruptions, advancements, politics, economies, and societies spanning centuries and shaping our future. Welcome to the world of supply chains. Like utilities—electricity, water, or internet—supply chains operate quietly in the background, delivering the goods that make modern life possible. We rarely notice them until they fail, much like we overlook the power grid until the lights go out. Global consulting firm McKinsey & Company defines a supply chain as "the interconnected journey that raw materials, components, and goods take before their assembly and sale to customers."

Yet, the term "supply chain" is a misnomer. There is no single supply chain; instead, millions of distinct networks crisscross the globe. For example, the supply chains for manufacturing vehicles in the auto industry differ vastly from those delivering fresh produce from fields to supermarkets. These dynamic systems underpin our daily existence, with a rich history that has evolved over centuries, transforming communities, nations, and regions worldwide. Though often unnoticed, supply chains tirelessly move goods, enabling the conveniences we take for granted.

However, supply chains, like utilities, are not flawless or without limits. McKinsey notes, "When any link in a supply chain isn't working optimally, the entire chain is disrupted." The COVID-19 pandemic vividly demonstrated this fragility, as global supply chains buckled under local and national shutdowns, causing shortages and delays. The public noticed empty shelves and prolonged wait times, much like a city becomes aware of a water main break when taps run dry. Such breakdowns are not unique to pandemics. Hurricanes, wars, and earthquakes routinely disrupt distribution networks, often out of public view. Only through the resilience of companies and their employees, leveraging advanced logistics, can supply chains be rebalanced, repaired, or rerouted to restore the flow of goods. This resilience was evident in 2020–21, raising public awareness of supply chains' critical role.

Looking ahead, supply chains demand our attention and deeper understanding. An estimated one-third of the global economy depends on supply chain-driven industries, which would cease without logistics. Modern life itself relies on these systems. Why? Our world is deeply interconnected, and logistics have grown increasingly complex. Since the end of World War II, and especially after the fall of the Berlin Wall, global trade has flourished, creating unprecedented prosperity for millions. Yet, this interconnectedness also makes us vulnerable. A disruption in one region can ripple across continents.

The U.S.-China trade war, launched in 2018 and escalating in 2025 under President Donald Trump's second administration, exemplifies these vulnerabilities and signals a second Cold War, with supply chains as the front lines. Initially aimed at addressing trade imbalances, intellectual property theft, and China's market practices, the trade war has evolved into a geopolitical struggle. Tariffs, export controls, and restrictions on critical goods like semiconductors and rare earth minerals have strained global supply chains, pushing some to near breaking points.

This rivalry, resembling a second Cold War, hinges on economic and technological supremacy rather than military might. Supply chains, like utilities in a blackout, reveal their importance when disrupted, as both nations leverage control over key resources and manufacturing. China, the "world's factory," produces about 70% of lithium-ion batteries for electric vehicles and smartphones, 80% of smartphones, and 90% of processed rare earths—minerals vital for computer chips, electric vehicles, and green technologies like wind turbines. The U.S. depends heavily on China, importing $540 billion in goods in 2023 while exporting only $150 billion, creating a trade imbalance that heightens vulnerability. A conflict, trade ban, or shipping disruption could halt supplies of critical materials, chips, or medicines, impacting the U.S. economy, healthcare, and national security.

China's dominance in key minerals, including lithium, cobalt, and rare earths, fuels this competition. It mines 60% of the world's rare earths and refines 85% into usable forms, with the U.S. sourcing over 80% from China. In 2010, China cut off rare earth exports to Japan during a dispute, spiking prices. In 2024, it banned antimony exports, used in batteries and weapons, doubling prices after U.S. tech restrictions. A total rare earths ban could halt U.S. production of fighter jets and solar panels, costing billions annually. The U.S. has one rare earth mine in California but sends ore to China for refining, leaving it exposed.

Competition over energy and resources drives this rivalry. China's Belt and Road Initiative has boosted trade with the Global South, reducing reliance on U.S. markets by importing soybeans from Brazil and expanding manufacturing in Vietnam and Cambodia. These shifts signal a move away from U.S. dependence, as both nations vie for control over the resources and networks powering the global economy.

The trade war's fallout extends beyond economics. President Trump's 2025 tariff policies have disrupted global supply chains, forcing companies to stockpile inventory or reroute trade through third countries. This volatility strains U.S. credibility with allies, as

As towns were founded along rivers and seacoasts, people started using water to move goods, and by the 1600s constructing dams and canals to control water, revolutionizing the movement of goods. These innovations allowed for more controlled and expansive trade routes, connecting distant regions and fostering economic growth. The legacy of these centuries-old initiatives remains evident in modern supply chains, which continue to rely on engineered infrastructure and strategic transport methods. The best place to start discussing modern supply chains is to start with the Roman Empire, which laid the foundation for the eventual development of the modern world.

ANCIENT ROME'S FOOD SUPPLY CHAIN

The Roman Empire, one of history's greatest, thrived due to its vast trade networks across Eurasia. The Silk Road was a vital part of this success, connecting Asia, Europe, and Africa. Started around 200 BCE during China's Han Dynasty, this 4,000-mile network eventually linked cities like Chang'an in China to Rome. Those who traveled it carried silk, spices, and other goods across deserts and mountains. Merchants used camel and horse caravans on land routes, while rivers and ports aided trade. The Silk Road was a web of trails through Central Asia, India, and the Middle East, protected by Han armies from bandits. Cities like Samarkand – a city in what is now southeastern Uzbekistan and that is among the oldest continuously inhabited cities in Central Asia – became hubs for trading goods. Beyond products, the Silk Road and other major trade routes helped to spread ideas, religions, and cultures. Though slow and risky due to bandits and harsh weather, the Silk Road helped empires like China and Rome prosper, illustrating the power of supply chains.

By the 2nd century CE, Rome and its surrounding areas had about one million people. Feeding so many without modern transportation or refrigeration was a major challenge. Local farms couldn't grow enough grain to sustain that many people, so Rome turned to distant regions for help. This led to the Cura Annonae, named after the Roman goddess Annona. It meant "care of Annona," and was the sys-

These man-made waterways connected inland areas to coasts, allowing cities far from the ocean to join trade networks. Dams also helped by redirecting rivers to prevent floods. This kept trade-focused cities safe from heavy rains or natural disasters, letting them focus on importing and exporting goods to grow their economies.

For example, Venice, Italy, used its coastal location and canals to become a trade powerhouse. Founded around the 1st century BCE in northeastern Italy, near the Adriatic Sea, Venice started as a Roman military colony. Its position by rivers and the sea made trade much easier. Over time, Venice grew, and its residents built 177 canals across 120 islands in a lagoon between the Po and Piave rivers. This network made Venice a major trading hub. **[FIG 1-2]**

Between the 14th to 16th centuries, Venice became a major center for trade, finance, learning, and the arts. The city dug more canals, boosting the buying and selling of goods and expanding its trade network. Its coastal location and canal system made it a hub for global commerce.

EARLY SUPPLY CHAIN BASICS

The stories of Rome, London, and Venice are certainly instructive and provide a glimpse into the beginnings of intricate trading networks. Still, let's keep in mind that most of the early supply chains were not terribly sophisticated. This is especially true when we compare them to the myriad of supply chains we rely on today.

In addition, early supply chains often catered to the whims of the elite. That is because, at first, only the very wealthy could afford to pay for special imported treats. Everyday citizens had to rely on what they could grow or purchase locally.

Over time, however, those involved figured out how to produce and send goods in bulk. As a result, supply chains began shipping commodities such as olive oil, wine, gold, and honey. As noted above, large amounts of grain were moved to Rome for centuries. Through its London docks, Great Britain imported tea, sugar, rum and more. Florence boomed in part because of wool imports.

The Silk Road brought goods like silk and spices from China, Turkey, and later Iran to London. Silk often reached England directly or through Italy and France, where tailors used it to make clothing and bedding. Like Rome's grain system, this supply chain supported London's growing economy. Spices, including salt, were also traded through supply chains. From the Norman conquest (1066) to the 17th century, salt was mined in coastal areas of England, France, or Scotland. It was then shipped to butchers in busy British towns and cities, mainly to cure meat for trade and storage, strengthening local food supply chains.

In 1602, the Dutch East India Company was formed and took the supply chain concept to another level. Acting on behalf of the Dutch government, the organization gained a monopoly on trade and commodities between Holland (and much of Europe) and the East Indies. Its network expanded to various ports in Asia and Europe, and eventually employed around 25,000 people.

Between 1602 and 1796, the Dutch East India Company sent nearly one million Europeans – a huge amount of people at that time – to establish and work in buying, trading and shipping more than 2.5 million tons of Asian goods – and enslaved people. In total, nearly 4,800 ships were used. In contrast, the rest of Europe combined (including the better-known British East India Company) sent only about 880,000 people to do similar work from 1500 to 1795. Moreover, the British East India Company's fleet – the nearest competitor in size to the Dutch East India Company – used fewer than 2,700 ships that carried only about 20% of the tonnage shipped by the Dutch. The Dutch East India Company generated huge profits from its monopoly on spices and its slave trading throughout much of the 17th century. The supply chains established by the Dutch were the most extensive and complex that had ever been created.

These beginnings, while simple compared to the complex supply chains of today, created a foundation on which to build. Over time, societies learned to move beyond a subsistent way of life. They could focus on specialization. If an area could create a very specific product or grow a crop that was in high demand in other regions, it no longer had to provide all its own food and goods. Instead, it could

MEDIEVAL TRADE ROUTES

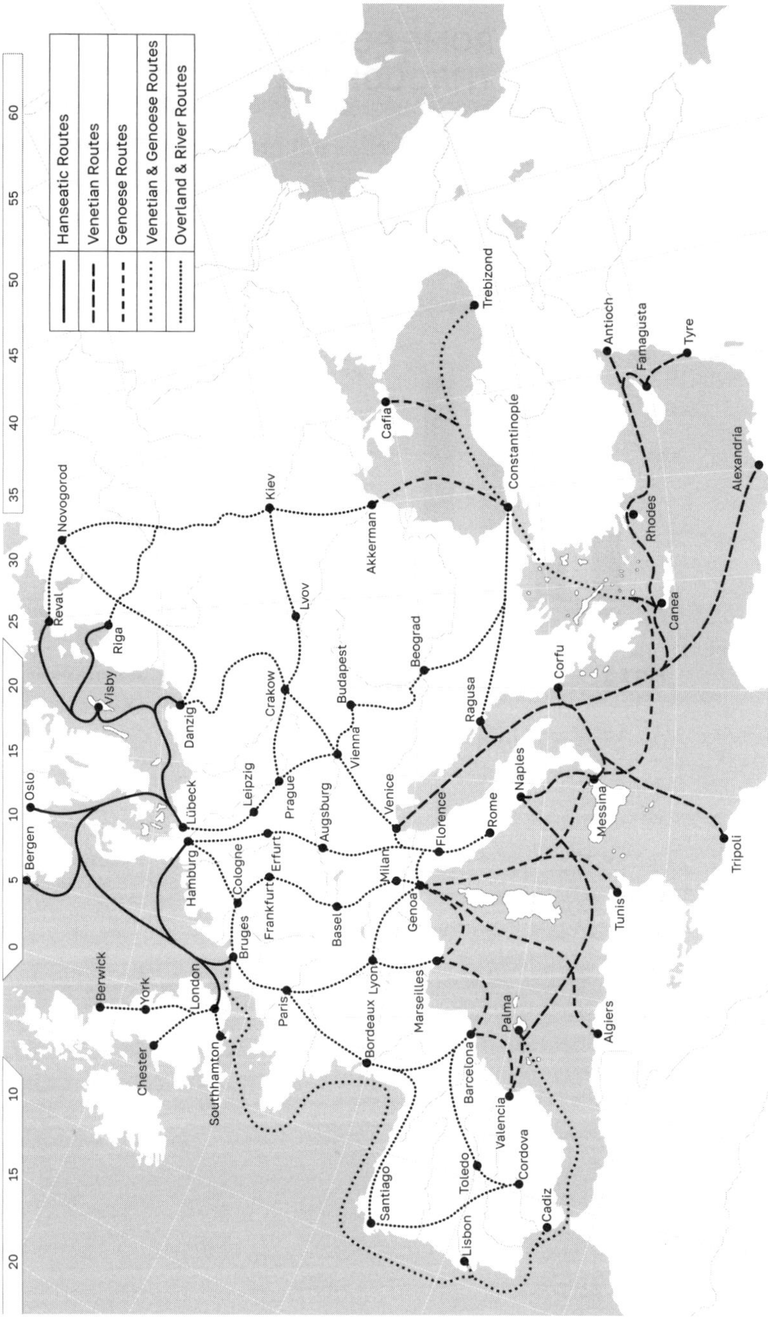

SOURCE: CREATOR "LAMPMAN"; PUBLIC DOMAIN

FIG 1-2

2

ENGINES REVVING CHANGE

The steam engine, born in the late 17th century, transformed supply chains from local markets to global networks, reshaping trade, industry, and logistics. This chapter traces the steam engine's evolution, focusing on railroads' pivotal role in America's economic rise, their adaptation to financial and regulatory challenges, and their modern contributions to energy independence and cross-border trade. From early innovations to today's intermodal networks, railroads have navigated monopolies, deregulation, and technological shifts, remaining a cornerstone of global commerce.

THE DAWN OF STEAM POWER (LATE 17TH TO EARLY 18TH CENTURY)

In the late 17th century, England's coal mines faced relentless flooding. Miners relied on horse-drawn pulleys to hoist water from deep shafts, a grueling and costly task. Thomas Savery, a military engineer born around 1650, envisioned a solution. In 1698, he patented a steam-powered pump, demonstrating it to the Royal Society in 1699. This crude device, harnessing fire to clear water from mines, was a marvel. Thomas Newcomen and James Watt later refined it, with Watt's efficient design inspiring the "watt" unit of power. By the early 18th century, steam engines powered factory machinery, enabling mass production of textiles and tools, setting the stage for the Industrial Revolution.

Before steam, trade relied on human and animal labor. Merchants hauled goods by foot, pack animals, or wooden ships, limited to small loads and short distances. Only empires could ship luxuries like spices across oceans, battling unpredictable winds. Steam shattered these constraints, driving Britain's urban mills and drawing rural workers to cities, creating hubs hungry for raw materials and finished goods. This industrial surge globalized supply chains, with cotton from America's South, carried by steamships, feeding British textile mills, whose fabrics reached markets worldwide.

STEAM-POWERED TRANSPORT EMERGES (EARLY 19TH CENTURY)

Steam's first leap into transport came with steamboats. In 1811, the New Orleans steamed down the Mississippi from Pittsburgh to New Orleans, proving steamships could haul heavy loads against river currents. By the 1830s, steamboats carried cotton south and coal north, forging river-based supply chains. However, dangers like boiler explosions—such as the 1858 Pennsylvania disaster, which claimed over 100 lives—highlighted their risks, pushing innovators toward railroads.

In 1825, England's Stockton and Darlington Railway debuted as the first public steam-powered line, inspiring America's Baltimore and Ohio Railroad in 1830. Railroads moved goods faster and cheaper than wagons or canals, transforming logistics. As production soared, the demand for efficient transport intensified, positioning railroads as America's economic backbone.

69

RAILROADS FUEL AMERICA'S EXPANSION (1830s–1860s)

Railroads revolutionized America, opening the West by connecting East Coast cities to new settlements. Before rails, a Pittsburgh merchant shipping flour to Philadelphia endured weeks of costly wagon travel; by 1850, railroads slashed the journey to days, cutting expenses. Chicago emerged as a rail hub, its 11 railroads by 1860 handling grain, livestock, and lumber, linking Midwest farmers to Eastern ports and cementing its role as the nation's breadbasket. Railroads enabled farmers to sell crops nationally, while Eastern factories accessed raw materials like iron ore, driving industrial growth.

By 1860, the North's 21,000 miles of track, compared to the South's 9,000, provided a strategic advantage during the Civil War. The 1869 transcontinental railroad united the nation, enabling rapid overland transport of large quantities, reducing reliance on rivers or canals, and making nationwide growth possible. Raw materials like timber and coal moved from forests and mines to ports by rail, then shipped worldwide. **[FIG 2-1]**

However, railroads' high costs—labor, construction, and maintenance—favored wealthy owners, creating disparities. Railroads dominated freight, often forming monopolies that charged farmers exorbitant rates for short hauls while offering secret discounts to large businesses like grain elevators or meatpackers. Cornelius Vanderbilt, controlling vast networks by the 1880s, epitomized the "robber baron" era, using rebates, predatory pricing, and service refusals to bankrupt competitors and acquire their assets, amassing wealth that shaped the industry.

REGULATION AND EARLY CHALLENGES (1880s–1930s)

The lack of competition left rural communities struggling, prompting the 1887 Interstate Commerce Act, which established the Interstate Commerce Commission (ICC) to regulate rates, curb discriminatory practices, and foster competition. The ICC reviewed railroad rates, investigated secret rebates, and penalized violators to protect small shippers, particularly farmers. However, early enforcement faced challenges: railroads exploited legal loopholes, mounted court challenges, and delayed compliance through lawsuits. The Supreme Court initially restricted the ICC's rate-setting power, and complex rate structures made proving discrimination difficult. The 1906 Hepburn Act strengthened the ICC's authority, but early setbacks limited its impact, though it set a precedent for government oversight.

By the late 19th century, coal powered locomotives and freight revenue, with railroads like the Chicago, Burlington and Quincy (CB&Q) and Union Pacific hauling massive volumes from mines to factories, power plants, and ports. Coal's steady demand made it a reliable revenue source, supporting railroads' financial stability.

In the early 20th century, railroads faced new pressures. By 1935, the U.S. rail network spanned 250,000 miles, operated by dozens of Class I carriers, handling 75% of intercity freight, including coal, grain, and manufactured goods. The Great Depression slashed freight volumes, pushing many railroads toward bankruptcy. The 1935 Motor Carrier Act, regulating trucking under the ICC, limited its long-haul growth, indirectly aiding railroads. Labor was critical, with over one million unionized workers in 1935 earning 20% above average industrial wages, though frequent strikes disrupted service.

WORLD WAR II AND POST-WAR GROWTH (1940s–1950s)

During World War II (1939–1945), railroads were vital, moving 90% of military freight and 97% of troops within the U.S., with the government seizing control to prioritize war efforts. Post-war, the industry surged, fueled by the economic boom of the late 1940s and 1950s. The 1956 Interstate Highway System expanded trucking's reach, but railroads retained dominance in long-haul freight, moving 1.5 billion tons annually by 1960, per the Association of American Railroads (AAR).

Technological shifts emerged. Diesel locomotives fully replaced steam by 1959, doubling fuel efficiency and reducing maintenance costs. Early computer systems aided scheduling, though ICC regulations hindered modernization. Railroads employed 540,000 unionized workers by the 1960s, earning 20% above industrial wages, but frequent strikes continued to disrupt service.

INDUSTRY CRISIS AND DEREGULATION (1960s–1980s)

By the 1960s, railroads faced a crisis. Overlapping routes, bloated workforces of 540,000, and ICC-mandated unprofitable services drained resources. The 1970 Penn Central bankruptcy, following the 1968 merger of the Pennsylvania and New York Central railroads, signaled industry distress, with freight volumes stagnating at 2 billion tons and trucking capturing 20% of intercity freight. Financial turmoil drove consolidation, building on 19th-century mergers under tycoons like Vanderbilt that formed regional giants.

The rail industry's struggles were rooted in decades of rigid ICC regulation, which fixed rates and required service on unprofitable routes, stifling innovation and pricing flexibility. By the 1970s, railroads faced mounting losses, with 20% of Class I carriers, including Penn Central, bankrupt. The broader U.S. economy, grappling with stagflation and fuel crises, spurred a push for deregulation to revive struggling industries. Railroads, losing market share to trucking—bolstered by the Interstate Highway System—needed freedom to compete. The 1976 Railroad Revitalization and Regulatory Reform Act began loosening ICC controls, but it was insufficient to halt the decline, setting the stage for comprehensive reform.

The Staggers Rail Act of 1980, signed by President Jimmy Carter, was a pivotal response to this crisis, deregulating the U.S. rail industry to restore financial viability. Named after Representative Harley O. Staggers, the Act addressed the ICC's restrictive oversight, which had left railroads unable to adjust rates or abandon low-demand routes. It granted railroads flexibility to set market-based rates, negotiate private contracts with shippers, and abandon or sell unprofitable lines, aligning operations with demand. The Act also streamlined merger approvals, encouraging consolidation to eliminate redundancies. By 1985, freight rates dropped 20% in real terms, making rail transport more competitive. Track mileage fell from 250,000 in 1935 to 140,000 by 2024, focusing on high-density corridors. The Staggers Act revitalized the industry, boosting revenues and enabling investments in infrastructure and intermodal systems. Critics, including some shippers, argued it favored large carriers and reduced service in rural areas, but its impact was undeniable, saving railroads from collapse.

The Staggers Act also reshaped competition with trucking, which faced its own deregulation through the Motor Carrier Act of 1980. This Act relaxed ICC controls on trucking rates, routes, and market entry, spurring a surge in new carriers and price competition. Trucking's flexibility and door-to-door service captured short-haul and time-sensitive freight, intensifying pressure on railroads. However, rail's ability to set competitive rates post-Staggers allowed it to retain long-haul and bulk freight dominance, while investments in intermodal systems countered trucking's gains. This dynamic forced railroads to innovate, paving the way for modern efficiency. Class I railroads dwindled from 40 in 1980 to seven by 2000 through mergers like Union Pacific-Missouri Pacific (1982), Burlington Northern-Santa Fe (1995), and Union Pacific-Southern Pacific (1996), which cost $500 million in lost revenue due to integration issues.

Deregulation spurred intermodal transport—containers transferable between ships, rails, and trucks. The 1984 introduction of double-stack trains doubled container capacity, moving goods from ports like Los Angeles to Chicago in 48–50 hours, outpacing trucks' 84–96 hours. Intermodal traffic grew from 3 million units in 1980 to 5.6 million by 1990, per AAR data. By 1990, railroads earned $28 billion, a 30% increase from 1980, with profit margins rising from 5–7% to 10–12%. Labor dynamics shifted, with unionized workers dropping from 540,000 in 1980 to 300,000 by 2000 after a 1991 strike by 17 rail unions led to a Congress-imposed settlement favoring railroads.

CONSOLIDATION AND TECHNOLOGICAL ADVANCES (1990s–2010s)

The 1990s saw further consolidation. The 1995 Burlington Northern-Santa Fe (BNSF) merger led in intermodal freight from West Coast ports, while the 1996 Union Pacific-Southern Pacific merger created the largest U.S. railroad, with 35,000 miles of track. By 2000, railroads moved 9 billion ton-miles of freight, a 50% increase from 1980, with operating revenues of $34 billion and margins of 10–12%.

Technological advancements reshaped the industry. Positive Train Control (PTC), mandated by Congress in 2008 and implemented by 2020 across 58,000 miles at a $15 billion cost, reduced derailments by 38%. GPS tracking, automated inspections, and fuel-efficient locomotives cut emissions by 20% since 2000, per AAR data. Intermodal traffic reached 13.5 million units by 2015, driven by e-commerce and global trade.

The rise of U.S. energy production, driven by the shale boom, bolstered railroads. U.S. crude oil production grew from 5.6 million barrels per day (bpd) in 2008 to 12.9 million bpd in 2019, per the U.S. Energy Information Administration. Railroads bridged pipeline gaps, moving 9,500 crude oil carloads in 2010 to 493,000 by 2014, peaking at 1 million bpd. BNSF's 32,500-mile network hauled crude from North Dakota to Gulf Coast refineries, supporting exports. However, crude-by-rail declined post-2014 as pipelines expanded, and safety concerns, like the 2013 Lac-Mégantic derailment, prompted stricter tank car regulations.

MODERN RAILROADS: EFFICIENCY AND CROSS-BORDER TRADE (2010s–2025)

Precision Scheduled Railroading (PSR), pioneered by Canadian National's Hunter Harrison and adopted industry-wide by 2018, emphasized longer trains and fewer stops, slashing costs. Between 2016 and 2022, Class I railroads cut their workforce by 29% to 150,000 and spent $196 billion on stock buybacks and dividends. Union Pacific, founded in 1862, reported record profits in 2021, and BNSF achieved its highest operating margin in over two decades in 2022. Railroads' profitability, with margins soaring from 15% in 2001 to 41% by 2021, rivaled tech giants like Microsoft, per AAR data. However, labor disputes, like the 2022 strike threat, strained operations.

Coal, once a rail cornerstone, declined from 44% of freight tonnage in 2008 to 25% by 2024, a 15% drop from 2020, due to natural gas and renewables. Railroads like BNSF, reliant on coal for 25% of tonnage, diversified into intermodal, which grew from 3 million units in 1980 to 14.5 million in 2024, up 5% from 2023, driven by e-commerce and global trade. Coal exports stabilized in 2024, with railroads hauling 15,000-ton unit trains from Wyoming's Powder River Basin.

Railroads support U.S. energy independence, with crude oil production peaking at 13.1 million bpd and natural gas at 34.1 trillion cubic feet in 2024, reducing net petroleum imports to near zero. Railroads moved 900,000 chemical and petroleum carloads in 2024, up 5% from 2020, and remained vital for energy logistics, moving a ton 500 miles on one gallon of diesel to refineries, power plants, and export terminals.

A landmark in modern consolidation was the 2021 battle between Canadian Pacific (CP) and Canadian National (CN) for Kansas City Southern (KCS). The resulting Canadian Pacific Kansas City (CPKC) network, formed on April 14, 2023, created North America's only single-line rail connecting Canada, the U.S., and Mexico. KCS's 6,700-mile network, the shortest route from Kansas City, Missouri, to Mexican ports like Lázaro Cárdenas, Tampico, and Veracruz, supports automotive, grain, and intermodal traffic under the USMCA, with U.S.-Mexico trade reaching $974 billion in 2024. CPKC's cross-border traffic doubled since 2012, fueled by near-shoring as manufacturing shifted to Mexico, where costs are 20% lower than China's.

Amid U.S.-China trade tensions and U.S. reindustrialization, driven by the 2022 Inflation Reduction Act and CHIPS Act, CPKC handles 10–12% of U.S.-Mexico trade, supporting Mexico's automotive and electronics sectors. For Canada, CPKC facilitates $7 billion in wheat and $8.3 billion in fertilizer exports, serving as a "land bridge" for Canada-Mexico trade, bypassing U.S. tariff risks, including 2025 threats of 25% tariffs on Canadian/Mexican goods. In 2023, CPKC reported a 10% increase in cross-border intermodal traffic, with automotive and grain volumes up 12% and 8%, respectively. The Mexico Midwest Express, launched in May 2023, moves freight from Chicago to San Luis Potosí in four days with 95% on-time performance. By 2024, cross-border revenue ton-miles rose 15%, with CPKC capturing $350 million in new business, 41% from cross-border shipments.

A FOUNDATION FOR THE FUTURE

Steam engines and railroads turned local trade into global commerce, fueling America's rise from the transcontinental's golden spike to CPKC's north-south routes. Early railroads overcame monopolistic practices through regulation, while consolidation, from Vanderbilt's mergers to modern giants, resolved pre-1980s chaos, enabling intermodal's rise. The shift from coal to intermodal, support for U.S. energy independence, and resilience amid global trade shifts underscore rail's adaptability. With operating margins at 41% by 2021, railroads remain vital, though PSR, labor challenges, and high capital costs persist. As later chapters explore, supply chain professionals navigate these complexities, building on rail's legacy to drive an innovative future.

GROWTH OF THE U.S. RAILROAD NETWORK

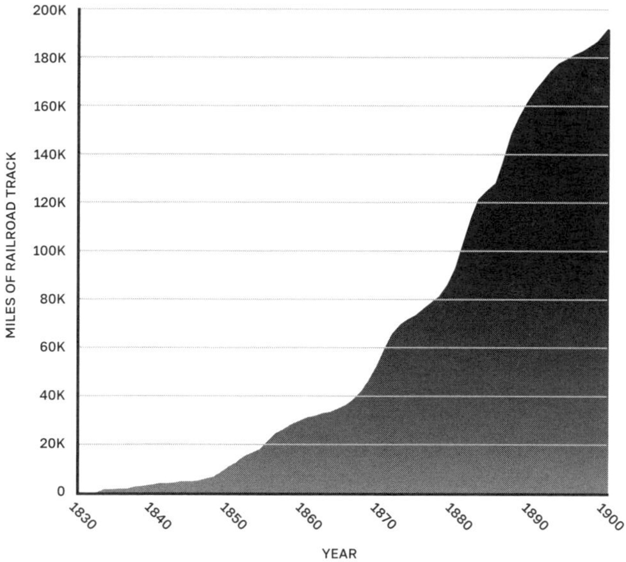

FIG 2-1

COMPILED FROM AGGREGATE DATA FROM UNITED STATES STATISTICAL ABSTRACT–1899-03

3

GOING POSTAL

Long before emails or delivery trucks, sending messages across vast distances was a challenge. The ancient Persian Empire, around 550 BCE, solved this with the world's first organized postal system, called the Angarium or Royal Road. This network, built under King Cyrus the Great and expanded by Darius I, stretched over 1,700 miles from Susa to Sardis, connecting the empire's far-flung regions. Like a modern supply chain, it moved information quickly and reliably (for that time), strengthening Persia's economy and government.

The Royal Road used a relay system of mounted couriers, called pirradazis, who carried messages in leather pouches. Stations, spaced about 15 miles apart, provided fresh horses and riders, allowing nonstop travel. A message could cross the empire in seven days, a speed unmatched for centuries. These couriers braved weather and bandits, ensuring royal orders, tax records, and trade deals reached their destinations. The system was mainly for official use, but merchants sometimes used it to send trade information, boosting commerce.

This postal network was a supply chain for information, much like today's delivery networks move goods. It helped Persia manage its vast empire, from Egypt to India, by keeping rulers informed. Governors sent reports, and kings issued commands, maintaining control over millions. The system's efficiency supported trade, as markets relied on timely updates about goods and prices. It was, perhaps, the first Price Reporting Agency (PRA) in history. Without the Angarium, Persia's empire would have struggled to function.

The Persian postal system set a model for later societies. Its relay stations inspired postal networks in other empires, showing how organized communication drives progress. The Pony Express in the U.S. operated in a very similar manner; more information about it is below.

THE JOURNEY OF THE U.S. POSTAL SERVICE: A TALE OF CONNECTION ACROSS TIME

In a bustling colonial tavern in 1775, amidst the clinking of mugs and whispers of rebellion, Benjamin Franklin stood tall as the Second Continental Congress named him the first Postmaster General. The 13 colonies, on the brink of the Revolutionary War, needed a way to stay connected – letters carrying battle plans, family news, and hopes for freedom had to travel fast. Franklin, with his sharp mind, mapped out routes from the pine forests of Maine to the humid marshes of Georgia, turning a patchwork of trails across the 13 colonies into a lifeline. His postal system became the nation's first supply chain for information, binding a new nation together as stagecoaches rattled through muddy roads, delivering mail that fueled the fight for independence.

By the 19th century, the U.S. Post Office Department (USPO) was expanding as rapidly as the nation itself. The Postal Service Act of 1792 had established the USPO as a permanent institution, and low newspaper rates spread ideas like wildfire, linking distant towns.

Postage stamps, introduced in 1847, simplified paying for mail, and the postal service eventually extended delivery to rural addresses nationwide. As railroads expanded and connected towns, they enabled faster and farther-reaching mail delivery to cities and remote areas across the country.

THE PONY EXPRESS: A LEGENDARY RELAY

In the spring of 1860, the U.S. frontier stretched from Missouri (at that time the end of the line for railroads) to California. Mail took weeks by creaky stagecoach – or months by ship around South America – far too slow for a nation on the brink of the Civil War and hungry for news and connection. Three bold businessmen, William Russell, Alexander Majors, and William Waddell, saw an opportunity. On April 3, 1860, they launched the Pony Express, a daring horse relay system to carry mail from Missouri to California – a 1,900 mile journey in just 10 days, creating a blazing-fast network for urgent information that tied a divided country together. Moreover, the Pony Express was a private venture, not part of the U.S. Post Office.

Imagine a teenage rider, barely 16, galloping out of St. Joseph, Missouri, with a leather mochila slung over his saddle, holding 20 pounds of letters, newspapers, and dispatches. He is one of 80 young riders, each racing 75 to 100 miles across prairies, mountains, and deserts to Sacramento, California. Every 10 to 15 miles, he swaps his sweating horse for a fresh one at one of 190 stations, and dodges bandits, Indians, storms, and rattlesnakes. For $25 a month, these riders – some as young as 14 – braved the frontier. They delivered hope and headlines, such as news of President Lincoln's 1860 election, in record time. A letter from New York to San Francisco, which once endured at least a month-long journey, now took two weeks, letting merchants send orders and families share words across the divide.

The Pony Express was a marvel, but it could not last. At $5 per half-ounce, it was extremely expensive, and its $700,000 annual cost far outstripped earnings. After 18 months and 35,000 letters, the Pony Express was replaced with a technological marvel – the transcontinental telegraph. Beginning in October 1861, the telegraph sent messages in minutes and ended the short history of the Pony Express. But its legacy endured, proving what grit and speed could achieve. Those legendary riders, racing through history, inspired innovations like airmail and left behind a symbol of the Wild West's untamed spirit.

MODERNIZING THE POST OFFICE

In the late 1960s, the U.S. Post Office Department faced inefficiencies, deficits, and labor strife. In 1969, it incurred a $1.1 billion deficit ($8.3 billion in 2025 dollars), driven by rising labor costs, outdated infrastructure, and surging mail volumes. A 1970 postal strike by 200,000 workers in cities like New York halted delivery, prompting Congress to pass the Postal Reorganization Act (PRA) on August 12, 1970. Signed by President Nixon, the PRA transformed the Post Office into the U.S. Postal Service (USPS), an independent agency tasked with self-sustaining operations and universal service nationwide, including Alaska, Guam, and Hawaii.

The PRA established the primary supply chain role of the USPS as mail delivery. The act granted the USPS autonomy to manage operations, set rates, and borrow funds, while mandating six-day delivery to 167 million addresses under the Universal Service Obligation (USO). It established collective bargaining for 525,000 workers, easing labor tensions. By prioritizing efficiency, the PRA ensured the USPS remained a national lifeline, connecting communities with its motto: "Neither snow nor rain nor heat nor gloom of night stays these couriers."

SERVING REMOTE REGIONS

The innovative methods of the USPS are often overlooked. For example, Alaska, the largest and most sparsely populated U.S. state, relies on unique delivery solutions. Since 1869, when mail delivery began in the Alaska Territory, mail reached coastal towns by ship, then dog sleds to villages, enduring harsh conditions. Air mail began in the 1920s, and today, airplanes serve 265 communities, many that survive without roads. Guam and Hawaii, with 160,000 and 1.4 million residents, depend on costly air and sea transport for mail services. These high-cost routes, vital for connectivity, burden USPS finances, but the USO requires service to every address.

USPS CHALLENGES AND REFORMS

The U.S. Postal Service (USPS) faces ongoing financial challenges while serving as a national lifeline. Since 2006, it has accumulated deficits, including a $6.5 billion loss in 2023. However, in the first quarter of 2025, the USPS reported a $144 million profit, a significant improvement from the $2.0 billion loss in the same period the previous year, driven by cost controls and increased package revenue. Declining mail volume, rising costs, regulatory constraints, and competition from UPS, FedEx, and Amazon continue to hinder profitability. The 2021 "Delivering for America" plan aims for a break-even budget by 2031 through transportation reforms, despite the USO.

First-Class Mail volume, the USPS' most lucrative product, has dropped 53% since 2006 due to digital alternatives. Despite generating $78 billion annually, the USPS struggles against private carriers dominating urban markets, leaving less profitable rural routes. Transportation restructuring has consolidated operations into regional centers, saving $1.8 billion yearly. Shifting to surface transport cuts $1.5 billion annually, and optimized routes are planned to save $36 billion over a decade, maintaining five-day delivery for most First-Class Mail.

Regulatory price caps, Congressional oversight, and labor costs (77% of total USPS expenses, with 90% of 525,000 workers unionized) limit progress. The USPS has exhausted its $15 billion borrowing limit and skipped $5 billion in 2023 retirement payments. Proposals like four-day delivery risk undermining the USO, especially in remote Alaska, Guam, and Hawaii. **[FIG 3-1]**

ECONOMIC IMPACT

The USPS is vital to the economy, supporting small businesses and e-commerce through cost-effective shipping like USPS Ground

Advantage. For example, the wares of Alaska artisans can reach Guam affordably, unlike private carriers. Large retailers like Walmart and subscription services like HelloFresh rely on USPS for efficient delivery. Mail-order pharmacies serve rural areas, and banks use First-Class Mail for secure documents. The 31,000 USPS post offices bolster rural economies, contributing $20.4 billion to GDP and 7 million jobs annually, according to a 2020 study.

THE RISE OF UNITED PARCEL SERVICE

Imagine bustling Seattle in 1907 – horses clop along cobblestone streets, and the air carries the scent of fresh rain and sawdust from nearby lumber mills. In this vibrant city, two teenage boys, Jim Casey and Claude Ryan, are poised to launch a significant venture with just $100 that they borrowed. Although only 19 years old, they have a dream to deliver packages more quickly and efficiently for all. This is the story of how their small company, United Parcel Service (UPS), grew from a couple of youths with bicycles into a global giant that transformed logistics – a pivotal chapter in the history of supply chains.

Jim Casey was no stranger to hard work. He had been employed since age 11 to support his family after his father died during the Klondike Gold Rush. In 1907, Seattle's population had nearly tripled in a decade to approximately 200,000 residents. However, communications remained challenging. Most homes lacked telephones, and the two local telephone companies did not even connect to each other. People relied on messengers to carry notes, packages, and even hot lunches across the city.

With their $100, Jim and Claude established the American Messenger Company in a tiny basement beneath a saloon. Envision a 6-by-17-foot room, damp and dimly lit, where a handful of teenage boys stood ready to run or bike anywhere in the city. Jim's younger brother George was among them. They charged a few cents per delivery, promising the "best service and lowest rates." When a store needed a package delivered or a message sent, these boys were the delivery service – rain or shine – dodging horses and navigating muddy streets.

As a result, by 1913, Jim and Claude partnered with Evert McCabe, who operated a motorcycle delivery business. They merged and renamed their company Merchants Parcel Delivery, focusing on retail store deliveries. That year, they acquired their first vehicle – a Ford Model T converted into a delivery car. It was transformative. No longer running or biking, they could transport more packages faster.

In 1916, Charlie Soderstrom joined the team. He proposed painting the delivery cars brown, as the color appeared clean, professional, and concealed dirt effectively. Soon, those brown vehicles became a symbol of reliability. By 1919, the company adopted a grander name: United Parcel Service. "United" reflected their merged services, "Parcel" denoted the packages they carried, and "Service" underscored their commitment. They expanded to California, delivering in Oakland and Los Angeles.

The 1920s and 1930s brought significant challenges for UPS. During Prohibition (1920–1933), when alcohol was illegal, some might speculate that UPS engaged in illicit deliveries. However, founder Jim Casey prioritized integrity, and UPS focused on legal goods, such as clothing and household items, for retail stores. No evidence suggests involvement in illicit activities; the company was dedicated to expansion. As early as 1924, UPS introduced conveyor belts to sort packages more efficiently, marking an early advancement in automating supply chains.

The Great Depression, beginning in October 1929, strained finances and caused many businesses to falter. UPS experimented with United Air Express, an air delivery service using passenger aircraft, but the Depression made it unsustainable, leading to its closure in 1931. Despite these setbacks, Casey persevered, steering UPS through economic hardship.

In the 1950s, as UPS expanded to serve the general public—not just retail stores—it began competing directly with the U.S. Post Office, which had long dominated letter mail and held a strong position in parcel delivery through its Parcel Post service, established in 1913.

The Post Office viewed UPS's growth as a threat, especially since UPS offered faster, more reliable service with features like daily pickups and automatic returns for undelivered packages.

THE POST OFFICE AND UPS GO TO COURT

To protect its dominance, the Post Office leveraged its government-backed authority, collaborating with state authorities to impose strict licensing requirements and advocating Interstate Commerce Commission (ICC) oversight to restrict private carriers like UPS. These regulations required UPS to prove its services were in the public interest—a costly and time-consuming process. The Post Office scrutinized UPS's rates, routes, and package sizes, arguing that private companies should not compete with a government service. These obstacles slowed UPS's growth, forcing the company to navigate years of regulatory hurdles to expand nationwide.

Despite these challenges, UPS persevered. By 1975, it achieved a major milestone with the "Golden Link," becoming the first package delivery company to serve every address in the continental United States. This milestone followed decades of legal battles, including a landmark 1974 ICC decision that granted UPS broader interstate operating authority, dismantling many Post Office barriers. The Post Office's efforts to hinder UPS ultimately spurred innovation in both organizations: UPS focused on efficiency and technology, while the Post Office, reorganized as the U.S. Postal Service (USPS) under the 1970 Postal Reorganization Act, pursued modernization. This rivalry helped shape a dynamic supply chain landscape.

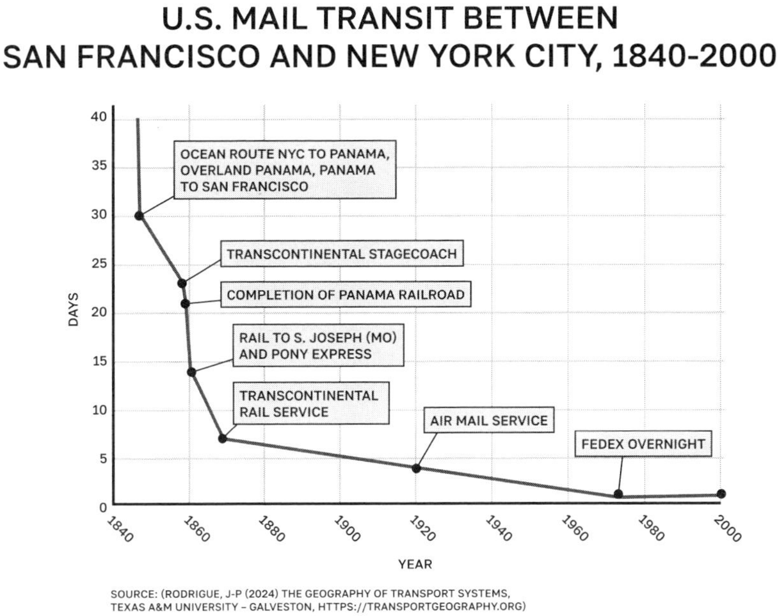
U.S. MAIL TRANSIT BETWEEN
SAN FRANCISCO AND NEW YORK CITY, 1840-2000
DAYS
YEAR
OCEAN ROUTE NYC TO PANAMA, OVERLAND PANAMA, PANAMA TO SAN FRANCISCO
TRANSCONTINENTAL STAGECOACH
COMPLETION OF PANAMA RAILROAD
RAIL TO S. JOSEPH (MO) AND PONY EXPRESS
TRANSCONTINENTAL RAIL SERVICE
AIR MAIL SERVICE
FEDEX OVERNIGHT
SOURCE: (RODRIGUE, J-P (2024) THE GEOGRAPHY OF TRANSPORT SYSTEMS, TEXAS A&M UNIVERSITY - GALVESTON, HTTPS://TRANSPORTGEOGRAPHY.ORG)

FIG 3-1

4

AVIATION'S DAWN

Imagine a world trapped in slow motion, where crossing an ocean took weeks by ship and ordering goods from across the globe was unthinkable. Communities, isolated and reliant on local produce, had no view of the world from above. Life felt small, disconnected from distant places and grand ideas. Then, in 1903, the Wright brothers' fragile flying machine took flight, setting the stage for a smaller, faster, and more connected world.

By the 1920s, airmail revolutionized letter delivery, speeding communication across the United States. In the 1930s, industries began relying on airplanes to transport goods and ideas, transforming early supply chains. Beyond cargo, airplanes carried military and economic influence, enabling the United States to project global authority in ways ships or armies could not. This aerial revolution reshaped commerce and connectivity, laying the groundwork for a new era.

Over decades, airplanes evolved from novelties to indispensable networks, shrinking the globe into a single marketplace. Today, they underpin global supply chains, delivering strawberries from California or abroad in January, rushing repair parts from Asia to doorsteps in days, and stocking shelves with sneakers, laptops, and countless goods. Airplanes make remote regions accessible, reunite families across oceans, and enable children to explore new countries, fostering a truly global community.

Without airplanes, the world of instant online orders, year-round fresh produce, and weekend getaways would not exist. Supply chains would falter, stores would lack diverse goods, and travel would remain a luxury for the few. Airplanes have woven the fabric of modern life, ensuring that the speed and connectivity we take for granted remain within reach, far removed from the slow, disconnected past.

THE WRIGHT BROTHERS AND FIRST FLIGHTS

Dawn broke over North Carolina's Outer Banks on Thursday, December 17, 1903, with a bitter chill that stung Orville Wright's face. At Kill Devil Hills, he and his brother Wilbur stood beside their fragile flying machine, a patchwork of wood, muslin, and metal gleaming faintly under a gray sky. The wind howled at 25 miles per hour, whipping sand across the dunes. It was no day for flight, yet the brothers' eyes burned with steely resolve. For years, they'd toiled in their Dayton, Ohio, bicycle shop, sketching wings, testing gliders, and dreaming of soaring like the hawks above. Today, they could etch their names in history – or crash into oblivion.

Three days earlier, disaster had struck. Wilbur, in their fragile craft, had lost control during takeoff, crumpling a wing. Repairs had been time-consuming, and now the weather taunted them. Across the country, failure loomed large – Samuel Langley's Aerodrome, backed by the Smithsonian Institute, had twice plunged into the Potomac River, its pilot Charles Manly lucky to survive. Farther back, dreamers like Portugal's João Torto had paid the ultimate price, his cloth wings no match for gravity as he plummeted to his death from a cathedral tower. Death was a real possibility, but Orville and Wilbur exchanged a glance – wordless, resolute. They would fly.

With five helpers, including lifesavers from a nearby station, the brothers positioned their craft. Orville climbed aboard, heart pounding. The engine sputtered to life, and the Wright Flyer lurched forward. For 12 seconds, it danced with the wind, skimming 10 feet above the sand before touching down. A fleeting moment, yet it shattered centuries of doubt. Kites in ancient China, da Vinci's sketches, Lilienthal's gliders – all had led to this. The Wright brothers had conquered the sky, launching a new era of supply chains where goods, ideas, and people would cross continents in hours, binding the world in ways once unimaginable.

SWIFT CHANGES

The Wright brothers' historic 1903 flight laid the foundation for a transportation revolution. Initially, Orville and Wilbur envisioned their airplane serving military purposes, such as reconnaissance or message delivery during conflicts, rather than commercial uses like passenger travel or freight transport. However, the U.S. Post Office quickly saw its potential for speeding mail delivery. By 1918, just 15 years later, the Post Office launched airmail service, using its own fleet of propeller-driven aircraft with open cockpits to carry letters from Washington, D.C., to New York and Philadelphia in hours rather than days. Early pilots braved harsh weather, and over time, the Post Office introduced navigational aids like radio beacons and safety measures to improve reliability and reduce risks, paving the way for modern aviation.

The U.S. Post Office's airmail program expanded rapidly, thanks to postal contracts that spurred innovation and broadened air routes. In the 1920s, the government began awarding contracts to private companies to transport mail by airplane, and encouraged them to develop superior aircraft and establish consistent flight schedules. These contracts proved transformative, providing stable revenue for nascent airlines and enabling them to establish new routes across the country, from Chicago to San Francisco and beyond. For instance, companies like Boeing Air Transport utilized postal funds to design faster airplanes and employ skilled pilots. This system not only accelerated mail delivery but also established the groundwork for commercial aviation, as airlines subsequently utilized these routes to transport passengers and cargo, and transformed how goods and individuals moved across America.

Early pilots, often called "daredevils" for braving hazardous conditions, proved aviation's potential through bold feats. In 1921, Amelia Earhart became one of the first women to solo a flight, climbing higher than any woman before her. In 1927, Charles Lindbergh completed the first solo transatlantic flight, from New York to Paris, capturing global attention. These achievements were not mere stunts; they demonstrated that airplanes could reliably cross vast distances, inspiring confidence in air travel's future.

Lindbergh's flight, in particular, transformed aviation. Within six months, airmail volume surged by 50%, pilot license applications tripled, and U.S. airplane production soared. His success spurred investment in aviation infrastructure, and Lindbergh himself helped establish transcontinental and intercontinental air routes, laying the groundwork for commercial air travel. These developments marked aviation's rise as a central force in global connectivity. **[FIG 4-1]**

Beyond practical impacts, flight offered a new perspective on Earth. Pilots soaring thousands of feet above ground gained unprecedented views of landscapes, revealing patterns invisible from below. Their observations drove advancements in agriculture, such as crop monitoring, and in surveying, military reconnaissance, and meteorology, reshaping how humanity understood and interacted with the planet.

Flight reshaped human perspectives, offering a new view of Earth from above. In the early 20th century, this aerial vantage point inspired cultural shifts, particularly in modernist art, which celebrated technology, motion, and innovation through bold depictions of machinery and progress. Aviation's transformative power soon extended beyond culture, revolutionizing global logistics and geopolitics.

WORLD WAR II'S AVIATION REVOLUTION AND THE BIRTH OF GLOBAL SUPPLY CHAINS

World War II (1939–1945) was a pivotal moment for aviation, not only as a tool of combat but as the backbone of unprecedented global supply chains. The war's demand for rapid, reliable transport across vast theaters transformed aircraft production and logistics, laying the foundation for modern air cargo networks and globalized supply chains. The industrial scale of WWII aviation and its logistical innovations—mass production, strategic airlifts, and coordinated supply networks—redefined how goods and resources move across the world, a legacy still evident today.

UNMATCHED AIRCRAFT PRODUCTION: FUELING WARTIME SUPPLY CHAINS

The war's global scope required an industrial effort unlike any before, with aviation at its core. Major belligerents collectively produced over 800,000 aircraft, a feat driven by the need to supply troops and sustain operations across continents. The United States led with 300,000 military planes, including 97,000 bombers (e.g., B-17 Flying Fortress) and 29,000 transports (e.g., C-47 Skytrain), per U.S. Army Air Forces records. By 1944, U.S. factories, such as Boeing and Lockheed, churned out 96,000 planes annually, with assembly lines optimized for speed and scale, often staffed by women dubbed "Rosie the Riveters." Other nations followed suit: the Soviet Union built 157,000 aircraft, Britain 131,000, Germany 119,000, and Japan 76,000, per aviation historian Richard Hallion.
[FIG 4-2]

This production boom was not just about combat; it was about logistics. Transport aircraft like the C-47 became the workhorses of supply chains, delivering fuel, munitions, and food to remote fronts. The war demanded synchronized production and distribution networks, linking raw material suppliers, manufacturers, and military logisticians. For example, aluminum and steel supply chains were streamlined to feed aircraft factories, while global shipping routes delivered critical components to assembly plants. This integration of production and logistics set a precedent for post-war supply chain management, where efficiency and scale became paramount.

AIRLIFT OPERATIONS: PROVING AVIATION'S LOGISTICAL POWER

WWII showcased aviation's ability to maintain supply chains under extreme conditions, a turning point for global logistics. Air transport bridged gaps where ground and sea routes faltered, delivering supplies across oceans and treacherous terrain. The C-47 Skytrain, for instance, airlifted 1.8 million tons of supplies over the Himalayas to China, sustaining the Burma Campaign despite monsoons and enemy threats, per USAAF records. In Europe, Douglas C-54s supported the 1944 Normandy invasion with 1,000 daily flights, delivering fuel and munitions to advancing Allied armies. These operations demonstrated aircraft's unique ability to provide rapid, flexible logistics, bypassing traditional infrastructure limitations.

The war also introduced scalable airlift models. The U.S. Army Air Forces developed airfields in remote regions, from Pacific islands to North Africa, creating ad hoc logistics hubs. These hubs, supported by radio navigation and weather forecasting, enabled continuous supply flows. The coordination required—between pilots, ground crews, and supply planners—foreshadowed modern just-in-time logistics systems. By war's end, aviation had proven it could sustain global operations, a concept that would shape post-war air cargo and commercial supply chains.

POST-WAR LEGACY: FROM MILITARY AIRLIFTS TO GLOBAL SUPPLY NETWORKS

The war's logistical innovations had a profound post-war impact, catalyzing the global air cargo industry. Surplus transport aircraft, like the C-47 (civilian DC-3), were repurposed for commercial use, offering affordable airfreight options. The Berlin Airlift (1948–1949), a direct descendant of WWII logistics, saw C-47s and C-54s deliver 2.3 million tons of supplies to West Berlin, proving air transport's reliability for large-scale civilian needs. This operation, per USAAF records, solidified aviation's role in crisis logistics and inspired the development of global air cargo networks.

WWII also left a physical and organizational legacy. Military airfields were converted into civilian airports, expanding air transport infrastructure. The war's global supply chains, which linked North American factories to European and Pacific theaters, evolved into commercial trade routes. Companies like Boeing and Douglas, veterans of wartime production, adapted their expertise to build commercial airliners (e.g., Boeing 707, Douglas DC-6), enabling faster, longer-range cargo transport. By the 1950s, airfreight was a growing sector, with global supply chains relying on aviation to move high-value goods, from electronics to pharmaceuticals.

World War II transformed aviation into a cornerstone of global supply chains, proving aircraft could deliver critical goods across vast distances under pressure. The war's mass production, strategic airlifts, and logistical networks not only won battles but reshaped how the world moves goods. From the Berlin Airlift to today's air cargo hubs, WWII's aviation legacy endures, underpinning the speed and reach of modern global trade.

THE JET AGE AND PRESSURIZED FLIGHT

The first operational jet aircraft, the German Messerschmitt 262 and the British Gloster Meteor, were deployed sparingly near the end of World War II. They represented the world's most advanced fighters when they took to the skies, but could not be manufactured in sufficient quantity. Consequently, they entered the conflict too late to influence the war's outcome, and their overall impact remained minimal.

Nonetheless, they established the foundation for subsequent advancements in aircraft, and the 1950s were dominated by jets. By that time, jet engines had become standard for combat aircraft. During the Korean War, the first jet-to-jet dogfight in history occurred. In this engagement, U.S. Air Force Lieutenant Russell J. Brown piloted an F-80 and engaged two North Korean MiG-15s near the Yalu River. Brown successfully shot down both North Korean airplanes. As a result, he was recognized with the first jet-to-jet dogfight victory in global history.

Jet engines provide swifter transportation over extended distances. They operate most efficiently when utilized at higher speeds and higher altitudes than propeller-driven aircraft. For comparison, consider a late World War II variant of the propeller-driven P-51 Mustang. It achieved a record speed of 487 miles per hour in a dive. The Gloster Meteor, equipped with a jet engine, could consistently exceed 600 mph. The P-51 Mustang required nearly 10 minutes to ascend to an altitude of 30,000 feet. The Meteor could accomplish the same ascent in half the time. The jet engine, with its fuel efficiencies at elevated speeds, significantly extended the range of air travel.

These attributes created novel opportunities for the application of jet aircraft in civilian life. Thanks to the velocity of the jet engine, supply chains and consumer networks could be restructured. For instance, fresh flowers could be transported thousands of miles and arrive at their destination intact and in a condition that made them worthy of purchase. Electronics could be manufactured on demand and shipped across continents. Supplies produced in Asia could be loaded onto an airplane and delivered to the United States on the same day. This precursor to the modern Just-in-Time supply chain diminished the time necessary to travel from one location to another by days and, in some instances, weeks.

PRESSURIZED AIRCRAFT: DEMOCRATIZING THE SKIES

In the 1950s, jet travel was an aspiration for most, with tickets costing as much as a new automobile. Only the affluent could afford to fly. Today, millions board commercial airliners annually, and traverse continents for work, vacations, or family reunions. Pressurized aircraft rendered this possible, and transformed jet travel from a luxury into an everyday convenience. By enabling aircraft to fly high, fast, and safely, this technology not only united people but also established robust supply chains that transport goods around the world.

Flying at high altitudes posed a challenge before pressurized aircraft. Above 10,000 feet, the air is too thin to breathe comfortably, and necessitates oxygen masks. Early airplanes, such as those used in World War I and in World War II, remained at low altitudes, and endured turbulent rides and consumed more fuel. The aircraft that were able to fly above 10,000 feet meant their crews were tethered to oxygen masks at higher altitudes and if the system failed the aircraft would have to descend to under 10,000 feet. Pressurized cabins revolutionized this by pumping air into the aircraft, and replicated conditions at 6,000-8,000 feet, even when flying at 30,000 feet. This ensured passenger comfort without masks and allowed airplanes to soar above storms, resulting in smoother and faster flights.

The Boeing 307 Stratoliner, introduced in 1940, was the first commercial airplane equipped with a pressurized cabin, and offered a preview of high-altitude travel. By the 1950s, jet-powered aircraft like the Boeing 707 refined this technology, and reduced travel times. A flight from New York to London, previously a 12-hour trip in a propeller-driven airplane, required just seven hours by jet. Pressurization, combined with jet engines, rendered long-distance travel practical, and laid the foundation for a new era of aviation.

Flying at high altitudes conserved fuel and avoided turbulence, thereby reducing airline costs and making jet travel accessible to the middle-class. Jets like the Boeing 707 could accommodate 150 passengers, significantly more than the 40 on older airplanes, and distributed expenses across more tickets. In the 1960s, airlines introduced "economy class" fares, and reduced prices by 30% compared to 1950s luxury flights. A New York-to-Paris round-trip ticket, formerly $1,000 (approximately $10,000 today), decreased to $300 by 1970.

This affordability transformed lives. Families embarked on international vacations, students pursued studies abroad, and workers traveled for employment opportunities. By 2025, over 4 billion passengers fly annually, with budget airlines offering $100 transatlantic flights. Airports evolved into bustling hubs, and manage millions of travelers yearly. Pressurized jets rendered air travel a commonplace choice, and connected individuals across the globe, thereby fostering a sense of a more compact world.

PRESSURIZED JETS AND GLOBAL TRADE

Pressurized aircraft have revolutionized supply chains by expediting global commerce. Pressurized cabins protect delicate cargo, such as electronics and pharmaceuticals, at high altitudes, and ensure their quality. Major airports handle millions of tons of cargo annually, encompassing everything from computer chips to fresh produce, and sustain enterprises worldwide.

This swift pace is vital for modern economies. Companies transport factory components, such as automotive parts, within a day. Perishable goods, like flowers or seafood, arrive at markets fresh, and promote export opportunities. These supply chains keep stores well-stocked and industries operational, and illustrate how pressurized aircraft drive global commerce, functioning as an exceptionally efficient delivery system.

AIR CARGO'S VITAL ROLE IN GLOBAL SUPPLY CHAINS

Air cargo's strength lies in its ability to swiftly transport a wide range of goods, meeting global demand with speed that ocean shipping can't match. From fresh seafood to high-tech electronics, air freight ensures products reach markets quickly, preserving quality and capitalizing on jet-powered velocity. This adaptability makes air cargo a cornerstone of modern supply chains, balancing cost with the need for rapid delivery.

Consider fresh seafood, like Alaskan salmon or Norwegian cod, which is flown to markets in Tokyo or London within 24 hours of being caught. This speed keeps the fish fresh and flavorful, unlike ocean shipping, which takes weeks and risks spoilage. Similarly, fresh fruits such as Peruvian avocados or Chilean cherries arrive ripe in North American or European supermarkets year-round, despite seasonal harvests. Air freight makes this possible by cutting delivery times to days, not months.

High-value goods also rely on air cargo's speed. Electronics, like semiconductors from Taiwan or smartphones from South Korea, are airlifted to meet tight production deadlines or product launches. Pharmaceuticals, such as vaccines or insulin, require precise temperature control, which modern jets provide, ensuring life-saving drugs reach hospitals worldwide without spoiling. Fashion retailers use air freight to rush luxury clothing from Milan or Shanghai to New York boutiques, staying ahead of fast-changing trends.

Even live animals, like racehorses or zoo-bound pandas, travel safely in climate-controlled jet compartments, arriving healthy across continents. These diverse examples highlight air cargo's specialized role in delivering goods that demand speed, precision, or care.

In 2024, air freight moved about 60 million tons of cargo globally, with perishables (e.g., seafood, fruits) and high-tech goods (e.g., electronics, pharmaceuticals) accounting for roughly 40% of the total cargo value. While air cargo is more expensive than sea transport, its speed and reliability make it indispensable for keeping global markets vibrant and responsive, ensuring fresh, timely, and critical goods reach consumers worldwide.

While contemporary air transportation offers considerable advantages, it also entails significant limitations. For numerous industries, air transport is not cost-effective. Shipping goods by cargo ship across oceans is substantially less costly – often a mere fraction of air freight rates. Air transport's swiftness facilitates urgent overseas deliveries, such as medical supplies or high-value electronics, but its high costs constrain its use for everyday supply chains, and compel enterprises to rely on slower, more cost-effective ocean shipping.

Air cargo's cost becomes apparent when evaluating expenses as percentage differences for overseas routes. In December 2024, the cost to transport a 1,100-pound shipment from China to the United States by air was approximately $2,250-$3,000 ($2.05-$2.73 per pound), whereas ocean freight costs were approximately $500-$750 ($0.45-$0.68 per pound for less-than-container-load). This means that air freight is 300% to 500% more expensive than ocean freight per pound. For an 11,000-pound shipment, air freight at approximately $20,000 ($1.82 per pound) is 600% to 700% more costly than ocean freight at approximately $2,500 ($0.23 per pound). Farmers exporting produce, retailers transporting consumer goods, or manufacturers shipping equipment overseas select ocean freight to realize substantial savings, and reserve air cargo for time-sensitive goods, such as seafood, pharmaceuticals, or highly valued products like semiconductors. These marked percentage differences underscore air freight's restricted role in global supply chains, where cost often supersedes speed for most commodities.

Despite its expense, air cargo outstrips all other transport modes in speed. Air cargo guarantees that certain goods arrive fresh and/or on-time. For industries in which every hour is crucial, such as medical supplies or electronics, air freight's unrivaled speed establishes it as the preferred option, even at a premium price, and solidifies its place in global supply chains.

This advantage of speed becomes even more important when supply chain disruptions arise. In the automotive industry, for instance, components are typically transported by truck and rail. When these systems fail, whether due to a carrier service breakdown, damaged goods, or an incorrect shipment, air transportation emerges as a feasible alternative. In certain instances, it literally "saves the day." In the United States, production plant shutdowns are prevented daily because of prompt air cargo deliveries. These are generally coordinated at the last minute. When another mode of transportation encounters a problem, a plant operator might identify the impending delay. To avert a halt in production, an aircraft is deployed. The supplies arrive, and workers on the assembly line continue their duties. Customers receive their orders, and remain largely unaware that a flight intervened to facilitate a last-minute delivery.

THE HISTORY OF DHL: A JOURNEY FROM A SMALL IDEA TO A GLOBAL LOGISTICS EMPIRE

In the late 1960s, the parcel shipping sector was sluggish and inefficient, particularly for international deliveries. Documents dispatched by sea from the United States to destinations like Hong Kong could require weeks, and were hindered by customs delays and port congestion. Three young entrepreneurs in San Francisco – Adrian Dalsey, Larry Hillblom, and Robert Lynn – identified an opportunity to transform this process. In 1969, they established DHL, a company that would redefine global logistics and emerge as a cornerstone of contemporary supply chains. The DHL name utilized the initial letters of their surnames.

Hillblom, who had served as a courier between Oakland and Los Angeles airports for an insurance company, invested $6,000 of his student loan savings as initial capital. Dalsey contributed his sales expertise and client connections, while Lynn was supposed to assist with financing but soon withdrew, doubting the venture's viability. Undeterred, Dalsey and Hillblom persevered, and drove a worn Plymouth Duster around San Francisco to collect documents in suitcases, then hastened to the airport to secure flights using corporate credit cards – a pioneering approach at the time.

Their first client was Seatrain, a shipping company that required bills of lading couriered between Los Angeles and Honolulu. Dalsey and Hillblom personally managed the deliveries, and flew the documents themselves to guarantee speed. The strategy succeeded; what once took weeks now required days, reduced unloading times and saved shippers money. Word spread, and within a year, DHL was managing shipments for 40 clients, and expanded to Guam, Los Angeles, and Portland, Oregon. By 1971, they targeted the Far East, and established offices in Hong Kong, Japan, and Singapore, thereby laying the groundwork for a global network.

The 1970s marked a period of remarkable growth for DHL. Unlike its competitors, which concentrated on domestic markets, DHL focused on international deliveries, a largely unexploited niche. In 1974, they opened their first European office in London, followed by the Middle East in 1977 and Sub-Saharan Africa in 1978. DHL's early triumphs were not without obstacles. The company encountered formidable resistance from national postal monopolies, which had dominated mail services for centuries. In 1982, for instance, the French post office attempted to enforce a 15th-century monopoly law, and ordered DHL to suspend operations outside Paris – despite the company holding an 80% share of the French market. Dalsey and Hillblom navigated these challenges with determination, and often worked tirelessly around the clock. Hillblom, who was preparing for the bar exam, even slept in airports between flights to sustain the business, while Marge, Dalsey's wife, managed the financial records from their dining room table.

By the end of the 1970s, DHL had become a genuine international leader, and delivered to over 70,000 destinations in 227 countries and territories. It had evolved into a vital lifeline for businesses requiring swift, dependable document delivery across borders, from the Pacific Rim to Europe.

REVOLUTIONIZING GLOBAL DELIVERY: THE RISE OF FEDEX

In the 1960s, documents – even those of great importance – moved slowly throughout the United States by passenger jet, truck or train, taking as long as days to cross the country.

But Frederick W. Smith had an idea to change the system, one he outlined in a 1965 paper for his economics class at Yale University. Smith proposed a visionary system – a delivery network designed to manage time-sensitive shipments, such as documents and medical supplies, by channeling them through a central hub and employing a fleet of airplanes to deliver them overnight. Smith's professor deemed the concept impractical and famously gave Smith's paper a C.

Despite the grade he had been assigned on his economics paper, Smith recognized the transformative potential of his idea.

After graduating and serving in Vietnam with the United States Marine Corps , Smith inherited $4 million from his father's enterprise. He utilized this, along with $90 million in venture capital – an extraordinary sum for the era – to transform his idea into reality. In 1971, he established Federal Express Corporation in Little Rock, Arkansas. (He used "Federal" in the name to evoke a national, government-like reliability.)

Smith acquired a modest fleet of 14 Dassault Falcon jets, modified to transport cargo, and implemented a hub-and-spoke model, wherein all packages would converge at a central hub for sorting before being flown to their destinations. The jets would fan out by dawn, ensuring next-day arrival.

Federal Express officially commenced operations on April 17,

1973, after Smith relocated its headquarters to Memphis, Tennessee, selected for its central location and minimal weather disruptions.

On its inaugural night of service, Federal Express delivered a mere 186 packages to 25 U.S. cities, a tentative beginning that highlighted the challenges ahead. The company depleted Smith's cash rapidly, and incurred $29 million in losses during its first two years. Fuel costs escalated dramatically during the 1973 oil crisis, and Smith struggled to persuade businesses to trust his unproven business model.

At one critical juncture, with only $5,000 remaining in the company's account, Smith traveled to Las Vegas, wagered the $5,000 on blackjack, and secured $27,000 – enough money to cover the Federal Express payroll for a few additional days.

Despite a rocky start, Smith's grit and determination paid off. By 1975, Federal Express delivered 20,000 packages nightly, and achieved its first profit in July 1975. That year, the company generated $75 million in revenue and posted an $11.5 million profit.

Smith's jets didn't just deliver cargo and critical papers – they delivered a logistics revolution. Federal Express used barcodes and computers, rare in the logistics industry at that time, enabled tracking, while overnight delivery slashed supply chain delays. A Chicago hospital received urgent medical supplies; a New York lawyer got critical contracts. By 1977, the Federal Express public offering fueled global dreams, raising $17 million to support further expansion. From its Memphis hub, Smith's vision shrank the world, proving speed could outpace doubt, weaving a network where businesses thrived and time gave way to innovation.

Federal Express, a name now synonymous with overnight delivery, revolutionized the logistics industry and established itself as a cornerstone of modern supply chains. From an untested concept in a college paper to a global powerhouse delivering millions of packages daily, the Federal Express journey embodies innovation, risk, and perseverance. The company pioneered the express delivery model, and fundamentally reshaped how goods traverse the world.

By the way, Federal Express did not begin using "FedEx" as a marketing term and nickname until 1994. In 1998, the parent corporation changed its name to FDX, and then in 2000 the company's name was officially changed to FedEx. Because most people know the company simply as FedEx, I will begin using that as its name going forward.

REGULATORY SHIFTS AND RIVALRY

The 1970s introduced pivotal regulatory shifts that heightened the competition among UPS, FedEx, and DHL.

The 1977 Airline Deregulation Act proved transformative for the air cargo industry, particularly for FedEx and DHL. Prior to deregulation, cargo airlines had to deal with stringent restrictions on routes and pricing, which constrained their capacity to expand. The Act enabled FedEx to acquire larger aircraft, such as Boeing 727s, and operate additional routes, thereby accelerating its growth. By 1980, FedEx was delivering 65,000 packages daily, and capitalized on the demand for overnight delivery. DHL also profited, as deregulation alleviated constraints on international air routes, and permitted it to expand its fleet and serve more countries. In 1979, DHL launched DHL Air Cargo in Hawaii. This unit had 100 employees and operated inter-island services with DC-3 and DC-6 aircraft (although this venture subsequently ended in 1983 due to financial difficulties).

Meanwhile, UPS confronted a distinct regulatory struggle. Throughout the 1970s, it was embroiled in legal disputes with the USPS, which sought to safeguard its monopoly on parcel delivery. The ICC rigorously enforced its oversight powers over UPS, and mandated that the company substantiate its rates and routes – a process that crimped its expansion. Despite these obstacles, UPS capitalized on its ground network to maintain a cost advantage. Ground delivery was substantially less expensive than air transport, and the company's emphasis on retail and consumer parcels provided it with a broad customer base. By 1975, UPS employed 50,000 workers and was delivering to every address in the continental United States, a scale neither FedEx nor DHL could rival at the time. However, UPS was slow to enter the overnight air market, which gave its two competitors a distinct edge in that profitable segment.

DHL's international orientation gave it a unique distinction. While UPS and FedEx vied for U.S. dominance, DHL was the leader internationally (although it continued to encounter opposition from national postal monopolies). DHL navigated these challenges by forging robust local partnerships and concentrating on the rising demand for the rapid movement of international business documents. By the late 1970s, DHL was transporting critical financial papers and legal documents across continents, a service neither UPS nor FedEx could fully replicate at the time. However, DHL's U.S. presence remained limited, and positioned it outside the direct domestic rivalry between UPS and FedEx for the time being.

THE BATTLE FOR MARKET SHARE: INNOVATION AND EXPANSION

The rivalry in the 1970s among the delivery services was not solely fought against government regulation; it also centered on innovation and strategic market positioning. The FedEx overnight delivery model targeted a specific market – businesses prepared to pay a premium for rapid service. Its slogan, "When it absolutely, positively has to be there overnight," encapsulated this strategy, and by 1978, FedEx was serving 75 cities with a fleet of 32 jets. The company also introduced the overnight letter in 1979, a flat-rate envelope for documents that proved immensely popular with law firms and corporations. FedEx's early adoption of technology, such as automated sorting at its Memphis hub, enabled it to manage increasing volumes efficiently, and the company processed 35,000 packages nightly by the end of the decade.

Meanwhile, UPS dominated the ground sector. Its extensive network of trucks and distribution centers permitted it to offer lower rates, and appealed to retailers and consumers shipping less urgent items. In the 1970s, UPS handled approximately 1 billion packages annually, vastly outstripping FedEx's volume. However, UPS acknowledged the competitive threat posed by FedEx's air service and DHL's international expansion. In 1976, UPS began lobbying for its own regulatory relief, and sought to broaden its air operations. It also began experimenting with expedited ground services, such as two-day delivery, to rival FedEx's speed without the elevated cost of air transport. UPS' scale and efficiency – refined over decades – provided a robust foundation, but its delayed entry into air delivery left it playing catch-up in the express market.

DHL, meanwhile, innovated on the global stage. It was among the pioneers to implement computer-based package tracking across borders, a vital feature for businesses requiring visibility into international shipments. DHL's emphasis on express air delivery for documents – such as contracts and financial reports – made it essential for multinational corporations. In 1979, DHL delivered over 50 million shipments, a testament to its swift growth. Although it did not directly compete with UPS and FedEx in the U.S. market during the 1970s, DHL's global achievements pressured both companies to consider markets beyond the borders of the United States. UPS began international operations in 1975, opening a Canadian hub in Toronto in 1975. FedEx initiated international deliveries in 1981, also beginning in Canada. Both initiatives were influenced by DHL's early dominance in cross-border logistics.

CULTURAL AND OPERATIONAL CONTRASTS

The rivalry also highlighted stark contrasts among the three companies. UPS, with its roots in early 20th century delivery, had a disciplined, almost militaristic culture. Its drivers wore crisp brown uniforms, and its operations were meticulous, with strict protocols for everything from package handling to vehicle maintenance. This culture, instilled by founder Jim Casey, emphasized reliability and cost-efficiency, making UPS the go-to for bulk retail deliveries. In 1979, UPS delivered around 1.5 billion packages, generating $2.4 billion in revenue, compared to $415 million in revenue at FedEx.

In contrast with UPS, FedEx was a daring upstart. Smith's willingness to take risks (like gambling company funds in Las Vegas to make payroll in 1973) defined its early years. The company's culture was entrepreneurial, with a focus on speed and innovation. Its employees, often young and tech-savvy, embraced the challenge of building a new industry. The FedEx Memphis hub became a symbol of this innovation, sorting packages at a pace UPS couldn't match in the air. By 1979, FedEx had 12,000 employees and was delivering to 90 cities, a rapid ascent that pressured UPS to rethink its strategy.

DHL brought a different flavor to the mix. Its founders, particularly Larry Hillblom, were relentless in their pursuit of global reach, often sleeping in airports during the company's early years to keep operations running. DHL's culture was scrappy and adaptive, focused on navigating the complexities of international shipping. In the 1970s its small team of couriers worked with a sense of urgency, hand-delivering documents across continents. Despite a minimal presence in the United States, its global network – spanning 227 countries by 1979 – set a benchmark for international logistics, pushing both UPS and FedEx to consider global expansion sooner than they might have otherwise.

Having achieved the "Golden Link" in 1975 – serving every address in the continental U.S. – UPS turned its attention in the early 1980s to air delivery to compete with FedEx. In 1982, UPS launched Next Day Air, using commercial airlines to offer overnight service, a direct response to FedEx's dominance in this space. By 1985, UPS expanded internationally, starting with air service to Europe a decade after starting operations in Canada.

In 1988, UPS received FAA approval to operate its own airline, UPS Airlines, which quickly grew into one of the world's largest cargo airlines, with a fleet of 500 aircraft by 2025.

But UPS faced labor challenges in the 1980s. Its workforce, members of the International Brotherhood of Teamsters, demanded better wages and conditions. The company's disciplined culture, rooted in Jim Casey's principles, helped it maintain efficiency, but it had to adapt to its changing workforce. Technologically, UPS began investing heavily in automation (which the union did not always like), spending $1 billion annually by the late 1980s on systems like package tracking and the Delivery Information Acquisition Device (DIAD), introduced in 1990, which allowed drivers to capture delivery data digitally. By 1989, UPS was generating $10 billion in revenue, delivering to 175 countries, and employing 200,000 people, cementing its status as a global logistics leader.

FedEx, meanwhile, was riding the wave of its overnight delivery success. Airline deregulation had allowed FedEx to expand its fleet, and by 1983, it hit $1 billion in revenue, becoming the first U.S. company to do so without mergers or acquisitions. After expanding into Canada in 1981, it launched services in Europe and Asia in 1984, directly challenging DHL's international dominance. The 1980s saw FedEx innovate aggressively, including automated sorting systems and handheld scanners. However, not all its ventures succeeded – ZapMail, a fax-based document delivery service launched in 1984, had flopped by 1986, costing FedEx $190 million as fax machines became widely affordable.

Nonetheless, by 1989, FedEx was serving 90 countries, delivering 1.2 million packages daily, and generating $3.9 billion in revenue. Its Memphis hub, now called the "SuperHub," was sorting 1.5 million packages nightly, making Memphis the world's busiest cargo airport. FedEx's acquisition of Flying Tiger Line in 1989, a cargo airline with extensive Asian routes, bolstered its Pacific Rim presence, putting it on a collision course with DHL. FedEx's entrepreneurial culture, driven by its founder, kept it agile, but its high-cost air model faced pressure from the cheaper ground services offered by UPS.

DHL'S RAPID GROWTH

DHL, which had pioneered international express delivery, was thriving globally by 1980. Operating in 227 countries and delivering 50 million shipments annually, DHL held a commanding lead in cross-border logistics. In 1983, it expanded into the U.S. domestic market, opening a hub at the Cincinnati/Northern Kentucky International Airport to compete with FedEx and UPS. It also became the first express service to operate in Eastern Bloc countries like Latvia, a bold move during the Cold War. DHL also entered challenging markets like Vietnam, China, and Kuwait during the Gulf War, showcasing its adaptability. By 1989, DHL Worldwide was the 84th largest company in the U.S., with 18,000 employees, 50 million shipments, and service to 184 countries.

DHL's innovations in international tracking were critically important to global businesses. However, it continued to face resistance from national postal monopolies. By the decade's end, DHL's revenues were estimated at $1.5 billion, trailing UPS and FedEx but leading in international express. In 1990, DHL's rapid growth in the 1980s culminated in a Global Transport Alliance with Lufthansa Cargo, Japan Airlines, and Nissho Iwai, securing $500 million in capital to expand its air freight network and strengthen its global supply chain capabilities.

DHL, already a global leader, faced a transformative shift in the 1990s. In 1995 Deutsche Post (Germany's national postal system, with roots going back to medieval times) was privatized, and became a fully independent company in 2000. Deutsche Post began acquiring shares in DHL in 1998, gaining full control of the company in December 2002. This merger created a logistics powerhouse, combining DHL's international expertise with Deutsche Post's infrastructure, which handled 61 million daily letter deliveries in Germany.

DHL expanded its U.S. presence with the 2003 acquisition of Airborne Express, integrating it alongside other units like Danzas and EuroExpress. By 1999, DHL was delivering to over 220 countries, with revenues of $5 billion and 60,000 employees, but its U.S. domestic operations struggled against the better known FedEx and UPS.

DHL leveraged e-commerce through its focus on international and B2B deliveries. Its 2005 acquisition of Exel for €5.5 billion expanded its supply chain services, and by 2016, DHL Group's revenues reached €57.3 billion, with a net profit of €2.64 billion. However, DHL still struggled against UPS and FedEx in the U.S. domestic market, and pulled back after losses in 2008.

Deutsche Post took the name of its DHL subsidiary in 2023; DHL became the international brand for all of what had been Deutsche Post's holdings.

Despite its lack of U.S. market share, DHL excelled globally, delivering 1.7 billion parcels annually by 2025. With 600,000 employees, DHL's five divisions – Express, Global Forwarding, Supply Chain, eCommerce, and Deutsche Post – made it the world's largest logistics company in 2022.

UPS' STRIKE AND IPO

UPS rapidly grew through the 90's, but not everything was positive. Its employees who were members of the Teamsters went on strike in 1997. The strike lasted 15 days, beginning on August 4 and ending August 19. The strike significantly impacted the nation's supply chain, cost UPS $850 million, and caused a backlog of over 7 million packages. It was one of the most successful labor actions in modern U.S. history and forced UPS to meet many of the Teamsters' key demands. The company bounced back, however. By 1999 UPS was delivering 3.1 billion packages annually, generating $27 billion in revenue, and serving 200 countries with 360,000 employees.

UPS went public in 1999 with one of the largest IPOs in history, raising $5.2 billion (although most voting shares stayed with employees, preserving its employee-owned culture). UPS also expanded through acquisitions, buying Mail Boxes Etc. in 2001 (rebranded as The UPS Store) to grow its retail presence.

The 2000s brought the e-commerce boom, reshaping logistics. Due in large part to the COVID-19 pandemic, e-commerce grew even bigger. UPS delivered 6.3 billion packages in 2020, and the company's revenues were $85 billion. It had grown to 500,000 employees, a fleet of 147,000 vehicles and 500 aircraft. However, in 2023 UPS once again faced labor challenges, narrowly averting a strike, with workers securing a $30 billion wage and benefits package, raising full-time driver pay to $170,000 annually by 2028.

FEDEX DELIVERS OVERNIGHT GROWTH THROUGH ECOMMERCE

As noted earlier, Federal Express rebranded to FedEx in 1994, reflecting its broader scope. FedEx's 1998 acquisition of RPS (rebranded as FedEx Ground in 2000) allowed it to challenge UPS in ground delivery, a move that paid off as e-commerce grew.

FedEx thrived in the e-commerce arena, delivering 8.5 million packages daily by 2010, with revenues of $34.7 billion. Its 2001 deal with the USPS to transport mail boosted its air network, while the 2004 acquisition of Kinko's (rebranded as FedEx Office) expanded its retail footprint. The company acquired TNT Express for $4.8 billion in 2016, strengthening its European ground network. However, a 2017 cyberattack on TNT cost FedEx $300 million. Nonetheless, by 2024 FedEx's revenues had swelled to $90 billion, with 424,000 employees delivering 15 million packages daily, supported by 700 aircraft and 200,000 vehicles.

FROM GARAGE TO GLOBAL GIANT

In 1994, in a cramped Bellevue, Washington, garage, Jeff Bezos packed books into cardboard boxes, dreaming of building an online bookstore. With no trucks or airplanes, his nascent Amazon leaned on the brown vans of UPS, FedEx's jets, and the rural reach of USPS to deliver its first orders.

Three years later, in 1997, Amazon went public, and its growth surged as it expanded beyond books into CDs, electronics, and additional product categories. By 1999, Amazon was shipping millions of items annually, and relied heavily on UPS for ground deliveries, FedEx for expedited air shipments, and USPS for last-mile delivery, particularly in rural regions. The postal system was especially vital for Amazon's early strategy – its flat-rate pricing and capacity to deliver to every U.S. address made it very cost-effective for lighter packages. A 2001 agreement with the postal service enabled Amazon to utilize USPS for "last-mile" deliveries, wherein USPS carriers deposit packages at customers' residences, a partnership that strengthened over the years.

THE EVOLUTION OF AMAZON'S LOGISTICS: FROM DEPENDENCY TO DOMINANCE

Despite long-term relationships with UPS, FedEx and USPS, Amazon's dependence on third-party carriers was problematic and became a bottleneck to the company's growth. In 1997, Amazon began to invest in its own infrastructure, beginning with fulfillment centers (FCs). Amazon began operations at its first FC in Seattle that year.

By 1999, Amazon was becoming a juggernaut, and millions of packages were being shipped by the e-commerce giant. During the 1999 holiday season, UPS, which processed the majority of Amazon's ground shipments, grappled with the surge in demand, and this resulted in delayed deliveries and dissatisfied customers. This incident underscored the vulnerabilities of depending on third-party carriers, particularly during peak seasons. FedEx, although faster for air deliveries, was costly, and eroded Amazon's profit margins. This led Bezos to continue to plan; he saw a future where speed was king.

Since then, Amazon has evolved into a global e-commerce titan, and delivers billions of packages annually. Its logistics journey represents a remarkable saga of transformation.

In 2005, Amazon introduced Prime, a subscription service promising free two-day shipping for a $79 annual fee. Prime's success with the Amazon customer base – membership expanded to 4 million customers by 2007 – imposed significant pressure on UPS, FedEx, and the USPS to fulfill Amazon's volume and speed requirements, which were often at discounted rates negotiated using Amazon's ever-increasing bargaining power. However, even with the carriers' discounted rates Amazon's profit margins were squeezed.

Amazon launched Fulfillment by Amazon (FBA) in 2006, and permitted third-party sellers to store products in Amazon's fulfillment centers for a fee. FBA not only enhanced Amazon's revenue but also amplified the volume of packages flowing through its system, and further strained the UPS and FedEx networks, as well as Amazon's relationships with the two carriers.

By 2010, Amazon's infrastructure had grown substantially; it maintained 40 FCs across the U.S. Each was strategically positioned near a major population center. These warehouses enabled Amazon to store inventory closer to customers, and reduced delivery times while also diminishing dependency on third-party carriers for storage and sorting.

That same year Amazon also hit a major milestone – shipping one billion packages. **[FIG 4-3]** UPS and FedEx continued to strain under Prime's volume, while at the same time their cost continued to cut into Amazon's margins. During the 2013 holiday season there was another delivery meltdown, with UPS once again failing to make thousands of deliveries on time.

For Bezos, this was the breaking point; UPS was jeopardizing Amazon's reputation. He publicly criticized UPS, and Amazon issued refunds to affected customers. This latest holiday debacle emphasized a critical lesson for Bezos and his leadership team – Amazon required greater control to fulfill Prime's commitment of swift, reliable delivery. Bezos vowed to control Amazon's delivery network.Therefore, the company had to accelerate its logistics ambitions.

In 2014, Amazon began experimenting with its own delivery network. It introduced "Amazon Logistics," a program that initially depended on small, local courier companies to manage last-mile deliveries in urban areas such as San Francisco and New York. This posed a direct challenge to the USPS, which had dominated last-mile delivery for Amazon, particularly for Prime packages.

Amazon also began leasing 20 Boeing 767 jets in 2015 under its Prime Air program, seeking to reduce reliance on FedEx's costly air services. They were branded with the Amazon logo and sent a message to both FedEx and its consumers.

By 2015, Amazon operated 65 fulfillment centers around the nation and was handling 40% of its U.S. deliveries through Amazon Logistics, although it continued to rely on UPS, FedEx, and the USPS for the majority of its volume, especially during peak seasons.

Amazon began to execute a pivotal shift in the mid- and late 2010s, aggressively developing its own logistics network. Bezos aspired to rival UPS, FedEx, and DHL.

It began by opening an air hub at the Wilmington Air Park, in Wilmington, Ohio. This hub, which was once an USAF base and then a key facility for Airborne Express and later DHL, became a crucial part of Amazon Air's network. It was and is a sorting center for packages, playing a role in supporting Amazon's air cargo operations and complementing the company's primary hub in Cincinnati. Wilmington is also unique – air-to-air operations are conducted there; it's not just a transfer point between ground and air, but also between aircraft.

By 2016, 40 aircraft were operating out of Wilmington; that number grew to 85 by 2023.

The 2016 fleet expansion directly threatened FedEx, which had served as Amazon's primary air carrier for many years. In 2017, Amazon terminated its relationship with FedEx for Prime deliveries, citing cost and reliability concerns. FedEx continued to handle some non-Prime shipments until 2019, when Amazon severed ties entirely after FedEx opted not to renew its contract, and chose instead to compete with Amazon.

Amazon also invested extensively in its ground delivery services. In 2018 it launched the Delivery Service Partner (DSP) program, and encouraged entrepreneurs to establish small delivery companies utilizing Amazon-branded vans. By 2020, Amazon worked with 1,500 DSPs using 100,000 vans, and they delivered 2.5 billion packages annually – surpassing FedEx's ground volume. This program not only diminished Amazon's reliance on UPS but also granted it greater control over the last mile, a crucial element of the delivery process. The USPS remained a collaborator, and made 30% of Amazon's last-mile deliveries in 2020, thanks to its cost-effectiveness and reach in rural areas, but Amazon was progressively shifting volume to its own network.

Technology played a pivotal role in Amazon's logistics ascent. In 2017, it inaugurated its first fully automated FC in Kent, Washington, and employed robots to move sort packages, thereby reducing labor costs and enhancing efficiency. Amazon also introduced Amazon Scout, autonomous delivery robots, in 2019, and began testing them in Snohomish County, Washington, to explore last-mile automation.

By the end of the 2010s, Amazon maintained 175 fulfillment centers around the world, 110,000 delivery vans, and 70 Prime Air aircraft. It delivered 4.2 billion packages – representing 20% of the U.S. parcel market – a staggering increase from its 5% share in 2015. The company's $90 billion in annual revenue rivaled that of the three logistics giants.

The COVID-19 pandemic (2020-2022) accelerated Amazon's logistics expansion. With most U.S. consumers confined to their homes, e-commerce and online shopping skyrocketed. In 2020 Amazon delivered 6 billion packages; its in-house network demonstrated resilience, while UPS and FedEx grappled with capacity constraints.

The Amazon expansion alarmed competitors – UPS and FedEx experienced declines in their market shares, while DHL, focused on international logistics, saw Amazon encroach on its business-to-business domain with services such as Amazon Freight.

Amazon also secured FAA approval in 2020 to operate drones in select U.S. cities, such as Lockeford, California, which is 16 miles from Stockton, 34 miles from Sacramento and 66 miles from Oakland. While it ended the program in Lockeford in April 2024, the company stated it would continue drone deliveries in College Station, Texas, and launch new locations in 2025, including Tolleson, Arizona. By 2025, Amazon drones were delivering 5% of packages in urban areas, a modest but expanding segment of its operations.

Because of COVID's effect on air travel, Amazon was able to acquire 11 Boeing 767s from Delta and WestJet in 2021. The aircraft were converted for cargo, and they further increased its air capabilities. That led to the launch of Amazon Air Cargo in 2022, a freight service competing directly with DHL and UPS Freight. By 2025, Amazon Air Cargo was transporting 10% of U.S. air freight volume, and had leveraged its scale to offer competitive rates.

In 25 years, Amazon had become a logistics titan. The company was managing 50% of its U.S. deliveries in-house. Its air hub network further expanded with the construction of a $1.5 billion facility at the Cincinnati/Northern Kentucky International Airport. This facility was capable of sorting 100 million packages annually.

By 2023 the Amazon Prime Air fleet had grown to 85 planes. Amazon's ground network also expanded significantly. By 2025, it operated 400,000 delivery vans, many of them electric-powered to align with its 2040 net-zero carbon objective. Its 2,000 DSPs employed 275,000 drivers. Amazon established "last-mile stations" in every major U.S. city; these enabled it to sort and dispatch packages directly to customers, thereby reducing reliance on the USPS to a mere

15% of last-mile deliveries.

Amazon's network of fulfillment centers had grown to 250 globally by 2025. Moreover, it was using 100,000 robots in these FCs. The company's delivery capacity had swelled to 10 billion packages annually. It became the largest parcel carrier in the U.S., surpassing UPS's 6.5 billion packages.

Amazon's logistics expansion has reshaped the competitive landscape. UPS, which delivered 60% of Amazon's packages in 2015, saw that share decline to 20% by 2025, and compelled it to re-focus on business-to-business and international markets because its revenue from Amazon will likely only continue to decline. FedEx, after losing its Amazon business, intensified partnerships with retailers, such as Walmart, but its U.S. market share decreased from 30% in 2015 to 25% in 2025. The USPS, although still an Amazon collaborator, shifted to serving smaller e-commerce entities as Amazon assumed greater control over its last-mile deliveries.

Over the course of a little over 30 years, Amazon has transformed itself from an online book seller to the world's preeminent online retailer – and also the preeminent logistics player. It manages more parcel volume than all other major parcel logistics operators combined.

When an Amazon package arrives, think of the Wright brothers, at least for a moment. Though they certainly could not foresee the full effect of their invention 100 years later, they changed the world in an untold number of ways. For those that look at the sky and wonder about flying, a ticket is just a purchase away.

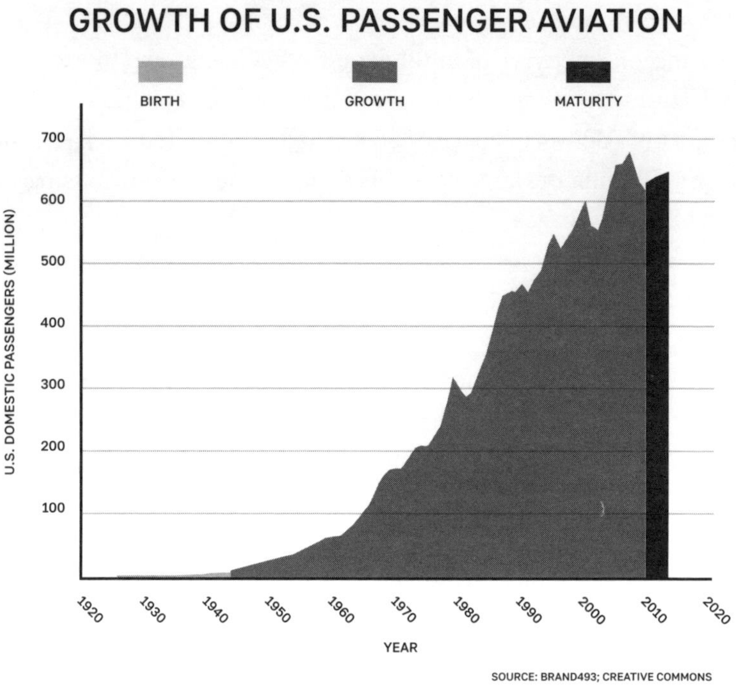
GROWTH OF U.S. PASSENGER AVIATION
BIRTH
GROWTH
MATURITY
U.S. DOMESTIC PASSENGERS (MILLION)
700
600
500
400
300
200
100
1920
1930
1940
1950
1960
1970
1980
1990
2000
2010
2020
YEAR
SOURCE: BRAND493; CREATIVE COMMONS

FIG 4-1

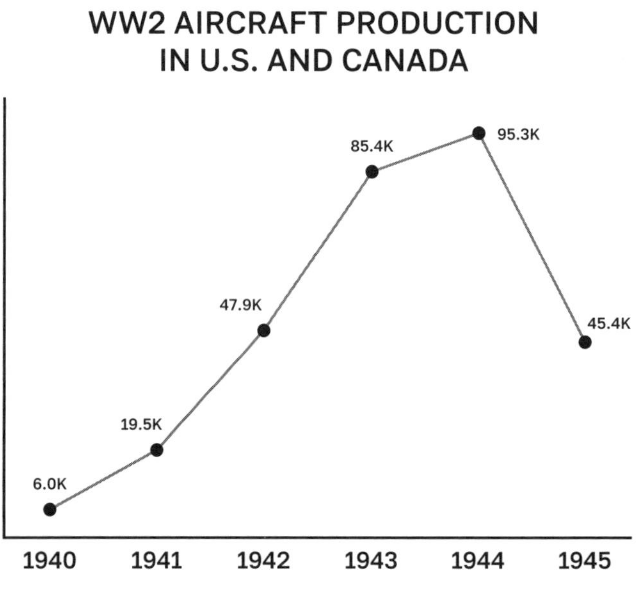
WW2 AIRCRAFT PRODUCTION IN U.S. AND CANADA
6.0K
19.5K
47.9K
85.4K
95.3K
45.4K
1940
1941
1942
1943
1944
1945
SOURCE: ARMY AIR FORCES STATISTICAL DIGEST

FIG 4-2

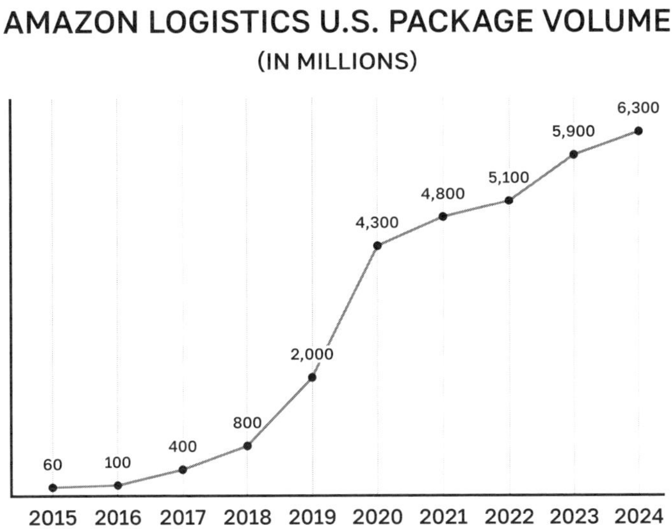

SOURCE: PITNEY BOWES SHIPPING INDEX

FIG 4-3

5

HIGHWAY HEROES

Chapter 4 explored how airplanes connected the global economy, but trucks arguably have a greater impact on moving products. Planes may race across skies, but they can't deliver door-to-door or match trucking's cost-effectiveness.

Trucking, a cornerstone of logistics, has evolved over a century from rudimentary vehicles of the early 1900s to sophisticated fleets, as Chapter 5 will explore. Its history reflects innovation, economic shifts, and regulatory changes that have shaped modern commerce.

Trucks transport over 70% of U.S. freight by value, fueling a $1 trillion industry that links manufacturers, retailers, and consumers. This network delivers fresh produce, medical supplies, electronics, and more, ensuring rapid market access and enabling just-in-time delivery systems vital to supply chains. Without trucks, e-commerce giants like Amazon would falter, grocery shelves would empty, and factories would stall, highlighting trucking's role as an economic lifeline.

Yet, trucking is a volatile business, with legendary boom-and-bust cycles and battles with regulators and unions, rivaling the drama of TV series like *Yellowstone*, *Landman*, or *Succession*. Few companies embody this saga like Yellow Freight, our next story.

THE LONG HAUL OF YELLOW TRUCKING: A TALE OF TRIUMPH AND TRAGEDY

In 1924, transportation entrepreneur A.J. Harrell launched a bold venture in Oklahoma City's dusty streets, founding Yellow Cab Transit Co. With a small fleet, he hauled less-than-truckload (LTL) shipments—freight under 10,000 pounds—between Oklahoma City and Tulsa. The roads, designed for horses, were rough, but Harrell foresaw businesses needing faster shipping than railroads could provide. His company grew steadily, pioneering LTL logistics by consolidating small shipments for efficient transport. By the early 1940s, Yellow had expanded into Kansas, Missouri, and Texas, serving the Midwest's growing markets. In 1944, after two decades of building a regional LTL leader, Harrell sold the company, passing the torch to new leadership.

POWELL'S ERA: RECOVERY AND GROWTH (1944–1957)

Under George E. Powell Sr., the new owner, Yellow Transit Co. entered a transformative phase. By 1949, the company operated 51 subsidiaries with nearly $7 million in annual revenue, but fierce competition and high leasing costs led to bankruptcy in 1951. Powell steered Yellow back to profitability by 1952, renaming it Yellow Transit Freight Lines. The 1950s were a golden era, driven by the postwar economic boom and the Interstate Highway System, launched in 1956, which sped up long-haul transport. Yellow expanded through acquisitions, reaching an estimated $15 million in revenue by 1957. Its hub-and-spoke system—collecting freight at local terminals, sorting it at central hubs, and dispatching it for delivery—revolutionized LTL shipping for small businesses moving 150–15,000 pounds, strengthening supply chain networks.

By the 1970s, Yellow Freight System, as it had been renamed in

1968, was a giant, earning $50 million with 300 terminals. But storm clouds gathered. The 1973 oil crisis sent fuel prices soaring, and Yellow's unionized drivers, part of the Teamsters, demanded better pay. Strikes loomed, and the union's strict rules made it hard to adapt quickly. Still, Yellow kept rolling, delivering millions of shipments across the U.S., its bright yellow trucks a familiar sight on the highways.

Then came 1980, a year that changed everything. The Motor Carrier Act deregulated trucking, stripping away rules that had kept rates high and stifling competition. Suddenly, new truckers and trucking companies flooded the market, offering cheaper rates. Yellow, with its higher union wages – drivers earned 50% more than their non-union peers – struggled to compete. Non-unionized carriers like Old Dominion Freight Lines sped ahead, while Yellow fought to keep up, opening new centers and expanding to 600 terminals by 1985. It covered all 50 states, even Alaska, and two-thirds of its business was LTL freight.

The 1990s brought innovation. And then Yellow launched MyYellow.com in 2000, letting customers track shipments online – a major technological improvement. But starting in 1999 under CEO Bill Zollars, Yellow took a risky turn. Zollars wanted to build a unionized LTL empire, so in 2003, Yellow bought Roadway Corporation, the nation's largest LTL carrier, for $1.05 billion. The resulting company became Yellow Roadway Corporation. In 2005, it snatched up USF Corporation, adding more regional carriers. The moves made Yellow huge, with $6 billion in revenue, but they came at a cost – over $1 billion in debt.

Because of its acquisitions, Yellow Roadway changed its name to YRC Worldwide in January 2006. This name change was part of a broader rebranding strategy to emphasize the company's global logistics capabilities. However, the 2008 recession hit the company hard. YRC Worldwide's revenue plummeted 40% to $5.3 billion by 2009, and it lost $974 million that year. Lenders took 94% of its equity to erase $470 million in debt, and YRC Worldwide sold Glen Moore, its truckload unit, in 2011 to stay afloat. The company tried to recover, but its debt and union costs were crushing. In 2020, a $700 million federal loan gave YRC a lifeline.

The end came fast. In 2021, YRC Worldwide became Yellow Corporation again, aiming to unify its network under "One Yellow." But the Teamsters, representing 22,000 of Yellow's 30,000 workers, resisted. They blocked plans to modernize, accusing Yellow of mismanagement. In July 2023, Yellow missed a $50 million benefits payment, nearly sparking a strike. Customers panicked, fleeing to rivals like FedEx, and Yellow's freight volumes dropped 80% in a week. On July 30, 2023, Yellow shut down, laying off all 30,000 employees. On August 6, it filed for Chapter 11 bankruptcy – the biggest in U.S. trucking history – with $1.5 billion in debt.

The Teamsters blamed Yellow's "greedy executives," while Yellow pointed fingers at the union for blocking change. In truth, Yellow's downfall was years in the making and was caused by multiple factors – risky acquisitions, heavy debt, and an inflexible union model that couldn't survive in a deregulated world where non-union carriers thrived. Handling as much as 7% of the nation's LTL freight, Yellow's collapse left a void, raising shipping rates and costing thousands of jobs. Its story, from a single truck in 1924 to a bankrupt giant just shy of 100 years later, is a cautionary tale of ambition and lack of adaptation in the ever-changing world of freight.

EARLY BEGINNINGS: PRE-20TH CENTURY FOUNDATIONS

The trucking industry's origins trace back to ancient transportation systems. In civilizations such as Mesopotamia, Egypt, and Rome, oxen, horses, and mules transported commodities, including grain, spices, and textiles along trade routes. These early logistics networks established structured freight transportation, and enabled caravans to facilitate long-distance trade.

The Industrial Revolution in the 18th and 19th centuries enhanced wagon design. In North America, the Conestoga wagon, with its robust frame and canvas cover, became emblematic of frontier transportation. In Europe, comparable wagons bolstered trade. However, animal-powered transportation was constrained by the speed that the animals could move and was further impacted negatively by weather and animal stamina.

Railroads, emerging in the 1820s in England and the 1830s in the United States, surpassed wagons pulled by beasts of burden by providing swifter, more efficient long-haul freight movement. By the late 1800s, railroads dominated transportation, and relegated wagons to local deliveries. The invention of the internal combustion engine established the foundation for a transformative transportation era.

THE DAWN OF MOTORIZED TRUCKING: EARLY 20TH CENTURY

In the gritty dawn of 1919, Amos Carter, a Michigan grocer, cranked the engine of his second-hand Liberty Truck, its exhaust spitting as he loaded crates of apples bound for Chicago. A decade earlier, such a journey meant depending on a railroad's schedule or trusting a horse's plodding hooves. But Carter's truck, a surplus relic of World War I, roared past rail depots, its pneumatic tires – born from Roy Chapin's wartime ingenuity – gripping new highways funded by the 1916 Federal Aid Highway Act. The truck wasn't just a vehicle; it was emblematic of free enterprise, stitching together small-town markets with city hubs.

In 1896, Gottlieb Daimler's gasoline-powered truck had sparked a revolution, followed in 1900-1901 by Mack Trucks' and White Motor Company's urban haulers. By 1914, 100,000 trucks rattled across America's muddy roads, outpacing horse-drawn carts but dwarfed by railroads' long-haul might.

World War I changed that. Trucks, hauling munitions to French trenches, proved their mettle, exposing rail's limits. Post-war, surplus trucks flooded the market, and diesel engines and tractor-trailers brought new opportunities. By 1920, over one million trucks rolled across the United States, fueled by better roads and the rise of LTL operators, consolidating shipments in hub-and-spoke networks. Carter's delivery wasn't just apples – he delivered the future, a new supply chain unbound by tracks, rumbling toward a world of endless roads.

TRUCKING'S RESILIENCE AND REGULATION DURING THE GREAT DEPRESSION

The Great Depression (1929–1941) wreaked havoc on the U.S. economy, devastating the trucking industry as demand for freight plummeted. Small operators, unable to weather the crisis, faced widespread bankruptcies. Yet, trucking's adaptability and lower costs compared to railroads made it indispensable for transporting perishable goods, such as produce, sustaining supply chains through the economic turmoil. This resilience highlighted trucking's growing role in delivering goods swiftly and flexibly, even in dire times.

Before regulation, the trucking industry was chaotic, with volatile freight rates destabilizing markets. Small truckers, desperate to compete, slashed rates to undercut larger firms and railroads, often using old, poorly maintained trucks that broke down or posed safety risks. Inexperienced drivers, hired at low wages, caused delays and accidents, endangering lives and damaging cargo. These practices led to unpredictable costs and unreliable service, frustrating farmers and businesses dependent on consistent transport. Railroads, losing freight to cheap truckers, argued that such practices undermined public safety and economic stability, pushing for government intervention to level the playing field.

In response, railroad leaders lobbied Congress throughout the 1930s, citing trucking's low rates and lax safety standards as threats to equitable competition. Their efforts culminated in the Motor Carrier Act of 1935, which placed interstate trucking under the Interstate Commerce Commission (ICC), the same agency regulating railroads. The ICC required trucking companies to obtain permits, meet safety standards, and publish uniform rates, stabilizing the industry by reducing accidents and ensuring reliable deliveries. The Act also supported fairer wages for drivers, especially unionized ones, by curbing cutthroat competition. However, regulation came at a cost: permits were hard to secure, blocking new entrants, and small operators struggled with costly compliance. Railroads, hoping to limit trucking's flexibility, raised their own rates, impacting farmers still reeling from the Depression. While the Motor Carrier Act of 1935 fostered a safer, more dependable trucking industry, it favored large firms and stifled innovation, shaping supply chains for decades.

1935-1970s: THE GOLDEN AGE OF TRUCKING

Under the Motor Carrier Act of 1935 the ICC established a wide variety of trucking regulations, and mandated that new truckers obtain a "certificate of public convenience and necessity." This restricted competition, and rendered trucking highly lucrative for established carriers. The ICC's regulations prohibited other companies from transporting freight on routes already controlled by competitors, and further curtailed competition. Concurrently, these regulations elevated the trucking industry's status to that of a public utility, and conferred greater legitimacy upon it.

The LTL sector of the trucking industry became an indispensable component of the U.S. supply chain in the years following the Motor Carrier Act. LTL evolved from a fragmented, regional service into a structured, regulated sector, and was propelled by economic growth, infrastructure development, and regulatory transformations. The Act also legitimized LTL firms by establishing standards for rates and services, and fostered enhanced professionalism within the industry.

Carriers such as Yellow Freight System, McLean Trucking, Consolidated Freightways (CF), Old Dominion Freight Line, and others, played pivotal roles, and navigated labor challenges, fuel crises, and regulatory obstacles while capitalizing on post-World War II prosperity. The hub-and-spoke model became integral to LTL operations: local terminals (spokes) collected freight, transmitted it to central hubs for sorting, and redistributed it for delivery. This efficiency rendered LTL ideal for small and medium-sized enterprises, which typically handled shipments weighing between 150 and 15,000 pounds.

The post-World War II economic boom, coupled with the GI Bill and suburban expansion, stimulated demand for LTL services, as manufacturers and retailers required the transportation of smaller, more frequent shipments. The Interstate Highway System, being built out around the nation, further facilitated long-haul trucking by connecting cities and enhancing carrier efficiency while supporting the industry's growth.

During the 1970s new complexities developed in the LTL sector. The National Motor Freight Traffic Association (NMFTA), established in 1956, standardized LTL practices by establishing guidelines for pricing and packaging, which carriers widely adopted. However, the 1973 oil crisis escalated fuel costs, and compressed profit margins. Unionized carriers, such as Yellow Freight System and CF, confronted labor unrest. Deregulation loomed with the 1980 Motor Carrier Act, which would eventually relax ICC restrictions, but in the 1970s, carriers operated under stringent regulations, and were required to comply with rigorous operational standards.

During the 45 years that the trucking industry was regulated by the ICC, the LTL sector was a cornerstone of the supply chain. National carriers, such as Yellow, Roadway Express, and CF, led with expansive networks, while regional operators, including Old Dominion Freight Line, Ward Trucking, Southeastern Freight Lines, Watkins Motor Lines, New England Motor Freight, ABF Freight, Averitt Express, and Central Freight Lines, fulfilled critical niches. The postwar profitability, driven by economic growth and infrastructure development, established the foundation for the industry's modern era, despite the challenges of the 1970s. While many of the LTL carriers went out of business following deregulation, their legacies endure, and those that remain (and those that were founded after deregulation) continue to shape the efficient movement of goods across diverse markets.

DEREGULATION'S TRANSFORMATION OF LTL TRUCKING (1960s–2000s)

In the 1960s and 1970s, U.S. trucking expanded, but rigid ICC rules on routes and prices curbed innovation and increased costs for shippers. In 1980, President Jimmy Carter signed the Motor Carrier Act, lifting these restrictions. New carriers entered the market, setting their own rates and routes, igniting fierce competition. The number of U.S. trucking firms soared from roughly 20,000 in 1982 to over 500,000 by the early 2000s, streamlining supply chains with faster, more flexible delivery.

This competition hit unionized LTL carriers hard. Before 1980, the Teamsters union secured high wages and benefits for drivers at firms like Yellow and CF, sustained by fixed rates. After deregulation, non-union competitors offered lower prices, capturing customers. Union contracts, with steep wages and restrictive work rules—like limits on part-time labor—hindered these carriers' ability to adapt. By the late 1980s, many struggled financially or faced bankruptcy, and the Teamsters' influence waned as non-union drivers grew more common.

The 1980s brought a surge of mostly non-union carriers, doubling the number of licensed firms to over 40,000 by 1990. These low-cost competitors further pressured unionized carriers, who faced frequent labor disputes and strikes over contract changes. Economic challenges, including rising fuel costs and the 2008 recession, hit unionized firms harder than their non-union rivals, deepening their financial woes.

Over time, many unionized LTL carriers collapsed. CF went bankrupt in 2002, a major industry failure with 7,000 trucks. Yellow followed in 2023, burdened by $1.6 billion in debt. Meanwhile, non-union carriers like Old Dominion Freight Line and R+L Carriers thrived, leveraging lower costs to expand their supply chain roles. Unionized carriers, which held about 60% of the LTL market in the late 1970s, saw their share drop to 13% by 2002, with most large LTL bankruptcies post-1980 involving unionized firms.

While deregulation lowered shipping costs, benefiting supply chains, it devastated unionized workers and legacy carriers. Their rigid labor models buckled under the competitive pressure, revealing a divide between non-union winners and unionized losers. This mixed legacy challenges the notion that deregulation universally improved trucking, underscoring its complex impact on the industry.

THE RISE OF TRUCKLOAD TRUCKING

In contrast to the LTL sector post-deregulation, the truckload sector had fewer problems. Truckload carriers specialize in transporting full trailer loads for a single customer directly from origin to destination. This sector experienced remarkable growth after 1980, and transformed the logistics landscape in the United States. This period of rapid expansion was driven by a convergence of factors: trucking industry deregulation, the emergence of large national retail chains, and the substantial decline of union influence. These elements reshaped the supply chain, and created unprecedented opportunities for truckload (TL) carriers.

Deregulation eliminated barriers to entry, allowed new companies to join the market without ICC approval, and enabled carriers to establish their own rates and routes. The impact was immediate – the number of licensed carriers doubled from 20,690 in 1982 to over 40,000 by 1990. Most of these new entrants were small truckload carriers, often owner-operators with one or two trucks, who could now compete on price and service. This surge in competition reduced shipping rates; by 1985, TL rates had decreased by 20% in real terms – and rendered truckload services more attractive to shippers. Deregulation also facilitated greater efficiency for TL carriers, because they could now use direct routes without ICC-mandated detours, thereby diminishing fuel costs and delivery times.

The flexibility of the truckload model – delivering full loads directly without the consolidation required by LTL carriers – caused TL carriers to be particularly well-suited to the deregulated environment. Companies such as Schneider National, founded in 1935 but a prominent TL player by the 1980s, capitalized on this autonomy, and the company expanded its fleet to over 5,000 trucks by 1990. J.B. Hunt Transport Services, established in 1961, also emerged as a leader, and evolved from a modest rice hull hauler to a publicly traded company by 1983, with revenues of $150 million by the end of the decade. Deregulation unleashed a surge of innovation, as TL carriers adopted advanced technologies, such as satellite tracking and electronic data interchange (EDI), to enhance efficiency and customer service, while further propelling their growth.

As noted earlier, the 1980s and 1990s also witnessed the rapid proliferation of large national retail chains, such as Walmart, Target, and The Home Depot, which fundamentally altered the demand for freight transportation. These retailers revolutionized supply chains by implementing just-in-time (JIT) inventory practices, which necessitated frequent, reliable deliveries of full truckloads to distribution centers and stores across the country. Unlike LTL shipments, which involve multiple customers and stops, truckload deliveries were optimal for transporting substantial volumes of goods directly from suppliers to retail distribution hubs, and aligned seamlessly with the TL industry's capabilities.

Walmart, in particular, caused the transformation of the truckload sector. By 1990, Walmart had grown from a regional chain to a national powerhouse with over 1,500 stores, generating $26 billion in annual revenue. Its distribution model depended heavily on truckload carriers to transport goods from suppliers to its more than 20 distribution centers, which then supplied stores daily. This created an immense demand for TL services, as each distribution center required hundreds of full truckloads weekly. Walmart's emphasis on low costs also compelled carriers to offer competitive rates, a dynamic that deregulation enabled by permitting TL firms to undercut LTL carriers and railroads.

Other retailers followed suit. The Home Depot, which expanded to 100 stores by 1989, and Target, with 400 stores by 1990, also adopted centralized distribution models, and relied on truckload carriers to transport goods efficiently. The growth of these chains stimulated the development of dedicated TL services, wherein carriers, such as J.B. Hunt Transport Services and Schneider National, secured long-term contracts to provide consistent capacity for retailers. The symbiotic relationship between national retailers and TL carriers fueled the industry's expansion, with TL freight volume increasing from 2.5 billion tons in 1980 to 4 billion tons by 2000.

UNION DECLINE AND TL TRUCKING GROWTH

The decline of union influence in the trucking industry post-1980 was another pivotal factor in the truckload sector's rapid expansion. Prior to deregulation, the Teamsters represented approximately 60% of trucking workers, particularly in LTL companies. Union contracts ensured elevated wages and comprehensive benefits, while also imposing stringent work rules, which escalated operating costs. The union contracts and work rules severely hamstrung the carriers that had to comply with them.

However, deregulation severely disrupted the union influence. With rates now determined by market forces, unionized carriers struggled to compete against non-unionized TL firms, which could offer reduced prices due to their adaptable labor models. The collapse of unions lowered barriers to entry for new TL carriers, particularly owner-operators. By 1990, over 70% of TL carriers were non-unionized, and allowed them to hire drivers at market rates – often 20% to 30% less than union wages – and adjust staffing according to capacity demand. An example of a non-unionized, truckload carrier that was successful in the new environment is Schneider National, which increased its revenue from $100 million in 1980 to $1 billion by 1995, and leveraged its lower labor costs to secure contracts with major retailers, such as Walmart.

The post-1980 era also saw economic and technological transformations that amplified the TL industry's growth. The 1980s economic recovery, followed by the 1990s technology boom, heightened demand for freight, as manufacturing and consumer goods production surged. The North American Free Trade Agreement (NAFTA) in 1994 further augmented TL volumes by facilitating cross-border trade with Mexico and Canada.

Technological advancements played a crucial role. The adoption of onboard computers in the 1990s permitted TL carriers to optimize routes and track shipments in real-time, enhancing operational efficiency.

THE RISE AND CHALLENGES OF LONG-HAUL TRUCKING (1980s–2000s)

Long-haul trucking, spanning hundreds or thousands of miles to deliver goods, was once the trucking industry's most lucrative segment. After the 1980 Motor Carrier Act deregulated the industry, carriers thrived into the early 2000s, hauling automotive parts, apparel, and foodstuffs nationwide. Drivers earned high wages, outpacing slower railroads when alternative transport options were scarce. Owner-operators built prosperous livelihoods, and major carriers expanded vast long-haul fleets. Celebrated as the golden age of long-haul trucking, this era saw drivers as icons of the open road. Yet, from the 2000s onward, rising competition and changing business practices eroded profits, reshaping supply chain dynamics.

In the 1990s, long-haul trucking remained highly profitable, maximizing truck use over long distances and attracting skilled drivers. Carriers like U.S. Xpress Enterprises and Covenant Logistics dominated cross-country routes, serving manufacturers and importers from the West Coast to the South, Midwest, and East Coast. With U.S. factories still active, freight flowed steadily along Interstates 40 and 20, balanced in both directions. Growing trade with Mexico, especially for automotive components along Interstate 35, signaled new opportunities for carriers navigating an evolving global market.

The 1994 North American Free Trade Agreement (NAFTA) amplified this trend, boosting U.S.-Mexico cross-border commerce, particularly for automotive parts and produce. Carriers like Contract Freighters, Inc. (CFI) and Celadon Group seized these opportunities, with trade volume rising 20% from 1994 to 2000. However, U.S. carriers faced complex customs processes and competition from Mexican truckers offering lower rates due to cheaper labor. Safety and regulatory gaps, including Mexico's less stringent driver standards, sparked debates over cross-border access, delaying full NAFTA trucking integration until 2016. While NAFTA initially fueled profits for specialized carriers, it later intensified competition, pushing U.S. firms to invest in cross-border logistics or lose market share. Smaller operators struggled, fueling the industry's cycles of boom and bust.

INTERMODAL TRANSPORT'S CHALLENGE TO LONG-HAUL TRUCKING (2000s ONWARD)

Intermodal transport, combining trains and trucks, began eroding long-haul trucking's dominance in the early 2000s by offering cost savings and aligning with global trade trends. Containers move seamlessly from ships to trains to trucks, cutting expenses over long distances, as trains haul more cargo using less fuel than trucks. Railroads like Union Pacific and BNSF upgraded tracks and schedules, delivering faster, more reliable coast-to-coast services that undercut trucking rates. China's 2001 entry into the World Trade Organization (WTO) boosted intermodal rail use, as goods from Asian ports traveled by train across the U.S., reducing reliance on long-haul trucks.

This shift, driven by surging Asian imports and declining U.S. manufacturing, disrupted trucking's efficiency. Carriers hauled loaded trailers from West Coast ports, brimming with Chinese imports, but often returned empty, lacking westward cargo. Similar imbalances plagued U.S.-Mexico cross-border freight. Railroads, with lower operating costs per mile, gained an edge in these one-way flows. Containerization further favored rail by streamlining handling, minimizing damage or theft, and allowing sealed containers for inland transport—a preference for large retailers like Walmart managing vast distribution networks. While carriers like J.B. Hunt adapted by investing in intermodal services, generating significant revenue, others, like Celadon Group and CFI, struggled as NAFTA trade growth slowed. Celadon's 2019 bankruptcy underscored how these shifts reshaped supply chains, challenging traditional long-haul trucking.

TRUCKING'S TRANSFORMATION: DEREGULATION, TECHNOLOGY, AND MARKET VOLATILITY

The 1980 Motor Carrier Act revolutionized trucking by ending 45 years of ICC control over rates, routes, and freight types. While unionized LTL carriers struggled, truckload carriers thrived, and simplified brokerage licensing fueled growth. Firms like C.H. Robinson connected owner-operators with steady loads, fostering entrepreneurship despite volatile rates. Before 1980, fewer than 20,000 U.S. trucking firms operated under strict rules limiting backhauls, reducing the need for brokers. By May 2025, over 531,000 fleets were active, 99% with 100 or fewer trucks, creating a fragmented market where shippers, carriers, and brokers navigate diverse priorities.

By 1990, doubled carrier numbers and relaxed backhaul rules cut long-haul rates by an estimated 20%, boosting efficiency. Early brokerages like American Backhaulers (founded 1981, acquired by C.H. Robinson in 1999) helped small carriers secure profitable return loads. By 2000, brokers handled 6% of trucking shipments, a share that soared to 33% by the 2020s, reflecting their pivotal role in logistics. Modern brokers use technology and vast carrier networks to manage high-quality loads, supporting small fleets with sales and customer service—tasks most cannot handle alone.

FREIGHT BROKERS AS DAY TRADERS

Freight brokers operate like day traders in a high-stakes logistics market, selling trucking capacity to shippers often at fixed rates while buying it from carriers on the volatile spot market. This mirrors commodity trading, where brokers "buy low" from carriers at fluctuating spot rates—sometimes as low as $1.50 per mile during oversupply—and "sell high" to shippers under stable contract rates, pocketing margins of 10–20%. FreightWaves' SONAR platform provides real-time spot market data, enabling brokers to exploit rate swings, much like traders on Chicago's commodity floors. This fast-paced environment has cultivated a "bro culture" in trucking, attracting aggressive, risk-tolerant personalities akin to former commodity traders. Brokerages like TQL and Coyote (now RXO) target young, ambitious recruits, often ex-athletes or finance graduates, who thrive in the industry's competitive, testosterone-driven atmosphere, complete with open-plan offices and sales-driven incentives.

Brokers are critical in matching carriers with shippers, ensuring goods move efficiently, but their relationship with truckers is tense and co-dependent. While carriers haul freight, brokers move money, negotiating deals that can make or break a carrier's profitability. A broker might secure a $2,000 load for a shipper but pay a carrier $1,600, keeping the difference—a practice that frustrates drivers when rates are low. Carriers, especially small fleets without direct shipper contracts, rely on brokers for steady work, yet many resent lowball offers that cut into their margins. Despite this friction, brokers are indispensable, managing logistics complexities that keep supply chains fluid. Information gaps amplify these dynamics. SONAR's real-time data on supply, demand, and prices gives tech-savvy brokers an edge, while carriers often rely on outdated insights. Brokers, leveraging this data to match loads instantly, amplify volatility with their trading-like tactics, reshaping supply chain dynamics in an unpredictable market.

DIGITAL PLATFORMS DISRUPT LONG-HAUL TRUCKING

In the mid-2010s, venture capital firms discovered truck brokerage, investing billions into platforms like Convoy and Uber Freight to disrupt the market. These platforms offered shippers a digital interface to book freight, often at rates 10–20% lower than those of incumbent brokerages. The appeal was clear: streamlined booking and cost savings attracted major shippers seeking efficient supply chains. However, traditional brokerages like C.H. Robinson and Echo Global Logistics quickly developed or acquired similar technologies, leveling the playing field. The VC-backed platforms, despite early hype, struggled to achieve sustainable business models, as high operational costs and fierce competition eroded their margins.

CHANGING FREIGHT PATTERNS

By the 2020s, many goods traveled short-haul distances of 100–200 miles, driven by retail giants like Walmart and Amazon placing distribution centers near urban areas for faster deliveries, reducing long-haul demand by an estimated 15% from its 1980s peak. Long-haul drivers, paid per mile, earned less from shorter trips, while freight recessions in 2019 and 2022 drove up fuel, insurance, and repair costs. Owner-operators, facing slim margins, often took low-paying loads or exited the industry. Hours-of-service regulations, aimed at improving safety by limiting driving time, reduced flexibility, sometimes pressuring drivers to work fatigued to meet financial demands, underscoring long-haul's challenges in a technology-driven supply chain.

THE TRUCKING MARKET'S UNPREDICTABILITY

Since the 1980 Motor Carrier Act freed rates and routes, trucking prices have fluctuated like a stock market, driven by supply and demand. Rates shift daily based on load origins and market conditions, making trucking highly volatile. High demand raises rates, attracting new carriers; low demand lowers rates, risking bankruptcies. Economic shifts, trade policies, weather, and consumer trends fuel this instability. Social media and industry forums shape decisions, but the data surge since the 2000s has widened the gap between tech-equipped brokers and smaller carriers, intensifying market swings.

6

THE CONTAINER REVOLUTION

From dusty wagons to high-tech fleets, Chapter 5 explored how trucks became the backbone of domestic logistics. Chapter 6 delves into how standardized containers, moving seamlessly between ships, trains, and trucks, transformed global trade, shrinking distances and driving economic growth.

You've likely seen containers at a railroad crossing, waiting as a long line of railcars rolls by, or at a port, hoisted from ships by towering cranes. Trucks haul them too—cargo containers are ubiquitous along global shipping routes. Though rarely headline news, they quietly simplify our lives.

Welcome to container shipping, a system that has reshaped global trade in ways unimaginable a century ago. Standardized containers streamline the transport of goods, eliminating the need to handle individual items or adjust for varying sizes. This speeds up shipping, boosts profit margins, reduces cargo damage, and fuels globalization.

To grasp their impact, we'll start with the basics: what containerization is, its societal effects, and its challenges, including corporate control over capacity and pricing, as well as environmental concerns. With growing focus on cleaner fuels, containerization's future may be both more efficient and sustainable.

CONTAINERIZATION 101

Loading a truck—whether a pickup or a 53-foot trailer—takes effort to organize and secure cargo. For centuries, goods were shipped via "breakbulk" methods, handled item by item, loaded and unloaded piece by piece—a labor-intensive, time-consuming process. Ports relied on large workforces operating small cranes, securing nets, and lifting barrels, often performing hazardous tasks. Many workers belonged to longshoremen unions, some tied to organized crime, as depicted in the 1954 film On the Waterfront, inspired by The New York Sun's exposés of extortion and racketeering on New Jersey's docks.

This inefficiency, compounded by unionized labor and occasional corruption, made port operations costly. Companies faced high shipping fees, often passed to consumers, limiting exports and reducing import profitability. Containerization, emerging in the 1950s and expanding in the 1960s, changed that. Standardized containers replaced varied cargo shapes, enabling quick, uniform loading and unloading—like stacking LEGO bricks onto a ship. **[FIG 6-1]** Vessels could carry far more cargo than when goods were packed manually in mismatched containers. Mechanization reduced labor needs, making shipping faster, cheaper, and more reliable.

THE POWER OF INTERMODAL TRANSPORTATION

Containerization revolutionized global goods movement. Standardized containers pack large volumes into sealed units, unopened until their final destination, saving time, minimizing damage or theft, and enhancing efficiency. This behind-the-scenes system keeps the modern world running, often unnoticed until disruptions occur.

Its strength lies in seamless transitions between transport modes. A container can travel by ship, train, and truck without unpacking.

Imagine a container leaving Shanghai's port, rolling onto a train in Los Angeles, then reaching a Chicago warehouse by truck—all without touching its contents. This reduces delays, speeds deliveries, and bolsters supply chain reliability.

As global trade expanded post-1950s, containerization slashed shipping costs by nearly half by the 1990s, enabling just-in-time production and connecting Asian factories to North American and European markets. This fueled post-Cold War economic growth, lifting millions from poverty by linking more nations to trade. Today, over 90% of non-bulk goods move in containers, with ports like Singapore, Los Angeles, and Rotterdam handling millions annually.

Intermodal systems enhance resilience. During the COVID-19 pandemic, when ports faced delays, businesses rerouted shipments via trains and trucks. In 2021, the Suez Canal blockage prompted some cargo to shift to transcontinental rail routes across Europe and Asia. Amid U.S.-China trade tensions, companies relocated manufacturing to Mexico, using intermodal transport to reach U.S. markets. This adaptability mitigates global disruptions.

Intermodal transport evolves with technology. Smart sensors enable real-time container tracking, while electric trains and low-emission trucks cut environmental impact, critical as transportation accounts for ~30% of global emissions. As climate change and geopolitics shape trade, intermodal systems will remain vital for efficient, sustainable supply chains.

RAILROADS PLAY A KEY ROLE IN CONTAINER MOVEMENTIZATION

Railroads have also taken advantage of containerization, and intermodal rail freight plays a major role in modern supply chains. Intermodal containers have been increasingly transported along rail lines that historically were dedicated to industrial, commodity, and/or agricultural supply chains. As railroads handle lower volumes of coal and steel, they have shifted to transporting containers holding consumer and retail merchandise. Additionally, railroads have negotiated strategic partnerships with some of the largest trucking carriers in the U.S., which have simplified pricing negotiations.

Intermodal rail is cheaper than trucking – sometimes costing 20% to 50% less per ton-mile. The longer the distance, the greater the savings between rail and trucking.

Railroads are the optimal way to transport containers across the country. Trains can carry hundreds of containers in a single trip, are more fuel-efficient than trucks and produce fewer emissions per ton moved. The longer the distance, the greater rail's savings are over trucking.

For these reasons, intermodal rail is especially valuable when companies need to build up reserves of critical materials, a strategy known as "just-in-case" inventory. For example, retailers like Walmart use rail to move goods from West Coast ports to inland distribution centers, cutting costs while keeping their supply chains reliable.

Intermodal rail can also function as a kind of moving warehouse. Containers on trains provide secure storage while in transit, allowing companies to keep inventory flowing without relying on extra warehouse space. This approach proved useful in 2024, when companies began bracing for a potential Trump victory and the threat of renewed trade tensions with China. Anticipating possible tariffs or restrictions, many firms imported record volumes of goods – not for immediate use, but to prestock. In this case, intermodal rail offered two advantages: it served as a low-cost storage option and reduced transportation expenses compared to trucking.

By combining affordability with flexibility, intermodal rail has become a key part of making supply chains more resilient and better prepared for whatever comes next.

TRACKING CONTAINERS IS NOW COMMON-PLACE

During the last decade, the ability to watch and monitor containers has become more important to shipping companies. Containers have numbers assigned to them, along with electronic data connections. This allows the location of each container to be tracked and reported in real time if necessary. Important milestones in a shipment's journey, such as being cleared for pickup at a container terminal or being loaded onto a vessel, are increasingly updated automatically. Large importers monitor port conditions in near real-time so they can redirect shipments if needed to avoid congestion or delays. They also study the efficiency of their transportation providers and of their own facilities. Advancements in technology have made it possible to track shipments at nearly every point along the supply chain, and there are fewer "black holes" compared to several years ago. When the information is integrated into a data system, the results can be powerful. An alert from a visibility provider can set off a chain of events without human intervention. As such, transportation providers can dedicate their operation teams toward more pressing situations that need human intervention.

CHANGES FOR GOOD

Ports look very different today than they did in the 1950s and early 1960s. These busy gateways of international trade now require far fewer workers to operate effectively. They are also less crowded, thanks to specialized terminals with container cranes and storage yards that make handling containers fast and efficient. This speed and organization help reduce delays and traffic congestion.

In recent years, technology has further accelerated the movement of containerized goods. Automation, using machines instead of people to perform tasks, plays a major role. At many ports, robots now handle the loading and unloading of containers. Advanced tracking systems help manage inventory and monitor shipments. These tools speed loading and unloading, reduce mistakes, improve accuracy, and make the shipping process more streamlined.

Containerization has also significantly reduced costs. When the concept was introduced more than 60 years ago, it brought the cost of loading or unloading a ship down by 97% – from $5.86 per ton to just $0.16 per ton. When containers continue their journey by train or truck, the savings increase even further, since the container is not opened until it reaches a warehouse or distribution center.

From a global perspective, containerization has helped countries and regions specialize in the products they produce most efficiently.

A region can focus on manufacturing a specific item and send it anywhere in the world at a relatively low cost. Because shipping is more affordable, international markets have become more accessible. Trade is no longer limited to luxury items for the wealthy. Today, everyday consumer goods can be traded globally and reach a much wider audience.

For American consumers, containerization and intermodal shipping have made it easier to access a wide range of imported products. By purchasing goods from countries with lower labor costs, households can stretch their budgets and improve their standard of living. Furniture, clothing, electronics, and many other common items are now produced overseas. A walk through any home quickly reveals how deeply global supply chains are woven into daily life.

THE ERA OF ENORMOUS CONTAINER SHIPS

The rise of massive container ships has launched a new era in global shipping, revolutionizing ocean transport. In 1984, the largest ships held 4,500 TEUs (twenty-foot equivalent units, the standard measure for a twenty-foot container); since 2018, new vessels have grown to carry over 20,000 TEUs, a fivefold increase that dwarfs earlier designs. Driven by economic and competitive pressures, these mega-ships reshape port operations, infrastructure needs, and trade patterns, embodying the bold ambitions of leading shipping lines.

PORT UPGRADES AND OPERATIONAL CHALLENGES

Accommodating these giant vessels demands major port upgrades worldwide. Channels are dredged deeper to handle their bulk, requiring costly excavation. Taller cranes unload towering container stacks, and improved rail connections move shipments inland swiftly. These investments, often costing hundreds of millions, are essential for ports to stay competitive and attract mega-ship traffic.

Yet, mega-ships' unwieldy, top-heavy design makes them prone to instability in storms or rough seas, where high winds or waves can jeopardize crew and containers. Despite these risks, their economic benefits are significant, carrying vast volumes with fewer crew members to cut labor costs and boosting revenue per voyage. However, their size triggers uneven container flows, overwhelming ports and causing congestion. In 2021–2022, over 100 ships queued offshore at Los Angeles and Long Beach, a bottleneck echoed at East Coast ports as routes shifted. Data shows delays when thousands of containers unload at once, straining terminal operations.

Only ports equipped for their scale can host mega-ships, concentrating traffic at hubs like Singapore and Rotterdam. This stresses infrastructure beyond terminals, affecting warehouses, distribution centers, rail ramps, and drayage truck operators. Smaller ports, unable to support these vessels, lose trade to urban centers, reshaping regional economies.

THE SHIPPING ARMS RACE

Leading shipping lines are in an "arms race" to build larger vessels, vying for market share. Bigger ships carry more containers per trip, increasing revenue and strengthening control over trade routes and pricing in a cutthroat industry. Firms like Hapag-Lloyd and Evergreen spend over $200 million per vessel, banking on long-term contracts with retailers and manufacturers to cement dominance.
[**FIG 6-2**, PG. 110]

Critics warn that this trend worsens port congestion and burdens local budgets, as ports compete with costly upgrades to lure shipping lines. Cargo concentration at hubs creates supply chain bottlenecks, delaying goods to warehouses and rail ramps. Drayage truckers face congestion, raising delivery costs and times, as seen in Los Angeles and Long Beach during 2021–2022.

SMALLER PORTS AND SPECIALIZED TRADE

Smaller ports, unable to host mega-ships, focus on smaller vessels—still larger than those of 25 years ago—and niche cargoes. The Port of Baltimore, for example, imports automobiles, farm machinery, and bulk commodities like salt, while exporting coal and vehicles. The Port of Oakland handles electronics, furniture, and batteries as imports, and agricultural products like nuts and wine as exports. These ports remain key trade hubs despite missing mega-ship traffic.

DANGERS AHEAD

Mega-ships drive efficiency but strain global logistics, causing port congestion and limiting access to key waterways like the Suez and Panama Canals, where some vessels are too large to pass. Industry consolidation amplifies these challenges. Exempt from U.S. antitrust laws under the 1984 Shipping Act, major container lines have acquired rivals, with the top 10 controlling 85% of global capacity by 2025—surpassing OPEC's 40% oil market share.

Shipping alliances, agreements to coordinate schedules and cap capacity, consolidate power further. By using "blank sailings"—cancelling voyages for half-empty ships—alliances maintain high rates, a practice since the 1990s. The U.S. government accuses alliances of cartel-like price-fixing, harming businesses and consumers. The 2022 Ocean Shipping Reform Act expanded the Federal Maritime Commission's (FMC) authority to probe late fees and cargo refusals but lacks antitrust enforcement power.

As the world's largest container importer, the U.S. is a minor player in shipping, with no top-20 global carriers. Matson, the largest U.S.-based carrier, ranks 28th, holding under 0.2% of global capacity. Foreign giants dominate: China's state-owned COSCO, the fourth-largest, plans military use of ships in wartime, while Denmark's Maersk, the second-largest, drives 15% of its nation's GDP. This leaves the U.S. vulnerable to disruptions, as conflicts could restrict access to vessels for essential goods, exposing a critical weakness in global supply chains.

THE ESCALATING VULNERABILITY OF CONTAINER SHIPPING: A DECADE OF EVOLVING THREATS

In the early 2010s, attacks by Somali pirates off the Horn of Africa were the primary threat to container shipping. Between 2005 and 2011, Somali pirates seized 149 ships and over 3,700 crew members, extracting ransoms estimated at over $300 million. These attacks, often executed with small boats, AK-47s, and rocket-propelled grenades, targeted vessels in the Gulf of Aden and Indian Ocean. Pirates exploited the region's weak governance and proximity to critical shipping lanes, such as the Suez Canal, through which 12% to 15% of global trade passes.

The industry responded effectively. International naval coalitions, including contributions from the U.S., China, and the EU, launched counter-piracy operations like Operation Atalanta, reducing incidents significantly by 2014. Ship operators adopted Best Management Practices (BMP), such as high-speed transits, armed guards, and long-range acoustic devices, to deter boardings.

However, vulnerabilities persist. Somali pirates accessed navigational data online, exploiting Automatic Identification Systems to track vessels. While these attacks were low-tech compared to today's threats, they exposed the industry's reliance on predictable routes and limited onboard defenses. The success of counter-piracy measures masked underlying risks, as the industry remained unprepared for more sophisticated threats emerging from geopolitical conflicts.

THE RISE OF HOUTHI ATTACKS: A NEW PARADIGM OF THREAT

Since November 2023, Yemen's Houthi rebels have launched over 130 attacks on commercial ships in the Red Sea, using drones, anti-ship ballistic missiles (ASBMs), and cruise missiles, severely disrupting maritime trade. Unlike Somali pirates seeking ransoms, the Iranian-backed Houthis claim solidarity with Palestinians in Gaza, targeting vessels linked to Israel. In reality, their strikes hit ships from over 40 nations indiscriminately, sinking two, killing four crew members, and seizing the Galaxy Leader in November 2023, still held off Yemen's Hodeidah port.

The Houthis' advanced arsenal, supplied by Iran and aided by Hezbollah's intelligence, marks a leap in maritime threats. ASBMs like the 'Asef' and 'Tankil'—potentially the first used in combat—along with drones, cruise missiles, and unmanned surface vehicles (USVs), enable precise, long-range strikes at sea. The July 2024 attack on the container ship Pumba with a USV highlights their ability to target vessels far from shore, unlike pirates' limited reach. **[FIG 6-3]**

Geospatial intelligence, reportedly from China's Chang Guang Satellite Technology Corporation and Russia's GRU, extends attacks into the Arabian Sea and Indian Ocean, endangering crews and cargo.

These at-sea assaults have crippled trade routes, slashing Suez Canal transits by an estimated 72% and Bab al-Mandab Strait traffic by over 60% from November 2023 to November 2024. Major carriers like Maersk and Hapag-Lloyd reroute around the Cape of Good Hope, adding 7–14 days and up to 47% to transit times from Southeast Asia to Europe. Container rates from China to Europe have soared from $1,000 to over $4,700, with Red Sea insurance premiums spiking 250% for some ships. Factory shutdowns, notably in automotive sectors, and strained supply chains underscore the crisis's toll on maritime logistics.

Israel's June 2025 airstrikes on Iran's nuclear and military sites, killing commanders and scientists, have escalated tensions, threatening Red Sea and Persian Gulf shipping. Iran's retaliatory missile strikes on Israel, combined with its control over the Strait of Hormuz—handling 20% of global oil and significant container traffic—raise fears of further maritime disruptions. If Iran or its proxies, like the Houthis, target vessels in response, shipowners may avoid these waters, effectively slowing or halting trade, as seen with Houthi attacks. The Persian Gulf's Jebel Ali port, a transshipment hub, faces risks, potentially bottlenecking South Asia and East Africa trade. This vulnerability, unprecedented in recent decades, is heightened by a new era of kinetic conflict at sea. Rising geopolitical rivalries, proxy wars, and advanced weaponry make maritime attacks more likely, endangering crews, inflating costs, and destabilizing supply chains critical to global trade.

MILITARY-GRADE TECHNOLOGIES: A GAME-CHANGER

The technologies and weaponry used by the Houthis pose challenges for commercial shipping, which lacks defenses against missiles or drones. Unlike warships equipped with advanced missile systems, merchant vessels rely on passive measures like citadels or water cannons, ineffective against high-altitude ASBMs. The U.S.-led

Operation Prosperity Guardian and EU's Operation Aspides have intercepted many Houthi weapons, but their defensive posture cannot protect every ship, forcing rerouting. U.S. and UK strikes on Houthi targets, including over 60 sites in January 2024, have degraded some capabilities but failed to deter attacks, as the Houthis' cost-benefit calculus favors low-cost drones over expensive naval defenses.

RESURGENT PIRACY AND EMERGING THREATS

While Houthi attacks dominate headlines, piracy has resurfaced. In December 2023, Somali pirates hijacked the bulk carrier Ruen, the first successful hijacking since 2017, followed by three attacks in January 2024. The Houthis' alliances with al-Shabaab and Somali pirate networks, providing financial and logistical support, have revitalized piracy along Red Sea and Indian Ocean routes. These groups exploit the chaos of Houthi attacks, increasing risks for vessels avoiding rerouting.

Cyber threats also compound vulnerabilities. In 2017, a German container ship's navigation system was hacked, rendering it uncontrollable for 10 hours, and the 2018 ransomware attack on Maersk's 'Petya' caused $300 million in damages. GPS jamming and AIS spoofing, reported in the Strait of Hormuz and Red Sea, disrupt navigation, exposing ships to attacks. These cyber risks, absent a decade ago, amplify physical threats, as vessels' reliance on connected systems creates new vulnerabilities.

COMPARING VULNERABILITIES: THEN AND NOW

For the reasons outlined above, container shipping is significantly more vulnerable today than a decade ago. Somali piracy, while disruptive, was manageable due to naval patrols and onboard defenses, with attacks confined to specific regions. Houthi attacks, leveraging military-grade technologies and geopolitical motives, are harder to deter, affecting a broader area and critical chokepoints like the Red Sea. The economic impact is stark – piracy in the early 2010s cost $300 million in ransoms over six years, while Houthi attacks have cost global trade $200 million daily since 2023.

The industry's reliance on just-in-time delivery exacerbates these vulnerabilities. Rerouting adds delay and cost, disrupting supply chains for electronics, automotive parts, and consumer goods. Piracy was a relatively localized issue; today's threats are intertwined with global conflicts, involving state actors like Iran and non-state groups with advanced weaponry. The lack of anti-missile defenses on commercial ships and the high cost of naval escorts leave the industry exposed.

NAVIGATING NEW RISKS: THE IMPACT OF CONTAINER SHIPPING VULNERABILITIES ON GLOBAL SUPPLY CHAINS

The escalating vulnerabilities of container shipping will significantly re-shape global supply chains in the coming years. With over 90% of global trade dependent on maritime routes, disruptions from military-grade technologies like ASBMs and drones pose unprecedented risks. Companies must now account for potential cargo delays, seizures, or losses when planning logistics.

This uncertainty is driving further interest in domestic sourcing and nearshoring strategies. Businesses are reevaluating long-distance supply chains, prioritizing proximity to minimize exposure to geopolitical conflicts and piracy. Calculating these risks involves assessing transit times, costs, and the reliability of routes through chokepoints like the entrance to the Red Sea. As companies invest in regional manufacturing hubs, particularly in North and South America, this shift could reshape trade patterns, enhance resilience, and mitigate the economic impact of maritime threats, ensuring supply chains remain robust amid growing global instability.

CLEANER AND HEALTHIER SHIPPING INITIATIVES

Historically, ships have used marine fuel, which contains a high level of sulfur. When burned, sulfur dioxide is released into the atmosphere and has a significant impact on the environment. This fuel is a major contributor to air pollution and can cause acidification of oceans, thereby harming marine life. It also leads to acid rain, which harms ecosystems, damages crops, and corrodes buildings and infrastructure. In addition, it is detrimental to human health and can lead to respiratory problems, especially for individuals with pre-existing conditions such as asthma.

In response to these damaging emissions, the International Maritime Organization (IMO), an agency of the United Nations, introduced a new set of global rules for ships that took effect in 2020. The purpose of the regulations is to reduce the amount of pollution that ships release into the atmosphere and sea and the damage they do to the environment. The rules limit the sulfur content of fuel used by ships to 0.50% mass by mass (m/m). This is a reduction from the previous limit of 3.50% m/m in most areas. The regulations also encourage the use of cleaner fuels, including low-sulfur marine fuels, or alternative technologies. These alternatives are primarily exhaust gas cleaning systems, often called "scrubbers," that remove sulfur dioxide from ship emissions.

An unanticipated outcome of the IMO 2020 regulations was a surge in radiant heat reaching the oceans and increasing their temperatures. While harmful in the ways described above, the sulfur dioxide that was in maritime fuel had a cooling effect, creating a layer in the atmosphere that kept some sunlight from reaching the oceans. The reduction in sulfur emissions has enabled a greater percentage of sunlight to reach the oceans, causing significant warming.

As ocean shipping companies work to meet the requirements of the IMO regulations, it's also likely that consumers will continue to buy goods from abroad, which in turn will continue to drive demand for shipping. Containerization and intermodal shipping have changed the way that goods are packaged and sent, all while reducing the manpower required to handle them and speeding up the delivery process.

From container ships crossing oceans to trucks navigating local roads, intermodal shipping has created global supply chains that deliver goods with unprecedented efficiency. Yet, as deglobalization and geopolitical tensions reshape trade, new policies are altering how these goods flow. In future chapters, the evolving challenges of global commerce in an era of tariffs and protectionism will be examined.

CONTAINER FREIGHT (MILLIONS OF TONS)

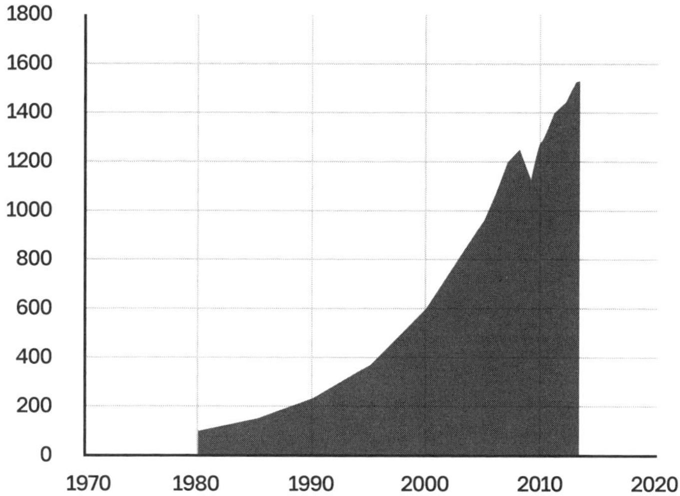

SOURCE: UNITED NATIONS CONFERENCE ON TRADE AND DEVELOPMENT

FIG 6-1

HOUTHI REBEL ATTACKS ON RED SEA SHIPPING VESSELS

Incidents from November 19, 2023 - June 15, 2024

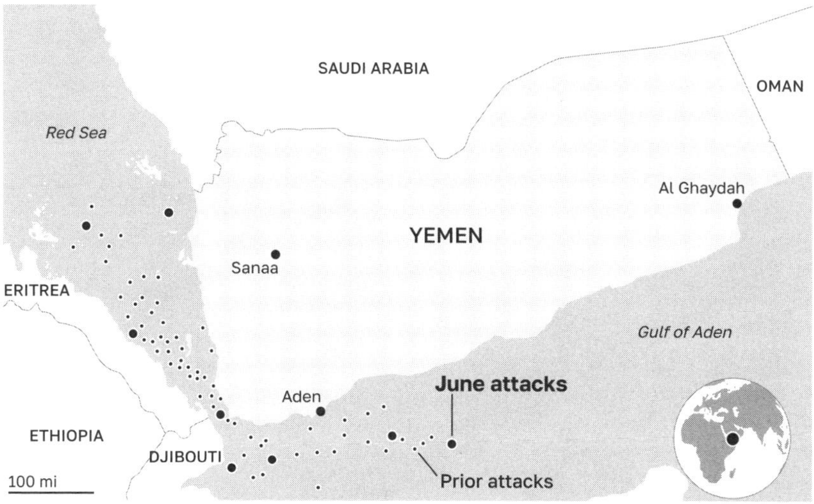

SOURCE: JOINT MARITIME INFORMATION CENTER

FIG 6-3

50 YEARS OF CONTAINER SHIP GROWTH

Container-carrying capacity has increased by approximately 1,200% since 1968

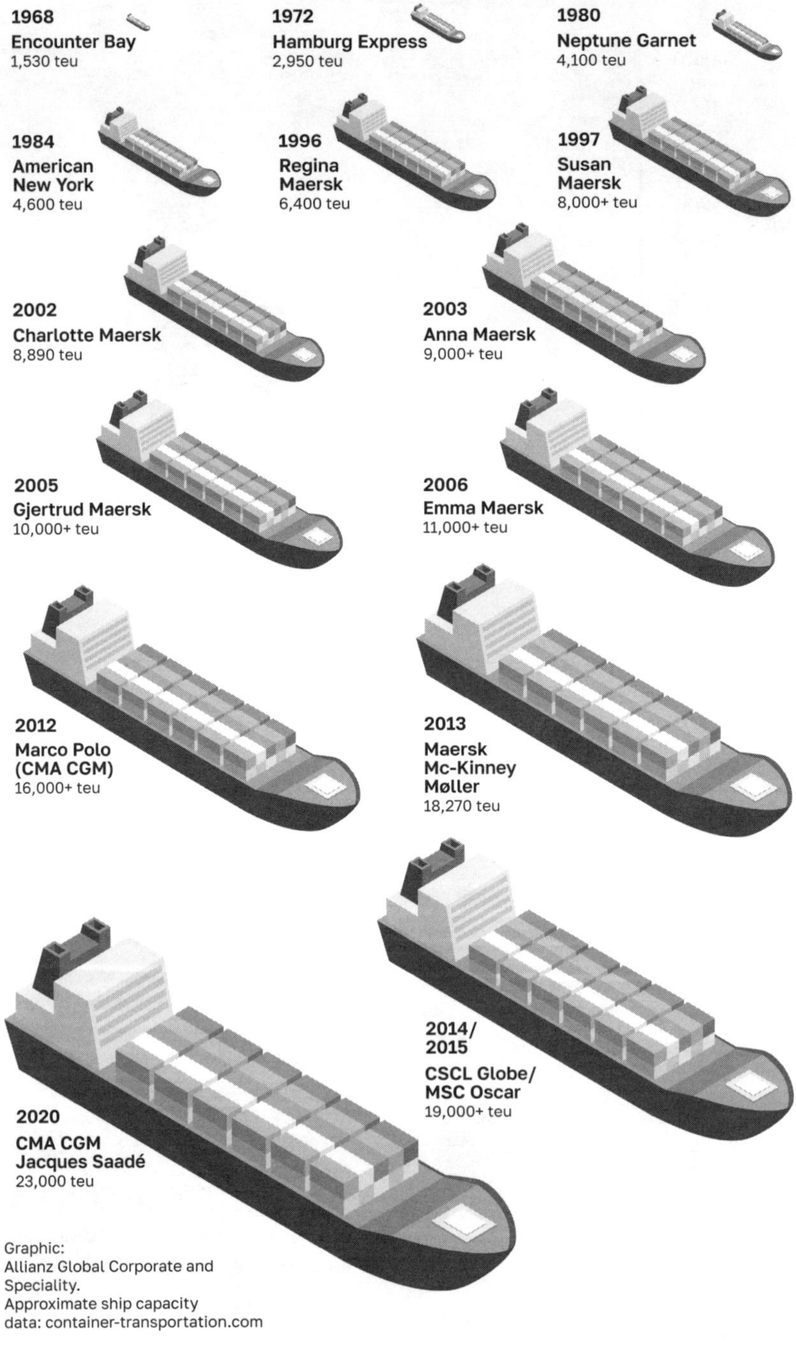

Graphic: Allianz Global Corporate and Speciality. Approximate ship capacity data: container-transportation.com

FIG 6-2

7

REFRIGERATION: THE UNSUNG HERO OF MODERN SOCIETY

As containers revolutionized global trade, moving goods seamlessly from ships to trains to trucks, another quiet hero ensured their freshness and safety – refrigeration. Chapter 6 showed how containerization shrank the world, enabling efficient transport of perishables. Now, Chapter 7 reveals how cooling technology, from ancient ice houses to modern freezers, transformed supply chains, diets, and lifestyles, making fresh food and comfortable living accessible year-round.

In February 2020, I saw signs of trouble in the global food supply chain. FreightWaves reported COVID-19 was causing chaos in Asia and Europe. Beyond the health crisis, I knew the U.S. food supply was at risk. Countries were closing borders, and trade routes were shutting down, threatening food deliveries. Shortages in my area seemed certain – not if, but when. To prepare, my wife and I bought 40 cases of rice and a large freezer for our garage. We stocked a year's worth of meat, fish, vegetables, and fruit to feed our (then) three children through potential disruptions. While grocery stores still looked normal, with full shelves of produce and meat, our relatives thought we were overreacting. To them, our stockpiling seemed unnecessary, but we were ready for the supply chain challenges that were on the horizon.

By April 2020, COVID-19 had disrupted North America's food supply chain. Shortages struck the U.S. that summer, with media highlighting the struggling trade network. As my family used our stockpiled food, relatives who once doubted us began to respect our foresight. When food is abundant, its source is rarely considered. You might take orange juice or grapes from the refrigerator no matter the season, or buy various fresh ingredients at a store. This convenience depends on refrigeration, a cornerstone of modern supply chains, like Rome's grain system more than 2,000 years ago. Cooling slows the growth of bacteria, preserving food and reducing spoilage, so households don't have to rely on local farms (unless they choose to do so). Refrigeration also enables global transport of medicines and vaccines, and air-conditioned homes and businesses improve comfort. Over the past 200 years, refrigerators replaced iceboxes, revolutionizing diets and trade. Meat, produce, and flowers now ship worldwide, making the term "in season" obsolete. Refrigeration has shaped modern diets and changed the way we live and work.

FROM ANCIENT TO MODERN TIMES

Civilizations from the past used various methods to chill and preserve food. Ice was often harvested from cold regions and stored in cellars or insulated buildings. Around 1775 BCE, the Sumerians, a civilization in southern Mesopotamia that flourished from 4100 to 1750 BCE, built "ice houses." These structures featured intricate drainage systems and shallow pools where water could freeze at night. While effective, the method had limitations. In warm weather, ice was brought out and sold to consumers and businesses, but outside its designated cooling spaces, ice melted quickly, losing its usefulness. In many areas, only the wealthy could afford ice due to the

labor involved in harvesting, storing, and delivering it.

These practices persisted until the early 1800s, when Thomas Moore invented the icebox. Moore, a farmer and cabinetmaker from Philadelphia, designed an oval cedar tub with a lid, lined with a tin chamber. Rabbit fur insulated the exterior, and ice was placed between the wood and the inner chamber. The icebox kept goods like butter cold, allowing Moore to transport cooled goods from his Maryland farm to sell in markets in the Georgetown area of the District of Columbia.

At that time, the icebox was truly revolutionary. It created a portable cool environment for food and medicine, extending storage and transport times. The byproduct, water, was also useful during hot summers.

As a result, ice grew in popularity as a tradable commodity. In the late 1800s, particularly from the 1830s to the 1870s, natural ice ranked as the second-largest U.S. export by value, behind cotton. Harvested from frozen lakes and rivers, primarily in New England, ice was shipped domestically and internationally to places like the Caribbean, South America, and even India. Entrepreneurs like Frederic Tudor, known as the "Ice King," pioneered this trade, making ice a valuable commodity for preserving food and cooling drinks in warmer climates. (Imagine the buzz on X if ice markets still existed – it would redefine a "cooling" or "hot" market!).

A series of inventions starting in the 1800s ushered in modern refrigeration. In 1834, American Jacob Perkins invented a machine using a vapor compression cycle to cool temperatures. In 1876, German engineer Carl von Linde patented a process for liquefying gases, a cornerstone of refrigeration technology. In 1913, American Fred Wolf invented the first home electric refrigerator, featuring a cooling unit atop an icebox. By 1918, American William Durant began mass-producing electric refrigerators, marking the dawn of a new era.

THE WORKINGS OF A REFRIGERATOR

Interestingly, the technology behind the refrigerator, in its basic form, has remained the same for the last century. A refrigerator functions on the principles of thermodynamics, and specifically the transfer of heat. The appliance removes heat from its interior and pushes it to the surrounding environment, thereby lowering the inside temperature.

The refrigerator contains a refrigerant, which is a substance with a low boiling point. In today's world, you'll often find refrigerants such as hydrofluorocarbons (HFCs) or hydrochlorofluorocarbons (HCFCs).

At the heart of the refrigerator system is the compressor. This is typically located at the back of the refrigerator. It uses energy to compress the refrigerant into gas, thereby raising its pressure and temperature. The gas, in turn, flows into the condenser, which is usually located on the back or bottom of the appliance. The condenser consists of a set of coils with fins that help dissipate heat.

As the refrigerant cools, it condenses into a high-pressure liquid. It then passes through the expansion valve, which is also called a throttle or metering device. The expansion valve reduces the pressure of the refrigerant, which causes it to quickly expand. The expansion, in turn, creates a drop in temperature.

The cold refrigerant then enters the evaporator located inside the refrigerator. The evaporator is a set of coils or tubes that are in contact with the interior space of the unit. There, the refrigerant evaporates into a low-pressure gas. In doing so, it absorbs heat from the interior, making it cool. The heat energy is transferred from the food and items inside the refrigerator to the evaporator coils. The low-pressure gas refrigerant then returns to the compressor, and the cycle begins again. The compressor increases the pressure and temperature of the gas, which restarts the cooling process.

While this fundamental technology and the thermodynamic principles behind it haven't changed in the last 100 years, there have been other advances. These tend to focus on design and energy efficiency. Modern refrigerators have updated features like fans to better circulate the air. There are mechanisms in place to better control the temperature. High-end defrosting systems keep food better preserved and reduce energy use. Some newer models have wi-fi capabilities and AI tools to help monitor inventory and plan meals.

THE REFRIGERATED SUPPLY CHAIN

I eat sushi about four times a week and consider tuna and salmon my go-to orders. Since I live in Tennessee, all the fish that I consume comes from faraway locations. Thinking about the path from its origin to my doorstep can give us a revealing look into the cold supply chain.

After being pulled from the ocean, fish like tuna and salmon are placed in the fishing boats' holds that are full of ice. They are then transported to a harbor, where they are transferred to a freezer. There, the fish is stored in a way to protect it from spoiling. It is then sent to a processing facility where it is butchered and prepared for shipment. The processed fish is then taken – often by air – to a regional distribution center. From that point, it is delivered by truck to my local grocery store (or sushi restaurant, as the case may be).

This process is only possible because of the power of refrigeration. Cooling technology has drastically changed the makeup of the global diet. Vegetables and fruit that are not in season in one region can simply be delivered from another place. Due to consumer demand and accessible pricing, refrigeration has made global food trade both possible and profitable.

The ability to cool and preserve food has transformed societies worldwide in unexpected ways. Traditional diets were often shaped by geographic limitations. Japan's centuries-long ban on beef, the evolution of European diets with refrigeration, and the development of the modern American diet all reflect the profound impact of cooling technology.

THE 1200-YEAR BAN

Whether it's a Kobe filet or Wagyu served teppanyaki style, Japanese beef has a certain level of prestige among meat eaters. The ingredient dominates the menu of Japanese restaurants around the world. Beef is both popular and prevalent in the country. I personally enjoy it and am fascinated by its preparation techniques.

Notably, beef was not always part of the Japanese diet. In fact, for twelve centuries all forms of meat were banned in the country. The only exception to this rule was seafood. The rule began around 675 CE and remained in place for nearly 1,200 years. It was based on both a belief system and for practical reasons. Japan comprises a number of islands in the Pacific Ocean; it was easy to access a variety of fish and preserve them, thus making fish a staple of the Japanese diet. Meat was hard to come by and based on religious beliefs that all living beings were sacred, was prohibited from consumption.

However, in 1872, the Emperor of Japan announced that he had eaten meat. This proclamation effectively ended the 1,200-year ban on its consumption. It also caused a huge stir. Buddhist monks, who held to the belief that all living animals were sacred and should not be killed, were particularly aggravated. Ten of them broke into the Imperial Palace and attempted to kill the emperor. They feared a meat-eating hysteria would change Japanese culture.

While beliefs certainly played a role in this decision, the geography of the country reveals another aspect to this story. As an island nation, Japan has very limited land available for farming and ranching. Only 20% of the country is suitable for cultivation. Since grazing animals require land – not to mention that they consume a vast quantity of resources – it hasn't always made economic sense to devote a large portion of land to raising livestock.

Thus, the country's population spent centuries abstaining from meat – while also fighting a series of Medieval civil wars. The nation didn't trade actively with other countries during this time; it was absorbed with internal events. Japan and the Japanese people remained isolated, and their diets reflected this.

All that changed after the emperor ate beef. The Japanese had been closed off from the outside world for centuries by then. However, that began to change in 1853. That year, U.S. Navy Captain Matthew Calbraith Perry led an expedition to Japan's harbors. He delivered a letter from President Millard Fillmore stating the U.S. was eager to break Japan's "seclusion policies" and "open" the nation to trade with the Western world.

The event brought an internal crisis for the emperor and his people, who had long avoided outside contact. It was feared that such contact would create internal disorder. However, with Perry's arrival, they were left with little choice. Trading with the West began.

With these new connections, Japan no longer faced the constraints of only consuming what could be produced locally or harvested from the sea. The trading that followed introduced new food items to the country. Many of these new foods came aboard ships packed with ice. Therefore, imports were incredibly expensive and inaccessible for most Japanese, who couldn't afford the luxury of these imports.

Over the following decades, that changed because of refrigeration. The new cooling technology democratized the food trade. With these advances, prices on many items dropped, including meat. Japanese markets could access beef from around the world, including Australia and the Americas, where there was more land for grazing and meat production.

Refrigeration, coupled with the shift to eating meat, caused further changes for Japan's cattle industry. Traditionally, cattle had been raised in Japan solely for labor purposes. They were used to work the land, pull logs out of forests, and transport goods and people.

LEANING INTO LIVESTOCK

While I am drawn to the Japanese diet, my roots are European. This continent also has remarkable ties to the cold supply chain and its impact. Before refrigeration, the people living in Europe also only ate locally available goods. This severely limited variety in their food selection.

Much of Western and Northern Europe is situated in a climate that does not lend itself to mass crop production. Rather than growing vegetables in abundance, citizens opted for livestock. Much of the limited crop farmland was used to grow food for the livestock. These animals, in turn, produced milk and meat. As a result, the typical European diet consisted of dairy products and protein for many years (the standard "meat and potatoes" diet).

In the 1900s, as cold supply chains developed, modern refrigeration changed daily life for Europeans. The people could now trade for perishable goods – and did so, readily gaining access to a wider array of food. They were able to access fruits and vegetables from places like Asia, Africa, and the Americas.

MOVING TO THE CITY

In 1900, nearly 40% of Americans lived on farms and nearly 60% lived in rural areas. People built their homes close to land where crops and livestock were raised. They needed to be near a food source to get their daily and weekly supplies.

That all changed with refrigeration. With electricity and electric appliances, some no longer considered it a disadvantage to live away from a farming community. Given this shift in mindset, many young people decided to leave the family farm and rural areas. They moved to cities, where they could get a job and enjoy the metropolitan culture. For food, they only needed to head to the city's shops and grocery stores.

Since perishable food could now be transported over longer distances, it encouraged regional specialization. Farmers no longer had to grow a variety of crops for their family or local market. They could choose to grow one or two crops. The output could then be sent to other places, where it would be purchased and consumed. This trend fostered the concept of industrial farming. With refrigeration, agricultural markets could shift from being only local to regional, national and eventually global. **[FIG 7-1]**

TODAY'S FOOD SUPPLY CHAIN

Without refrigeration, we would be living in a very different world. Cooling capabilities are a core part of the modern supply chain. From storing products for future sales to transporting them over long distances, refrigeration is an indispensable part of everyday life. Using refrigeration, supermarkets can extend the shelf life of their perishables. Consumers can purchase goods and store them at home to make them last.

Of course, like many other technologies, there is an ebb and flow to refrigeration. One of the recent developments impacting this segment is local delivery. With services like Instacart, Shipt, and Amazon Fresh, some consumers have opted out of in-person grocery shopping.

The concept of fresh food delivery became more accepted during COVID, when shoppers who may have previously shopped in-person preferred (or were required) to stay at home. This led to a growing number of households that opted for online ordering. For some consumers, a weekly grocery drop-off has replaced the weekly shopping trip to the store. In some cases, those deliveries occur every day.

From ice houses to air-conditioned megacities, refrigeration has reshaped how we eat, work, and live, enabling global supply chains that deliver fresh goods and comfort worldwide. Yet, as cooling technology fuels trade, it also raises questions about sustainability and resource use. The next chapter explores how modern supply chains navigate these challenges, balancing efficiency with environmental and economic demands to sustain a connected world.

WHO SHIPS AND RECEIVES THE MOST FOOD

(KILOGRAMS PER YEAR)

IN 2012, LOS ANGELES COUNTY BOTH SHIPPED (OUTFLOWS) AND RECEIVED (INFLOWS) MORE KILOGRAMS OF FOOD THAN ANY OTHER U.S. COUNTY. OTHER CALIFORNIA COUNTIES RANKED HIGHLY IN BOTH CATEGORIES.

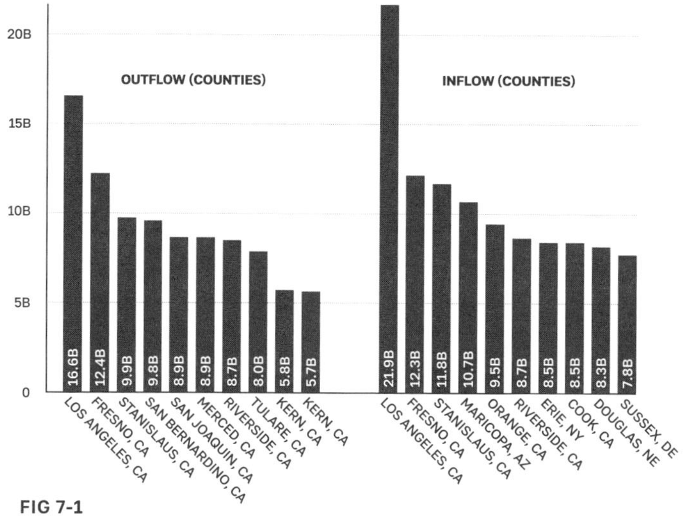

FIG 7-1

SOURCE: FOOD FLOWS BETWEEN COUNTIES IN THE UNITED STATES
XIAOWEN LIN, PAUL J RUESS, LANDON MARSTON AND MEGAN KONAR
PUBLISHED 26 JULY 2019 • © 2019 THE AUTHOR(S). PUBLISHED BY IOP PUBLISHING LTD
ENVIRONMENTAL RESEARCH LETTERS, VOLUME 14, NUMBER 8
CITATION XIAOWEN LIN *ET AL* 2019 *ENVIRON. RES. LETT.* 14 084011
DOI 10.1088/1748-9326/AB29AE

8

JUST-IN-TIME CHANGES THE GAME

Previous chapters highlighted technologies enabling modern supply chains. Chapter 8 shifts focus to how companies have built innovative business models, made possible by centuries of technological advancements in transportation.

When buying a smartphone, do you prioritize the latest features? Do you browse reviews for recent models, or would a device with components from five or ten years ago suffice? For many, checking the newest options is standard, even if they don't purchase them. We expect frequent upgrades and new features, and carrying a decade-old phone feels as outdated as the device itself. Customization—choosing color, size, or storage—has also become a consumer norm, turning shopping into a quest for tailored products.

How do companies meet this demand for novelty and variety? Those adopting Just-in-Time (JIT) philosophies, or lean manufacturing, fine-tune production to fulfill orders efficiently. Instead of stockpiling components in vast warehouses, they order raw materials, produce goods, and deliver them promptly. JIT ensures products, like smartphones or fresh produce transported in refrigerated trucks using heat pump technology—the same as air conditioning and refrigeration—feature the latest components. This minimizes inventory costs and enhances cash flow, unlike goods made from parts stored for months.

JIT began post-World War II in Japan, where manufacturers, constrained by limited capital and warehouse space after the war's devastation, developed lean production. This philosophy spread globally, including to the United States, enabling firms to meet customer demands with minimal delays. By monitoring costs and maintaining low inventories, companies streamlined operations.

However, JIT exposes vulnerabilities. The 2020 pandemic revealed risks of low stockpiles, causing shortages and delays, notably in the auto industry, where computer chip shortages halted assembly lines. Recent geopolitical tensions have prompted some firms to rethink global JIT supply chains, favoring local manufacturing for resilience.

To understand JIT's global impact, we'll trace its origins, explore its adoption across countries and industries, and examine challenges driving shifts to Just-in-Case strategies, fostering robust supply chains.

A NEW WAY TO MANAGE INVENTORY

Post-World War II, Japan's economy faced severe manufacturing constraints due to wartime destruction, including thousands of tons of conventional bombs and two atomic bombs. With limited capital, warehouse space, raw materials, and natural resources—compounded by high inflation and scarce technological development—firms couldn't afford excess inventory. Yet, an abundance of labor, with workers seeking jobs, provided a foundation for recovery.

Rebuilding under American occupation policies was challenging, but Japanese companies innovated to meet customer needs. Toyota pioneered a lean production concept, initially called the Kaizen

method, meaning "continuous improvement," later known as the Toyota Production System and Just-in-Time (JIT) delivery. JIT emphasizes maximum quality, waste elimination, and ongoing efficiency gains in equipment and processes.

JIT avoids holding raw materials and components until a customer order triggers production. This enables rapid conversion of resources into sales, reducing warehouse costs. Inventory is kept minimal, meeting only near-term demand, which cuts waste from overproduction and delays. For example, JIT ensures perishable goods, transported in refrigerated trucks using heat pump technology—the same as air conditioning and refrigeration—reach markets fresh, supporting efficient supply chains.

Workers in JIT systems develop simple, clear processes, taking responsibility for quality and using error-prevention methods. Clean, organized workspaces and multiskilled employees enhance flexibility and job satisfaction, fostering a culture of continuous improvement.

By 1970, Toyota led JIT adoption in Japan and began selling vehicles in the U.S., though its initial market share was small. General Motors sold nearly 39 million vehicles in the U.S. that year, Ford over 23 million, and Chrysler about 15 million, while Toyota sold just over 2 million. Despite this, Toyota gained a foothold, becoming the top foreign car producer in the U.S. by the late 1970s. Its U.S. market share grew from 3% in 1976 to over 10% in 2002, peaking at nearly 17% in 2009, showcasing JIT's global impact.

THE SPREAD OF JUST-IN-TIME DELIVERY

Toyota's guiding principles helped it gain leadership in a country recovering from a global war. **[FIG 8-1]** The JIT system solved a problem that had long plagued manufacturers – too much inventory. In particular, high levels of excess parts get pricey very quickly. Extra components that are stockpiled tie up capital. They can also cause inefficiencies, as it may be difficult to organize and label parts, find them, or use them before they expire, deteriorate or are no longer desired by consumers. If inventory isn't well managed, it can impact a company's ability to respond to market changes and consumer tastes. A plant might keep manufacturing the same electronic item over time, using up parts from its warehouses. If other companies produce new, more advanced models, customers might turn to the upgraded versions, passing over older, outdated options.

JIT resolved these issues and cleared the way for a more streamlined, cost-efficient system. It also helped to overcome market obstacles, including abrupt changes in supply. For instance, during the 1973 Arab-Israeli War, OPEC members imposed an oil embargo against the U.S. and its allies in response to aid the U.S. provided to the Israeli military. The crisis reduced the demand for cars, especially large vehicles that required more gas to run. Many auto manufacturers suffered negative effects from the oil embargo.

Among Japanese companies, Toyota was able to best withstand the repercussions and carry on. This was largely due to its JIT philosophy, which could quickly pivot and change its production levels. It could lower the number of vehicles it manufactured and not take a major loss. Furthermore, it could respond by improving the quality of its smaller vehicles, which were in greater demand because of the higher price of gasoline.

In a show of national pride, Toyota opted to share its production system with other Japanese auto manufacturers. These companies, after learning how JIT worked, adopted the methodology as well. Soon, Japanese manufacturers began to dominate global markets. They could offer products that cost less than competitors in other countries. Moreover, their vehicles were of higher quality. In the years immediately following World War II, "Made in Japan" meant cheap, inferior products. But over time, "Made in Japan" came to mean products of high quality and dependability. Japanese companies using JIT techniques were able to effectively respond to near-term demand changes. By 2022, Toyota was the world's largest vehicle manufacturer for the third year in a row.

MOVING BEYOND AUTOMOBILES

During the late 1970s and early 1980s, Japanese companies further developed and refined their JIT strategies. As a result, they began to take more market share from U.S. and European manufacturers. In addition to gaining dominance in auto sales, companies based in Japan increased their presence in the electronics industry. Soon the country became the world's semiconductor leader and was recognized for its technological superiority.

While U.S. manufacturers tried to compete against the Japan-led surge, they were largely unprepared. Most major American companies were big, bulky, and bureaucratic. Given this, they were unable to deal quickly or effectively with their Japanese competitors.

As a result, articles began to appear in U.S. business magazines and newspapers that explained the Japanese JIT manufacturing processes. By the late 1980s, U.S. manufacturers realized they had to adopt processes that were similar to their Japanese competitors, especially in the auto industry. They did so, and during the process adapted them to fit their own cultures and needs. When JIT techniques were implemented in the U.S., they became known as the Lean Manufacturing method.

One company in particular adopted Lean Manufacturing and used it to climb to the top of its industry. In 1984, Michael Dell founded PC's Limited. It went on to become Dell Computer Corporation in 1988 and then changed its name to Dell, Inc. in 2003.

After its start in the 1980s, Dell worked to improve the lean manufacturing process and adapt it to computer manufacturing. In the late 1990s, it initiated on-demand personal computer sales. Through the business model that Dell established, customers could buy PCs directly from catalogs and magazines. Over time, shoppers could purchase computers online too. This way, the company could receive orders and then produce the equipment. It didn't have to manufacture large quantities of PCs and send them to retailers, where they would sit on shelves, waiting for customers to choose them.

Then Dell rolled out custom-built PCs, which allowed customers to design the model with features they desired. If there was a component shortage in the supplier network, Dell would offer a different component instead of the one it didn't have on hand. This gave it an additional advantage. Essentially, Dell was able to avoid maintaining an inventory of components that it couldn't sell.

Dell also benefited significantly from the cash flow cycle of JIT. It collected payment before it ordered the needed components. Unlike the traditional method of paying for parts, building the product, and then waiting to sell it, Dell turned the process on its head. The company collected funds from consumers before it sent orders to its component suppliers. In doing so, it used the money it already had on-hand from consumers to pay its suppliers.

Many competing PC manufacturers weren't so lucky. The PCs they built were often considered to be top of the line. These models had the latest parts. Unfortunately, it took so long for them to be produced that when they hit the market, something new would have already come out that was better, faster, and cheaper. Dell's production model allowed for maximum flexibility, while other PC makers had systems that did not. As a result, Dell dominated the PC business in the late 1990s and early 2000s. Meanwhile, many other companies, including Packard Bell and Gateway, went out of business.

A LOOK AT VULNERABILITIES IN THE SYSTEM

While JIT creates efficiencies and reduces costs, it comes with drawbacks as well. Perhaps the main disadvantage is that manufacturers lose some control over their production processes. Since they keep only the raw materials and components on hand to meet near-term demand, they become dependent on their sources. In a JIT model, manufacturers must rely on their supplier networks, along with their transportation and logistics partners, to achieve high service levels.

To better understand this concept, suppose you run a manufacturing company that applies the JIT philosophy. You receive an order from a customer and begin the steps to produce the requested goods. Perhaps you schedule a truck to deliver the components needed to create the items on the day they are supposed to go on the production line. You'll need to be confident that the shipment will be complete and on time 99% of the time. (After all, no system is perfect, but the point is you'll depend on it to work normally.) This way you'll be able to stay on schedule and fulfill your customer's order. If the parts don't arrive, you'll need to readjust what goes on the production line or face delays.

With JIT, your suppliers must be able to deliver a steady stream of smaller orders over a greater amount of time. They won't have the option of sending a few larger orders during a short timeframe. You won't be stockpiling inventory, so it will be essential to have these ongoing, minimalistic deliveries from a dependable source.

The higher the number of separate components and materials involved in a manufacturing process, the more likely it is that a supplier or transportation provider will cause a disruption. There are simply more factors at play, and a greater number that could go awry. For manufacturers with a long list of parts needed and an extensive network of suppliers in different locations, it can be difficult to accurately orchestrate their supply chains.

Computerized systems that can automate orders sent to suppliers help to mitigate these risks. Digital tools can assist with manufacturing resource planning to further simplify complex processes. However, these also come with their own set of potential drawbacks. If systems fail or have irrelevant data, there could be delays and disruptions in the supply chain.

Because of these drawbacks, JIT management can make it difficult to be located far from suppliers. In many cases, the companies delivering goods to manufacturers must be physically close to their customers. In the modern automotive industry, many Tier 1 suppliers (direct suppliers) have a factory near the original equipment manufacturer, or OEM. (In the automotive sector, a car manufacturer is often referred to as an OEM. Ford, Tesla, General Motors, Toyota, BMW, and Mercedes are all examples of OEMs).

THE PANDEMIC DISRUPTS JUST-IN-TIME

By design, the JIT strategy eliminates the buffer stock or inventory that is held in warehouses and storage. In a normal market, this creates an ideal situation. Companies produce what customers will consume. They keep only the needed inventory on hand to fulfill current orders.

What happens, then, when there is a crisis? It is at this point that the lean manufacturing method can suffer. Recent history provides a clear example of how the system can falter. In early 2020, the world experienced the onset of COVID. This was the deadliest pandemic since the global influenza pandemic that affected populations in 1918-20.

During the 2020 pandemic, the demand for personal protective equipment, known as PPE, skyrocketed. Consumers, businesses, and medical institutions, among others, purchased vast amounts of hand sanitizer, cleaners, gloves, and masks. Hospitals had a great need for ventilators to accommodate higher levels of patients ill with COVID. This sudden surge of demand, largely unanticipated, drained buffer stocks as well as global inventories.

The U.S. government and businesses stepped in to meet the demand. Some manufacturers started to expand their production lines to fill near-term PPE needs. They didn't know how long the increase in production would last.

Moreover, the supply crisis soon moved beyond PPE. Consumers looked at dwindling supplies of toilet paper, paper towels, and other household goods on retailer shelves. Certain types of meat, produce, and other food products also were scarce at times. Buyers started to hoard products, which put further strains on inventories. This, in turn, caused widespread rationing at the retail level.

As the pandemic continued, shortages throughout the consumer economy were exposed. With most Americans confined to their homes, many changed the way they spent disposable income. They reduced their eating out, entertainment, and travel purchases. Instead, they shifted toward home improvement projects that they could carry out on their own. As a result, soon it was hard to find certain building products, furniture, and other household goods. In 2020 and 2021, it seemed at times as if everything was in short supply.

Then, in 2022, the nation began to normalize. The short-term demand shocks subsided in many categories. However, at the same time, many companies realized they had overcorrected. Even as fewer PPE and household products were purchased, manufacturers were fulfilling increased orders from retailers. The few months of shortages in certain goods soon turned into an over-supply of those products. This phenomenon is known as the "bullwhip effect," which refers to how small fluctuations in demand at the retail level can cause increasingly larger fluctuations for manufacturers.

The bullwhip effect wreaked havoc on the economy. Retailers went from too few products in their inventory to an oversupply. American consumers switched their disposable income back to pre-COVID patterns and stopped purchasing vast quantities of household improvement goods. They resumed their dining out excursions, entertainment expenditures, and travel.

These factors led to the Great Freight Recession, a significant downturn in the domestic freight market, which began during the first quarter of 2022 and has continued. At publication, the freight recession has not ended, although there are signs that the freight market may be recovering.

A SHIFT TO BOOST RESILIENCE

From the fall of the Berlin Wall in 1989 to the onset of COVID-19, the world experienced unprecedented economic growth, driven by globalization and efficient management of supply chains. JIT manufacturing played a pivotal role, enabling manufacturers to minimize inventory and rely on highly coordinated, liquid supply chains. As consumers worldwide gained access to affordable goods, global trade flourished, lifting millions out of poverty in regions like East Asia and Latin America.

However, when COVID-19 struck in 2020, this finely tuned global system collapsed. Businesses and consumers faced the harsh reality that JIT systems, optimized for efficiency, were highly vulnerable to disruptions. Supply chain breakdowns for products like semiconductors, medical supplies, and consumer goods caused widespread delays and shortages, leaving many uncertain about the future. The pandemic exposed the risks of over-reliance on single suppliers and distant manufacturing hubs, particularly in China.

Emerging from the pandemic, the world underwent profound shifts. Companies recognized that JIT techniques depend on trading nations adhering to shared international rules. When those rules are ignored, breakdowns swiftly follow, eroding predictability and consistency in supply chains. This became evident when geopolitical tensions disrupted global trade. In 2022, Russia's invasion of Ukraine, a key supplier of wheat for Europe and neon and palladium for semiconductor manufacturing, triggered shortages of critical materials. Concurrently, China's strict COVID-19 lockdowns halted production in major manufacturing hubs like Shanghai, further fracturing the global economy and signaling the onset of a second Cold War.

Raw materials, particularly commodities sourced from Russia and Ukraine, faced severe delays and shortages. Consumer goods previously produced in China became less accessible as factories shuttered or export restrictions tightened. In effect, leaders in Russia and China upended four decades of free-market trade and economic liberalism, prioritizing national interests over global cooperation. This marked a turning point, splitting the world into competing blocs and challenging the foundations of globalized supply chains.

We entered a new era, divided by regimes that place national self-interest above global trade. Since COVID-19 and the re-emergence of a more assertive Russia and China, supply chain decision-makers have had to reassess sourcing from potentially adversarial regions. Consequently, there has been a resurgence of North American manufacturing to mitigate geopolitical risks. Between 2021 and 2022, the U.S. added approximately 800,000 manufacturing jobs, and from 2020 to 2023, factory construction surged by 125%. In 2023, Mexico surpassed China as the United States' largest trade partner for the first time in over two decades, reflecting a shift toward regionalized trade.

Producing goods closer to consumption centers allows manufacturers to retain JIT benefits, such as rapid delivery to regional consumers, without managing lengthy, vulnerable supply chains. Some companies are also shifting to Just-in-Case models, increasing stockpiles of critical components. By proactively purchasing excess raw materials to cover demand spikes, they aim to avoid production disruptions, a lesson learned from COVID-19 and geopolitical tensions. However, excess inventory raises costs, requiring firms to balance resilience against financial risks.

The U.S.-China geopolitical rivalry, intensified by the trade war and export controls, has deepened uncertainty, pushing companies to prioritize supply chain resilience over efficiency. Sudden tariff hikes – like the 145% U.S. tariffs placed on Chinese goods in April 2025, followed by China's 125% retaliation – along with bans on critical materials like rare earths, have made China-centric supply chains risky. Global companies like Apple, Intel, and Tesla are diversifying suppliers, shifting production to Vietnam, India, and Mexico. Apple now produces 20% of its iPhones in India, up from 5% in 2020. Nearshoring and friendshoring have surged, with U.S. companies investing $200 billion in North American manufacturing since 2022.

Yet, resilience comes with challenges. China's dominance in critical materials – 90% of processed rare earths and 70% of lithium-ion batteries – leaves firms exposed, and building alternative supply chains takes years. Uncertainty from U.S.-China tensions discourages long-term investments, but it also spurs innovation. Technologies like 3D printing enable localized production, while green logistics align supply chains with sustainability goals. As companies adapt, their strategies will reshape global trade, balancing resilience with cost and competition.

Despite these shifts, JIT's benefits, particularly waste reduction, remain valuable. As the world seeks to lower carbon emissions, manufacturers will blend Just-in-Time principles with Just-in-Case resilience, favoring nearshore production with leaner inventories – and a touch extra for some. COVID-19 taught us that, like utilities, supply chains are only noticed when they fail, and it's wise to prepare for the unexpected.

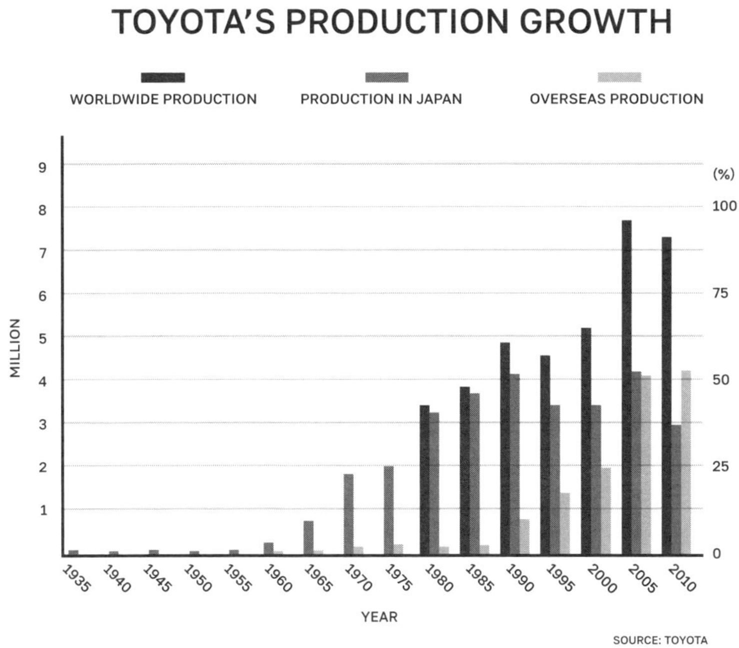
TOYOTA'S PRODUCTION GROWTH
WORLDWIDE PRODUCTION
PRODUCTION IN JAPAN
OVERSEAS PRODUCTION
MILLION
9
8
7
6
5
4
3
2
1
(%)
100
75
50
25
0
1935
1940
1945
1950
1955
1960
1965
1970
1975
1980
1985
1990
1995
2000
2005
2010
YEAR
SOURCE: TOYOTA

FIG 8-1

9

RETAIL REVOLUTION

To teach my 16-year-old son about business, I searched online for a real-world example of today's e-commerce. I wanted him to grasp how digital companies thrive in our modern economy. On Acquire.com, a platform listing businesses for sale, I found Aeroswag, a small e-commerce startup selling custom swag for pilots – items such as shirts, coffee mugs, phone cases, hats, and sweatshirts. Its print-on-demand model, which produces items only after orders are placed, eliminates inventory needs.

Aeroswag's operations are elegantly simple, relying on a trio of platforms to streamline commerce:

* **Stripe:** Processes credit and debit card payments with one integration.
* **Printful:** Handles on-demand printing, producing items as orders come in.

* **Shopify:** Powers the online storefront, connecting Aeroswag to a global audience.

This model frees merchants from managing inventory, collections, retail spaces, warehouses, or shipping. For my son, Aeroswag was the perfect part-time business (also known as a side hustle) for a 16-year-old while going to school. His focus was product design and marketing.

With Aeroswag he is generating around $400 of profit per week for about eight hours of work, or $50 per hour, plus he is learning how business works.

Aeroswag thrives on a century of telecommunications breakthroughs. The internet has transformed merchants into global sellers, with customers expecting personalized goods delivered in hours – or days at most. This shift reflects a revolution in how we shop, driven by technology that seamlessly connects buyers and sellers.

How did we get here? The modern economy emerged from 20th century innovations. World-class universities, the rise of capitalism, and entrepreneurs' ability to launch ventures that quickly succeeded or failed fueled progress. Cold War military technologies, like early computing, were critical. These foundations paved the way for digital marketplaces.

Recent decades reveal the internet's impact on trade and the rise of credit card payments. These changes reshaped retail, propelling brands like Amazon while others faltered. The communications revolution transformed supply chains, enabling customers to buy anything, anytime, from anywhere, without knowing the seller – like Aeroswag.

THE MOST INNOVATIVE RETAILER OF THE 20TH CENTURY

In the 1800s, conventional wisdom for retailers was that success depended on location – open a store in a high-traffic area, like a city center, and customers would enter, buy products, and take them home. The strategy was clear – proximity drove sales. A prime spot meant more foot traffic and transactions.

But one retailer had an innovative idea that upended the consumer market, catapulting it to become the largest and most innovative retailer of the 20th century, launching dozens of successful billion-dollar businesses, many thriving today – Discover, Craftsman Tools, DieHard batteries, Kenmore appliances, Allstate, Dean Witter, and Coldwell Banker. That company was Sears, the most disruptive retailer of the 20th century. Its innovation – the mail-order catalog. While other catalogs existed, Sears excelled with a diverse product range, from clothing to sewing machines, cars, medicines and even houses. Between 1908 and 1940, it sold over 70,000 Craftsman kit houses, enabling customers to build homes using materials delivered by train. The catalog's wide selection and dependable service attracted a vast customer base, boosting sales. Customers browsed pages, ordered items, and received them in four to six weeks.

The kit houses showcased Sears's precision. Each kit included thousands of parts, from screws to shingles, shipped by train. Sears's warehouses used detailed lists to ensure no piece was missing, enabling customers to assemble homes with clear instructions. This operation reached deep into rural communities, expanding Sears's influence.

Sears also ventured into real estate financing. For kit houses, it offered loans, managing payments across thousands of customers. Its real estate arm, which evolved into Coldwell Banker, handled property transactions, building on Sears' record-keeping systems. This financing supported its housing business, attracting more buyers.

Despite its great success, the catalog system had drawbacks. Delivery times, often weeks long, made it hard to adjust inventory based on demand. A holiday catalog was fixed for a year, limiting the ability to introduce new products quickly.

Sears's catalog revolutionized shopping by reaching rural America, where stores were scarce. The company's understanding of rail logistics was key. In the late 1800s, railroads were rapidly expanding, crisscrossing the nation and connecting remote towns. Sears saw the opportunity and partnered with railroads, an ideal move that brought the company along for the ride. Trains delivered everything from tools to entire house kits, making Sears a household name. For Craftsman kit houses, trains carried lumber, nails, and windows to local depots, where customers collected them. This partnership allowed Sears to serve millions, scaling its business with the railroads' growth.

Sears used its catalog to understand customer preferences. Order data showed regional trends – farm implements in the Midwest, fishing gear in coastal areas. Sears tailored its offerings, stocking relevant products to boost sales. Its mailing list enabled personalized promotions, driving purchases without excess inventory.

To support its catalog sales, Sears built massive warehouses, like its Chicago hub, to store diverse inventory. These facilities employed thousands, sorting goods for shipment. Sears used early demand forecasting to stock seasonal items – plows for spring, coats for winter – ensuring customer needs were met. This planning kept sales steady, even in far-flung regions.

To further broaden its reach, Sears opened physical stores for in-person purchases. Retail stores added a new dimension to Sears' business model. By the 1930s, its stores offered a hands-on shopping experience, complementing the catalog. Some locations served as pickup points for catalog orders, streamlining access. Sears tracked inventory with paper records, balancing stock between stores and warehouses to meet demand.

Cash-only transactions, however, restricted growth, as many customers couldn't pay immediately. Sears introduced an in-house payment (charge) card, extending credit to increase sales. This credit access fueled sales, particularly in rural areas. The payment card system expanded Sears's financial reach.

By offering credit, Sears enabled purchases of high-cost items like appliances or kit houses. Managing millions of accounts required tracking payments and defaults, a complex operation that grew over the decades into Discover.

Manufacturing private-label products, like DieHard batteries, gave Sears control of production processes. Operating its own factories, Sears managed raw materials and schedules, ensuring consistent quality. This in-house approach kept shelves stocked, even during supply shortages that hit competitors.

Sears also strengthened its offerings by working directly with manufacturers. For private-label brands like Kenmore appliances and Craftsman tools, it collaborated with factories to design reliable products. Cutting out middlemen lowered prices, making Sears competitive. This direct approach ensured a steady supply, meeting customer demand without delays.

Sears's non-retail ventures – Allstate Insurance, Dean Witter investments, Coldwell Banker real estate – diversified its portfolio – and made its relationships with its customer base "stickier." Allstate handled claims with organized record-keeping, serving millions of policyholders. Dean Witter processed financial transactions, and Coldwell Banker managed property deals, each relying on th Sears operational framework. These businesses broadened Sears's economic impact.

In addition, the Sears workforce was central to the company's success. By 1900, it employed thousands in warehouses, stores, and offices. Sears standardized training to maintain service quality, ensuring employees could handle diverse tasks, from catalog orders to store sales. This effective management of labor supported its growth.

Sears' employee benefits, like profit-sharing plans, fostered loyalty. These programs, innovative for the time, ensured a motivated workforce, critical for the volume of catalog and store operations. This focus on employees set a standard for retail – and other sectors as well.

Sears's advertising efforts also amplified its reach. Beyond catalogs, it ran ads in newspapers and magazines, targeting specific regions. Ads were timed with product availability, driving customers to stores or catalogs. This coordinated approach maximized sales impact.

Despite its innovations and advancements, Sears faced challenges. The catalog's slow updates couldn't keep pace with market shifts. Competitors like Montgomery Ward adopted similar models, narrowing Sears's lead. By the late 20th century, its reliance on physical stores and an outdated logistics network struggled against digital retail's speed and flexibility.

By 2018, Sears filed for bankruptcy, reduced to fewer than 700 stores and 68,000 employees. While online retail grew, Walmart's rise as America's retail leader, with its advanced business model, was the decisive factor. Walmart's innovations, building on Sears's historical groundwork, mark the next chapter of retail's evolution. **[FIG 9-1]**

WALMART TOPPLES SEARS

In 1995, as the decline of Sears began, I turned 16 and got my driver's license. My earliest memories of Sears centered on parking my car. On busy days at the mall, finding a parking spot was tough. When prime spaces were taken, I drove to Sears. As an "anchor" store at the mall's end, its parking lot was often nearly empty, a sign of its fading appeal.

Around then, Walmart started seriously cutting into Sears' market share. Walmart's no-frills stores spread quickly, except in the Northeast. Its aggressive discounting outshone Sears. Offering electronics, clothing, toys, and groceries at low prices, Walmart drew customers away from Sears.

Walmart's cash registers seemed to never stop. Targeting rural and suburban areas with little competition, it bought and sold household goods in bulk, passing savings to customers. This high-volume strategy built scale, making Walmart a leader in discount retail.

Walmart's logistics network became a cornerstone of its success. Manufacturers shipped products to regional distribution centers, where goods were sorted and placed on Walmart's trucks for delivery to stores. Shelves stayed stocked, ready for customers. Unlike Sears (and Kmart, which purchased Sears in 2005), Walmart built one of the nation's largest private trucking fleets, allowing quick responses to demand shifts and ensuring stores had the right products at the right time.

Initially focused on American goods, beginning in the 1980s Walmart soon embraced cheaper imports from China and Mexico under its "Always Low Prices" mantra. It leveraged China's cheap labor and became a key trading partner of the Communist nation. Sourcing from Mexico diversified supply, reducing reliance on U.S. manufacturers. Walmart's global sourcing drove its low prices. It soon became the world's largest container importer and a key trading partner of China.

The downside of Walmart's global sourcing model is that it shifted manufacturing of numerous products overseas, impacting U.S. jobs while keeping consumer prices low. And unless it was your job that was eliminated and you couldn't find a similar one, most shoppers liked the company's lower prices – drawing shoppers from Sears and a host of other retailers.

Because Walmart's low prices hurt Sears, Kmart, JCPenney, and other retailers, it forced them into defensive positions rather than being able to innovate as many had previously. In 1993, Sears dropped its catalog, focusing on physical stores to compete with Walmart – a key misstep.

Sears stopped publishing its general catalog, also known as the "Big Book," on January 25, 1993. This marked the end of an era; the iconic Sears catalog had been a cornerstone of the company for over a century. The decision to discontinue the catalog was part of a broader effort to restructure Sears and address declining sales and profits. In hindsight, had Sears kept its mail-order system and pivoted to e-commerce, it might have thrived.

As noted, Walmart's logistics prowess set it apart from Sears and reshaped the retail sector. Its private trucking fleet included over 9,000 tractors and 80,000 trailers by the early 2000s, operated by thousands of drivers. This fleet moved goods from distribution centers to stores with precision, covering millions of miles annually. Unlike Sears, which relied on third-party trucking companies, Walmart's in-house fleet controlled delivery schedules, cutting costs and delays. If a store in rural Texas needed more toys before Christmas, Walmart's trucks delivered within days, adapting to local demand. This ensured shelves were rarely empty, unlike the inventory struggles of Sears and other retailers.

Walmart's distribution centers were logistical marvels. By the 1990s, it operated dozens of facilities, each up to a million square feet, placed near highways for efficient trucking. These centers used the automation then available, like conveyor belts and barcode scanners, to sort goods quickly. Products arrived from manufacturers, were processed in hours, and loaded onto trucks, minimizing warehousing costs and keeping inventory lean, a model Sears couldn't match.

Moreover, even early on, Walmart's logistics leaned on data. The first inventory tracking systems used sales data to predict demand. If a product sold quickly in one region, Walmart adjusted shipments to avoid stockouts. This approach, advanced for its time, ensured efficiency, unlike the too-slow catalog updates that Sears had relied on.

In the early 20th century Sears became a logistics behemoth by understanding the power of the railroads and postal system. In the late 20th century (and to-date in the 21st century), Walmart's logistics prowess – in trucking, ocean logistics, and inventory systems – has created a supply chain model that dominates the retail landscape. Walmart's expertise gave it a massive edge. However, just as Walmart challenged and then eclipsed Sears and other more traditional retailers, a 21st century upstart that understood the power of air cargo, end-to-end logistics, and e-commerce is challenging Walmart's supremacy.

THE AMAZON PLATFORM

For most consumers, Amazon is the modern internet catalog of choice. Launched in 1995, just two years after Sears dropped its catalog, it began selling books online and initially wasn't profitable. Founder Jeff Bezos estimated a 30% chance of success – better than the one-in-10 odds for internet startups. By the time Amazon gained relevance in the early 2000s, Sears was deep in decline, its market share eroded by internal missteps and external competition.

Amazon's path to profitability differed from Walmart's. Both developed sophisticated logistics networks, but Walmart relied on global sourcing from China, India, and Vietnam, while Amazon focused on e-commerce, using third-party sellers to source products and managing payment and post-sale logistics. This online-first model drove Amazon's sales, unlike Walmart's stores and sourcing-heavy approach.

Walmart, like Sears, depended on physical stores for most of its revenue, offering in-store services – automotive, health, general merchandise and groceries – and leasing space to banks, eyewear retailers, and salons. Its private-label food and grocery brands lacked the devotion of the brands that Sears had created and nurtured. Amazon has private-label products but prioritizes its online platform, offering few in-store services compared to Walmart.

The irony of the collapse of Sears is striking: while Sears abandoned its iconic mail-order catalog, Amazon, the e-commerce giant, now publishes a printed Christmas catalog for kids. My youngest children spend hours poring over it each year, a ritual that echoes the Sears of Christmas past. When my son was five, we asked him to circle his Christmas wishes. An hour later, he had circled nearly every boy toy, his excitement a vivid reminder of the Sears catalog's enduring charm.

Amazon disrupted Walmart by mastering e-commerce in ways Walmart couldn't match (and still hasn't). Its intuitive platform – simple search, one-click checkout, hassle-free returns – made shopping effortless, pulling customers from Walmart's stores. Amazon's vast product range, from books to electronics, often at lower prices, eroded Walmart's urban and suburban market share by the 2010s. Unlike Sears, which failed to pivot online, Amazon's speed and convenience redefined retail.

Amazon's data-driven supply chain was key to this disruption. Its systems tracked millions of daily transactions, analyzing searches, purchases, and browsing patterns. If headphones surged in demand in Chicago, algorithms predicted restocking needs, alerting suppliers or redirecting inventory from nearby warehouses. This precision minimized stockouts, unlike Sears' slow catalog updates or Walmart's less agile store-based system. Amazon's Vendor Central platform enabled third-party sellers to sync with its supply chain, flagging low stock for immediate replenishment, streamlining sourcing compared to Walmart's manual supplier negotiations.

Amazon's logistics prowess rivaled Walmart's but emphasized speed. By the 2000s, it built million-square-foot fulfillment centers with robotics for rapid order processing, enabling same-day delivery via Amazon Prime. Unlike Walmart's 9,000-tractor, 80,000-trailer trucking fleet, Amazon used a hybrid model – thousands of branded vans plus third-party carriers like USPS – cutting costs and outpacing Walmart's delivery times. Data-optimized warehouse locations near urban hubs shortened shipping routes, a flexibility Walmart's highway-focused distribution centers lacked.

Amazon's dynamic pricing, powered by data, has further disrupted Walmart. Algorithms adjusted prices based on demand, competition, and customer behavior, undercutting Walmart's discounts instantly. Its lean global sourcing, focusing on high-margin private-label goods like AmazonBasics, contrasted with Walmart's millions of containers from Asia. Amazon's efficiency maximized variety while minimizing logistics costs.

Walmart countered with e-commerce acquisitions: Jet.com for $3 billion in 2016, Moosejaw for $51 million, and Bonobos for $310 million in 2017, plus Parcel for same-day delivery. The Moosejaw and Bonobos acquisitions failed, with Bonobos sold for $75 million in 2023, a loss of $235 million. To date, Walmart's e-commerce effort remains clunky compared to Amazon's seamless platform.

THE SHOPIFY GENIUS

Amid the rise of online shopping, Shopify stands out as a key e-commerce player. Based in Ottawa, Canada – far from Silicon Valley – it showcases how technology dismantles geographical barriers. Shopify's platform empowers small merchants who lack the logistics and supply chain resources of large retailers, providing tools that big companies easily access.

Founders Tobias Lütke and Scott Lake built Shopify from personal experience. In 2004, they tried creating an e-commerce site to sell snowboards but found no reliable tools for small businesses. This gap inspired a viable solution for entrepreneurs, offering a white-label website that managed backend operations like hosting and payments. Shopify launched in 2006.

Shopify's vision is to be the operating system for e-commerce businesses, creating a turnkey operation that simplifies every aspect of running an online store. Its business model eliminates barriers for small merchants, requiring no expertise in logistics, payments, or website development. A drag-and-drop website builder lets users create professional storefronts without coding. Shopify Payments processes transactions seamlessly, bypassing external gateways. Marketing tools, like email campaigns and social media integration, help merchants reach customers directly. This all-in-one platform allows entrepreneurs to focus on products and sales, not technical details, leveling the playing field against retail giants.

This vision reshapes supply chains by enabling micro-businesses to operate globally. Shopify's platform supports sourcing products worldwide through integrated apps for dropshipping and inventory management, unlike the rigid catalog system that Sears established in the 1890s. Data tools track sales in real time, alerting merchants to restocking needs, ensuring efficient delivery. These features create flexible supply chains tailored to small businesses, from artisanal crafts to tech gadgets, without the infrastructure of Walmart or Amazon.

Early success led Shopify to expand services. It introduced Shopify Payments and financial tools, like capital loans to stabilize merchants' cash flow, support growth without external financing. These offerings strengthened small businesses' ability to scale, enhancing their supply chain resilience.

Shopify initially developed a fulfillment network to provide logistics solutions, connecting merchants to warehouses for storage and shipping. In 2023, it sold this network, including Deliverr, to Flexport, acknowledging the complexity of logistics. Shopify wasn't too proud to exit this business, instead leveraging robust partnerships with Flexport to deliver the same logistics value. Merchants still access seamless shipping, but Shopify focuses on its core software, reinforcing its operating system role.

Shopify's app ecosystem further redefines commerce. Thousands of third-party apps for inventory, marketing, or analytics allow merchants to customize operations, adapting to unique needs. This flexibility contrasts with the inflexible Sears catalog or Walmart's store-centric model, enabling small businesses to compete globally. Shopify's data-driven insights optimize supply chains, predicting demand and streamlining sourcing, ensuring products reach customers quickly.

Entrepreneurs, like my son, run world-class e-commerce sites with Shopify's advanced tools, prioritizing growth over back-office tasks. The platform's global reach and partnerships, like Flexport, empower merchants to navigate supply chains effortlessly. In its heyday, Sears mastered railroads and postal systems; whereas Walmart excels in trucking and ocean shipping. Amazon has leveraged air cargo and e-commerce, but Shopify's platform has empowered small merchants, reshaping retail's supply chain.

Next up we will focus on two companies that are threatening Walmart, Amazon, and Shopify, along with all U.S. retailers. These companies are exploiting a little-known section of U.S. trade policy, combining social media, on-demand fulfillment, global logistics, sourcing, and AI to capture retail market share.

RETAIL'S TRANSFORMATION

	SEARS	WALMART	AMAZON
FOUNDED	1893	1962	1994
BUSINESS	CATALOG REATAILER	SUPERSTORE RETAILER	ONLINE RETAILER
2000 SALES	$40 B	$181 B	$2.7 B
2000 STORES	3,021	3,000	0
2005 SALES	$49 B	$312 B	$8.5 B
2005 STORES	3,500	6,200	0
2016 SALES	$22 B	$482 B	$135 B
2016 STORES	1,400	4,1777	20
RECENT M&A ACTIVITY	SALE OF CRAFTSMAN TOOLS	ACQ. JET.COM, BONOBOS, MODCLOTH, MOOSEJAY, SHOEBUY, HAYNEEDLE	ACQUIRED SOUQ.COM, ACQUIRING WHOLEFOODS
2017 STORES △	-180	NO CHANGE	+460

SOURCE: FIRST RETAIL INC.

FIG 9-1

10

AI AND ITS IMPLICATIONS FOR SUPPLY CHAINS

AI, machine learning, and analytics are transforming supply chains, helping companies operate faster, cheaper, and safer. While some, like Shein and Temu, use AI to bypass U.S. brands, its greatest potential lies in enhancing supply chain safety and efficiency. The COVID-19 pandemic exposed weaknesses in traditional supply chains, which struggled with sudden disruptions. Ernst & Young reports growing investments in AI, analytics, robotic automation, and control towers, alongside worker retraining to adapt to these tools.

Safety remains a challenge in transportation and logistics. Driver fatigue, equipment failures, and hazardous conditions cause accidents, injuries, and delays, raising costs and disrupting operations. The Federal Motor Carrier Safety Administration (FMCSA) notes thousands of fatigue-related truck crashes annually, often tied to long hours and tight schedules. Harsh weather, poor roads, and faulty equipment like worn tires or brakes increase risks. In warehouses, slippery floors and overloaded forklifts lead to thousands of injuries yearly, per the Occupational Safety and Health Administration (OSHA).

A key driver of AI's impact is "exhaust data"—unintentional data generated from digital activities, like IoT devices in vehicles and warehouses. Often overlooked, this data reveals patterns in logistics, safety, and economic trends, powering AI to optimize supply chains. My work at FreightWaves showed its value.

AI trained on exhaust data predicts shifts in fragmented supply chains, where no single player fully sees market trends. In April 2020, during COVID lockdowns, FreightWaves' SONAR platform, analyzing over 3.5 million daily logistics data points, predicted a V-shaped economic recovery. This bold call, doubted by many, proved correct as the economy rebounded swiftly. In March 2022, SONAR's data signaled a freight recession, with declining trucking activity and excess inventory. Despite skepticism, major retailers soon confirmed the downturn, dubbed the "FreightWaves Recession" by Bloomberg. In 2022, SONAR also foresaw a 36% drop in U.S. container imports, defying predictions of a surge. By September, volumes fell 40%, validating the forecast.

SONAR's accuracy stems from exhaust data, like "tenders" (shipper requests for trucks) and "tender rejections" (carriers declining loads). Rising rejections signal higher freight prices, while falling rejections indicate lower prices, reflecting market health. Similarly, safety data reveals risks.

AI uses exhaust data from IoT devices to prevent accidents and failures. Telematics in trucks monitor speed, braking, and driver behavior, with AI detecting fatigue signs like erratic steering. Companies like Samsara report a 30% reduction in safety incidents, aiding FMCSA compliance. AI integrates weather, GPS, and traffic data to identify hazards like icy roads, rerouting drivers to safer paths. Sensors monitor equipment health, predicting issues like tire blowouts for preemptive maintenance.

In warehouses, AI-powered sensors track forklift movements and load weights, reducing injuries by alerting managers to unsafe practices. Geotab notes a 25% drop in equipment-related incidents. Cameras and sensors detect hazards like blocked aisles or unsafe lifting, while AI predicts risks by analyzing near-misses, cutting OSHA-reportable injuries, as seen in Amazon's safety systems.

AI also bolsters security. Exhaust data from GPS, transactions, and networks flags anomalies, like shipment detours or suspicious payments, reducing theft and fraud. Identifying high-risk areas enables rerouting or extra monitoring, enhancing reliability.

AI leverages exhaust data and external feeds to create real-time risk profiles, enabling proactive safety and security. Machine learning refines predictions, learning from incidents, much like SONAR's market forecasts. By preventing accidents, failures, and theft, AI protects workers, streamlines operations, and strengthens supply chains. This data-driven approach builds resilience, ensuring supply chains withstand disruptions while prioritizing safety and efficiency.

THE SURGE IN FREIGHT FRAUD

Freight fraud is a growing threat to U.S. logistics, costing nearly $1 billion annually and undermining supply chains with sophisticated scams. The Transportation Intermediaries Association (TIA) reports a 65% surge in fraud from 2024 to 2025, with 22% of brokers facing significant losses. Organized crime groups, often operating cross-border, exploit digital platforms, disrupting businesses, eroding trust, and raising consumer costs.

Freight brokers, handling nearly one-third of U.S. trucking freight, fuel this problem. As intermediaries between shippers and carriers, brokers obscure direct relationships, creating openings for fraud. Since 2020, brokerages have grown 25%, with over 20,000 new entrants due to low barriers—a $1,000 bond and FMCSA registration. Inexperienced operators overwhelm vetting, allowing fraudulent brokers to infiltrate platforms with fake profiles, targeting high-value goods like electronics or perishables.

Fraud's profitability drives a vicious cycle. A stolen load, like electronics or pistachios, can yield over $100,000 for a $100 dark web ID. Double brokering alone generates $500–$700 million annually, per the TIA. Digital scams, mimicking white-collar crimes like wire fraud, carry low risk as fraudsters operate remotely, often from Eastern Europe or India, using stolen identities and dark web tools.

Prosecution is rare, with only 30% of cases solved and less than 10% of cargo thefts leading to convictions due to complex evidence and cross-border challenges. Unlike securities fraud, which has SEC oversight, freight fraud lacks dedicated task forces. Law enforcement's limited logistics expertise and training further hinder progress.

Load boards, operating like unsecured marketplaces, amplify risks. Brokers post loads to attract carriers, but offline email transactions resemble the early internet's vulnerabilities. Fraudsters pose as carriers, secure loads, and vanish with cargo or payments. The trucking industry's scale—thousands of carriers, brokers, and shippers—combined with regulatory gaps like the FMCSA's outdated registration system, leaves supply chains exposed.

MAJOR TYPES OF FREIGHT FRAUD:

- **Cargo Theft:** Criminals target high-value goods, such as electronics or perishables, often valued over $100,000 per load. Insiders leak load details, allowing thieves to pinpoint trucks at rest stops or warehouses. They may break into trailers, use forged documents, or create fake carrier profiles to steal goods. Track-and-trace technology is misused to track loads, and criminals will liquidate the cargo by selling it through platfoms like eBay and Amazon.

- **In Route Shrinking:** In this sophisticated scam, a load is stopped at an intermediate location, where thieves remove a portion of the cargo, such as a few pallets. The trailer is resealed, and paperwork is altered to reflect the reduced count. The receiving warehouse, unaware of the theft, believes it has received the full order.

- **Double Brokering:** Fraudsters pose as carriers, accept loads, and illegally subcontract them without consent, pocketing payments. Using stolen identities or defunct carrier registrations, they bid on platforms like DAT, subcontract to unsuspecting carriers, and disappear. Overseas groups use VPNs to hide locations.

- **Load Phishing:** Load phishing is a type of fraud targeting the freight industry, specifically load boards, where criminals pose as legitimate carriers to steal cargo. It's essentially a variation of wire transfer phishing, but instead of money, the target is valuable freight. The scam involves fraudsters creating fake email addresses or using compromised ones to book loads on load boards, then arranging for the cargo to be picked up by a driver under false pretenses, leading to the cargo being stolen.

- **Payment Fraud:** Criminals manipulate transactions using forged invoices or hacked accounts. They hack broker emails to send fake invoices with altered bank details or impersonate carriers with false payment proofs. Dark web tools exploit the speed of digital payments.

COMBATING LOGISTICS CRIME: CHALLENGES AND AI SOLUTIONS

Authorities face significant challenges in curbing logistics crime due to its global reach, fragmented enforcement, and limited resources. Many schemes originate overseas, beyond U.S. jurisdiction, which complicates prosecution. Although the FBI monitors these threats, understaffed agencies often prioritize violent crimes, leaving most logistics cases unresolved. Moreover, rapidly evolving criminal tactics outpace regulatory updates, and lax oversight of online platforms allows fake profiles to spread. As government efforts struggle to keep up, the logistics industry must take the lead in combating fraud.

To address this, businesses are adopting digital tools inspired by financial security to proactively identify fraudsters. For instance, non-transactional data—such as GPS tracks, payment logs, and user behavior—powers machine learning to detect threats before crimes occur. A carrier bidding on high-value loads outside its usual routes, for example, may indicate double brokering. By analyzing billions of daily data points, algorithms flag irregularities like suspicious payments or fake platform profiles, enabling early intervention.

This proactive approach is yielding results across the industry. Highway's Freight Fraud Index, for example, flagged over 400,000 fraud attempts in the first quarter of 2025 alone. Its algorithms, which detect invoice discrepancies, trigger instant alerts to prevent losses, streamlining trusted operations. Similarly, the RMIS compliance platform strengthens defenses through automated onboarding, monitoring, and verification. By checking licenses and insurance, RMIS blocks rogue operators, while its risk scoring—leveraging extensive data—catches 30% more threats by identifying patterns like frequent address changes or sudden operational shifts, with real-time notifications. Multi-factor authentication and behavioral tracking, adapted from financial protocols, further secure access, blocking thousands of illicit entities annually.

Other platforms are also making significant strides. Overhaul's FraudWatch, for instance, scores shipment risks in real time, saving $100 million by detecting fictitious pickups. Likewise, Verisk CargoNet's collaborative platform maps criminal networks, pinpointing thousands of fraud attempts since 2023. Its predictive analytics, akin to banking security, highlights behavioral anomalies—such as rapid account creation—often linked to Eastern European hackers. SaferWatch, meanwhile, has reduced losses by 20% through similar data-driven methods. OTR's E-Pay, processes numerous brokerage transactions and examines payment histories to verify carriers, much like credit card theft detection. Unusual patterns, such as sudden transaction surges, signal potential stolen credentials.

By preemptively identifying risks—such as cargo theft or fund diversion—these machine-learning tools disrupt schemes, countering the 65% surge in logistics crime driven by brokerage growth. Unlike reactive law enforcement, this data-driven strategy empowers the industry to safeguard operations and build resilience where traditional oversight falls short. Despite these advances, further innovation and collaboration are needed to fully address the evolving threat of logistics fraud.

AI AND ANALYTICS IN SUPPLY CHAIN EVOLUTION

Logistics companies use AI-driven tools to make freight transport more efficient and cost-effective. Machine learning streamlines workflows and addresses challenges in moving goods from origin to consumer. Industry reports indicate that half of logistics operations plan to invest in AI and analytics.

While AI reshapes retail for major players, its potential in logistics is even greater. Businesses are exploring how these tools enhance operations, supplier coordination, vendor relationships, and customer satisfaction. Key applications include warehouse automation, quality control, streamlined procurement, improved customer service, and optimized delivery routes. As adoption grows, companies will invest in customized solutions, making AI and analytics standard in logistics.

In warehouses, AI-powered robots handle picking and packing, freeing workers for oversight tasks. Wearable devices assist with lifting heavy items, reducing injuries, and RFID tags simplify tracking.

Consumers also benefit. Online shoppers experience smoother purchases, better product visualization, and faster global deliveries. These improvements will expand as companies enhance customer experiences with analytics.

Since the 1960s, innovations like computers and automation have revolutionized logistics, replacing paper-based processes in trucking, unloading, data analysis, and warehouse management. Looking forward, AI's growing role will continue to transform workplaces and benefit society.

EMERGING AI APPLICATIONS IN SUPPLY CHAINS

As AI advances, it transforms supply chain management, delivering efficiency and enabling robotics and autonomous trucks. Using real-time data and predictive analytics, AI tackles long-standing challenges. Below are key AI applications that boost resilience, sustainability, and automation in logistics.

- **Weather-Based Routing:** AI optimizes routes using real-time weather data for safer, faster freight transport. Unlike static maps, machine learning integrates weather feeds, satellite imagery, and traffic updates to reroute trucks around storms or icy roads. For temperature-sensitive goods like pharmaceuticals, AI ensures cold chain integrity by avoiding extreme heat. This reduces delays, enhances safety, and supports autonomous trucks, which rely on similar data for navigation.

- **Temperature-Based Inventory Planning:** AI revolutionizes inventory management for temperature-sensitive goods like produce or vaccines. Machine learning forecasts stock needs using weather, sales, and spoilage data. For example, a grocer stocks more ice cream during heatwaves. If a heatwave nears, AI signals extra refrigeration to protect vaccines. IoT sensors monitor warehouse conditions, cutting waste and supporting robotic systems for automated stock handling.

- **Disrupted Shipment Detection.** AI quickly identifies and resolves in-transit disruptions, like port delays or truck breakdowns. Machine learning analyzes GPS, port logs, and traffic data to flag issues instantly and suggest solutions, such as rerouting to another port. Real-time tracking provides visibility, reducing downtime. This supports autonomous trucks, which need disruption data for dynamic routing and robotic load coordination.

- **Reducing Waste, Fuel, and Emissions:** AI cuts supply chain waste, including fuel and emissions, for sustainability. Machine learning analyzes GPS, fuel sensors, and shipment patterns to reduce empty truck trips and idling. It suggests low-emission routes or modes, like rail, and optimizes warehouse layouts to minimize forklift use. These efficiencies align with autonomous trucks, which use AI for fuel-efficient routing, supporting greener logistics.

- **Automating Repetitive Tasks:** AI automates repetitive tasks like data entry, invoicing, and scheduling, reducing errors. Natural language processing handles invoices, while chatbots resolve customer queries. In warehouses, AI assigns picking tasks, saving time. These systems integrate with robotic pickers and autonomous trucks, streamlining tasks like loading or routing for fully automated logistics.

- **Freight Optimization:** AI maximizes cargo space and routing efficiency. Machine learning analyzes load sizes and vehicle specs to fill trailers fully, cutting costs. It matches shipments, like electronics and apparel, to avoid partial loads. Real-time traffic and customer data optimize routes, saving fuel. This supports robotic warehouses and autonomous trucks, which rely on precise load planning for efficiency.

- **Agentic AI in Logistics:** Logistics relies on human tasks like brokering and negotiation, but agentic AI—autonomous systems—changes this. AI platforms automate call centers, handling carrier negotiations and load updates, cutting costs. They learn tasks like scheduling, reducing errors and freeing workers for strategic roles. Agentic AI enables growth without heavy hiring, supporting robotic warehouses and autonomous trucks for efficient networks.

- **AI-Connected Cameras for Yards:** AI cameras enhance warehouse yard management and security. They identify trucks using optical character recognition, flagging unauthorized vehicles to prevent theft. Cameras track trailer visits to gauge retail demand, improving inventory planning. Machine learning assigns dock slots to reduce congestion. IoT ensures constant monitoring, supporting robotic yards and autonomous trucks with secure, efficient navigation.

- **Enabling Robotics and Autonomous Trucks:** These AI applications—weather routing, inventory planning, disruption detection, waste reduction, task automation, freight optimization, agentic AI, and camera analytics—pave the way for robotics and autonomous trucks. Weather and disruption data guide autonomous navigation. Inventory and freight optimization streamline robotic operations. Waste reduction and automation enhance efficiency. Together, these advancements build resilient, sustainable logistics networks, with autonomous trucks projected to cut costs significantly.

11

AUTONOMOUS VEHICLES AND ADAPTIVE MANUFACTURING

A common question in logistics is: When will autonomous trucks take over the industry? This is the focus of this chapter.

Imagine a truck driver navigating a freak thunderstorm, with hail denting the cab and gusts rocking the trailer. A pileup looms ahead, and a tire blows out, sending the rig skidding toward a strange sinkhole. This chaos isn't real—it's a virtual simulation designed to train autonomous trucks. The driver, too, is an AI construct, tested in a digital world filled with extreme scenarios like storms, accidents, and even fantastical hazards.

Tech companies use exhaust data—traffic reports, video feeds, weather patterns, and road incidents—to build these simulations. Data from truck sensors, highway cameras, warehouse logs, and social media enriches these virtual environments, mimicking real-world physics like road friction and wind resistance. Autonomous trucks "drive" millions of miles in these digital realms, facing fog, bridge collapses, or rare events, learning to handle risks like black ice or floods without human input.

Simulations provide a safe, cost-effective way to train trucks, unlike expensive real-world tests. Extreme scenarios ensure robustness, reducing failure risks. AI refines algorithms with each run, improving decision-making. These virtual tests also spark innovation, allowing firms to tweak designs or fleet strategies without physical prototypes. However, simulations require massive computing power, and covering every possible scenario remains a challenge.

Autonomous trucks, powered by AI, sensors, and machine learning, promise to revolutionize logistics by improving safety, efficiency, cost savings, scalability, and sustainability. Unlike human drivers, they eliminate risks tied to fatigue, illness, distractions, and regulatory limits, ensuring safer and more reliable freight transport.

OVERCOMING HUMAN DRIVER RISKS

Human drivers face significant safety challenges. Fatigue from long hours slows reactions, increasing collision risks. Illness, like flu or chronic conditions, impairs focus, while distractions—phone use or eating—divert attention. Regulatory hours-of-service rules limit driving time, delaying deliveries. Autonomous trucks address these issues with constant vigilance via lidar, radar, and cameras. AI processes data instantly, reacting to hazards like obstacles or lane changes faster than humans, promising fewer accidents and safer roads.

BOOSTING EFFICIENCY AND COST SAVINGS

Autonomous trucks drive non-stop without needing breaks, speeding up deliveries. AI plans the best routes using live traffic, weather, and road data to avoid delays. This makes deliveries reliable and reduces the number of trucks needed, simplifying logistics. Costs drop significantly by removing driver salaries, a major expense, which lowers shipping prices. AI also drives smoothly and predicts maintenance needs, saving fuel and repair costs, making businesses more competitive.

Autonomous trucks cut emissions by choosing efficient routes and fully loading cargo, reducing empty trips. AI can pick eco-friendly paths and work with electric or natural gas trucks to meet green goals. They solve driver shortages, letting companies expand fleets without hiring more people. Virtual training prepares trucks for tough conditions like storms, keeping operations steady.

TECHNOLOGICAL CHALLENGES FOR AUTONOMOUS TRUCKS

Autonomous trucks can improve logistics with better safety, lower costs, and sustainability. However, they face big technical challenges to work safely and reliably. These include issues with sensors, AI decisions, cybersecurity, internet connections, road systems, regulations, liability, and real-world testing. Below, we explain these challenges, their impacts, and what's needed to fix them.

- **Sensor Issues in Tough Conditions:** Autonomous trucks use sensors like lidar, radar, and cameras to "see" their surroundings. Bad weather, like rain or fog, can block these sensors, making it hard to detect objects and risking crashes. Low light affects cameras, and busy areas confuse radar. For example, a truck at a port might mistake a moving crane for an obstacle and stop. Solutions include combining sensor types to double-check data, improving reliability. AI can learn to handle rare situations, like icy roads, through virtual training. But building weather-proof sensors is expensive, and equipping entire fleets will take time, slowing use in harsh areas.

- **AI Decision Challenges:** AI guides trucks by analyzing sensor data, but it struggles in cities with pedestrians or unpredictable drivers. For instance, it's hard for AI to guess if a cyclist is turning or stopping. Rare events, like sudden roadblocks, are risky because AI doesn't think like humans. Training AI for unusual cases needs huge amounts of data and simulations, but it's tough to cover everything. AI must be careful but not too slow, or it causes delays. Advanced AI that mimics human thinking could help but needs powerful computers. Different state rules also make AI programming harder.

- **Cybersecurity Threats:** Autonomous trucks use internet connections to share data, making them targets for hackers. A hacked truck could be rerouted or have its brakes disabled, endangering people. Cybersecurity risks are expected to grow in logistics. Strong encryption and AI to spot unusual activity can reduce risks. Regular software updates are needed but tricky to manage across many trucks. Keeping up with hackers is a constant challenge.

- **Internet Connection Needs:** Trucks need fast 5G or satellite connections for live data like traffic updates or GPS. Rural areas often have weak signals, causing delays that could lead to mistakes, like a truck misjudging a turn. Using a mix of 5G, satellites, and truck-to-truck networks could improve connections. Onboard data processing can help when signals are weak, but it needs small, powerful hardware. Expanding 5G in rural areas is expensive and slow, delaying progress. Connections must also be secure, tying into cybersecurity issues.

- **Road System Compatibility:** Autonomous trucks need smart roads with digital signs and sensors, but most highways don't have these. Faded lane lines or non-digital signals confuse trucks. Construction zones with human workers are especially hard for AI to understand, risking errors. Adding digital signs and road sensors could help, but it costs a lot. Upgrading roads takes time, and different states have different rules, creating confusion. Training AI to follow human workers is in progress but hard to perfect. Poor road systems will slow down autonomous trucks, especially in rural areas.

REGULATORY HURDLES FOR AUTONOMOUS TRUCKS

State laws restricting autonomous trucks, such as proposed bans or human operator mandates, require costly technological solutions. AI must adapt to varied state rules, like safety plans or accident reporting, increasing development expenses. Remote monitoring systems meet "driver-in" requirements but add delays and costs, reducing labor savings. Federal mandates, like requiring warning triangles, demand innovations like automated beacons, complicating designs.

Navigating regulations is tricky due to overlapping local, state, and federal rules. City streets, controlled by local governments, often require human oversight in pedestrian zones, forcing companies to use expensive remote systems. States regulate highways, with some allowing testing while others demand human drivers or propose banning heavy autonomous trucks. Federal rules, set by the Federal Motor Carrier Safety Administration (FMCSA), lack clear standards, causing compliance issues. A few years ago, I asked FMCSA's General Counsel if hours-of-service rules would apply to autonomous trucks, given their cost advantages. He replied, "We don't have a rule stating whether a human driver is even required in the cab," highlighting the regulatory gap.

A truck crossing state lines might face conflicting rules—needing a human in one state but not another—requiring AI to adjust to local speed limits, safety protocols, and federal reporting. Compliance costs could rise 20%, industry estimates suggest, straining budgets. Companies face lengthy negotiations with city, state, and federal officials, delaying rollouts. Labor unions and safety advocates, worried about job losses and untested technology, slow progress. Solutions include AI systems that adapt to rules in real time and industry efforts to unify regulations for smoother operations.

LIABILITY IN AUTONOMOUS TRUCK ACCIDENTS

As autonomous trucks grow, accident liability becomes a major hurdle. Unlike human errors, which are easier to litigate, AI-driven crashes shift blame to manufacturers, developers, operators, or infrastructure providers. If a truck swerves to avoid a pedestrian but hits another vehicle, who's at fault? This uncertainty could delay adoption by discouraging investment.

High-stakes "nuclear" lawsuits—multi-million- or billion-dollar claims like aviation disasters—pose risks. A fatal crash could trigger massive lawsuits, exceeding insurance limits and targeting tech firms, stifling innovation. A faulty sensor misreading a sign might spark complex litigation, with parties deflecting blame.

UNPROVEN TECHNOLOGY IN REAL-WORLD SCENARIOS

Despite promise, autonomous truck technology remains unproven in unsupervised real-world scenarios, raising dependability concerns. Current pilot programs operate under tight supervision by expert engineers, using controlled routes and constant monitoring. These achieve high success rates, but supervision masks risks. In unsupervised settings, with chaotic traffic and unpredictable weather, reliability could drop significantly. Projections estimate a notable decline in performance without oversight, as AI struggles with variables like erratic drivers or debris.

The gap between pilots and real-world deployment is stark. Engineers intervene in pilots to correct errors, such as misjudging a construction zone. In unsupervised scenarios, these safety nets vanish, risking accidents. Virtual simulations train trucks for extreme conditions, but cannot replicate reality's infinite variability. Developing algorithms for these requires larger datasets and computing power, straining technology. Scaling demands robust fail-safes – remote overrides, emergency braking, and more – but these add costs, undermining efficiency. Dependability must match pilot performance to enable widespread use.

A PATH FORWARD: THE INEVITABLE RISE OF AUTONOMOUS TRUCKS

The technological challenges facing autonomous trucks – sensor limitations, AI complexity, cybersecurity, connectivity, infrastructure, regulatory fragmentation, liability, and unproven real-world performance – form a daunting gauntlet, yet they are not insurmountable.

Eventually, these hurdles will be overcome, though it may take a decade or two to achieve the seamless integration that proponents envision. Autonomous trucks will drive highways, navigating with precision beyond human capability, slashing labor costs, enhancing safety, and reducing emissions. However, the journey will be slower than enthusiasts hope, as each challenge demands rigorous innovation and collaboration. Sensor fusion will conquer weather barriers, neural networks will master urban chaos, and robust cybersecurity will shield fleets. Infrastructure will evolve, regulations will harmonize, and liability frameworks will clarify responsibility, mitigating nuclear lawsuit risks. Real-world testing will bridge the gap from supervised pilots, ensuring dependability.

Human drivers, with their various vulnerabilities, will remain a fixture for some time, coexisting with autonomous systems as the transition unfolds. This gradual shift will create new roles – engineers, analysts, technicians – while preserving human oversight when and where needed. Shippers will reap faster, cheaper deliveries, and logistics networks will gain resilience, aligning with the efficiency focus of prior chapters.

ADAPTIVE MANUFACTURING: FLEXIBLE SUPPLY CHAIN SOLUTIONS

Picture a factory that switches from car parts to medical devices overnight, instantly meeting customer demands. This is adaptive manufacturing, a flexible method using AI, robotics, and the Internet of Things (IoT) to build responsive production systems. When supply chains face disruptions like pandemics or chip shortages, adaptive manufacturing adapts to market shifts, customer needs, or supply problems. It enables fast changes, real-time tweaks, and local production, transforming how goods are made and delivered, saving costs, and strengthening resilience. This section covers its role, applications, technologies, challenges, and future in supply chains.

BOOSTING PRODUCTION FLEXIBILITY

Traditional factories rely on fixed assembly lines for mass-producing standard items. Adaptive manufacturing allows quick shifts. For instance, during COVID-19, General Motors retooled its Kokomo, Indiana plant in weeks to make ventilators, using flexible tools and AI-driven processes. This cuts downtime and inventory costs, crucial when supply chain delays cost millions.

In electronics, adaptive systems stand out. Flex Ltd. uses AI and IoT to adjust production at over 100 global sites, switching from smartphones to wearables based on demand. Live data from suppliers and customers reduces lead times by 30%. For supply chains, this means smaller, flexible batches, minimizing excess stock and waste.

USES ACROSS INDUSTRIES

Adaptive manufacturing serves many sectors. In automotive, BMW's smart factories use robotics and digital twins—virtual models of production lines—to test new setups, creating custom vehicles without pausing. In pharmaceuticals, Pfizer ramps up vaccine production, adjusting formulas based on trial data. In consumer goods, Unilever's plants switch detergent types to suit local preferences.

Local production is a big win. Adidas uses 3D printing to make custom sneakers near major markets, slashing shipping times and costs. These uses enhance supply chain agility, letting companies handle regional disruptions or demand spikes without distant suppliers.

TECHNOLOGIES DRIVING CHANGE

Adaptive manufacturing relies on advanced tools. AI forecasts demand and identifies bottlenecks, streamlining schedules. IoT sensors monitor machines, enabling maintenance that cuts downtime by 20%, according to McKinsey. Modular robots, like Fanuc's, tackle various tasks, while 3D printers craft parts on demand. Digital twins simulate processes, reducing mistakes.

These tools link to supply chains via enterprise resource planning (ERP) systems, syncing production with inventory and logistics. Managers get clear insights for better planning and supplier coordination, but need strong cybersecurity to protect connected systems.

CHALLENGES TO OVERCOME

Adaptive manufacturing has hurdles. Setting up AI, robotics, and IoT can cost over $10 million per factory, a barrier for smaller businesses. A shortage of skilled workers, like engineers for smart systems, is a problem, with two million unfilled manufacturing jobs projected by 2030. Outdated ERP systems often require costly upgrades.

Supply chain complexity adds issues. Adaptive systems need instant supplier data, but global disruptions, like the 2021 chip shortage, can interrupt flows. Managers must balance costs and benefits, often testing scalability with small pilot projects.

THE FUTURE OF ADAPTIVE MANUFACTURING

Deloitte estimates adaptive manufacturing could add $2 trillion to global GDP by 2030, driven by Industry 4.0 advances. AI may lead to fully autonomous factories, and 5G will boost IoT connections. Local micro-factories will expand, reducing reliance on long supply chains.

From GM's ventilators to Adidas's 3D-printed sneakers, adaptive manufacturing delivers value. For supply chain managers, it offers flexibility and savings but needs smart planning—picking scalable tools, training workers, and aligning with suppliers. As markets grow unpredictable, adaptive manufacturing will strengthen supply chains, delivering goods right on time.

12

ROBOTICS, DRONES, AND ADVANCED TRANSPORT

Robotic automation is revolutionizing factories and warehouses, reshaping logistics networks by enhancing efficiency, safety, and scalability. As supply chains face pressures from rising consumer demand, labor shortages, and global disruptions, robotics offers a solution to streamline operations, reduce costs, and improve resilience. From automotive assembly lines to retail fulfillment centers, automated systems – ranging from robotic arms to autonomous mobile robots (AMRs) – are critical for maintaining competitive supply chains. By automating repetitive, labor-intensive, or hazardous tasks, robotics frees human workers for more strategic roles, ensuring goods move seamlessly from production to delivery. This chapter explores the importance of robotic automation in factories and warehouses, its impact on supply chains, and specific applications across industries, building on prior discussions of AI, autonomous vehicles, and logistics challenges.

IMPORTANCE OF ROBOTIC AUTOMATION FOR SUPPLY CHAINS

Supply chains thrive on speed, accuracy, and adaptability, and robotic automation delivers on all these. Factories and warehouses are the backbone of these networks, transforming raw materials into finished goods and ensuring timely shipments and delivery to consumers. Robotics enhances these operations by automating tasks that humans find tedious, dangerous, or error-prone, such as material handling, assembly, or inventory management. Studies suggest robotic systems boost productivity significantly, reduce errors, and cut operational costs, making them indispensable for meeting modern demands like rapid e-commerce fulfillment or just-in-time manufacturing.

The labor landscape underscores robotics' importance. Human workers face fatigue, illness, and regulatory limits, as seen in trucking, while warehouses struggle with high turnover and the resulting labor shortages. Robots operate continuously, unaffected by these constraints, ensuring consistent output. Industry reports highlight that automation addresses labor gaps by taking on low-value tasks, allowing employees to focus on problem-solving or innovation. This shift improves efficiency and enhances safety by removing humans from hazardous environments, such as heavy lifting or chemical exposure. Robotics also supports scalability, enabling operations to expand without proportional hiring, a critical advantage in volatile markets.

Supply chains benefit from robotics' data-driven capabilities. Advanced robots, equipped with AI and sensors, collect and analyze data on workflows, inventory, and performance, providing insights to optimize processes. This aligns with the emphasis in prior chapters on AI-driven simulations and data platforms, enhancing visibility and resilience against disruptions like port congestion or shortages of raw materials. By automating factories and warehouses, robotics ensures supply chains remain agile, cost-effective, and responsive, cementing its role as a cornerstone of modern logistics.

EXAMPLES IN THE AUTOMOTIVE SECTOR

The automotive sector pioneered robotic automation, leveraging it to streamline manufacturing and supply chain operations. In factories, robotic arms perform precision tasks, ensuring consistent quality and high throughput. For instance, on assembly lines, robots weld chassis parts with pinpoint accuracy, reducing defects compared to manual methods. Robotic welding improves production speed while maintaining stringent safety standards.

Robotic automation extends to material handling, where AMRs transport parts across factory floors. These robots navigate dynamically, avoiding obstacles and delivering components to assembly stations, eliminating fixed conveyor belts. Industry outcomes indicate AMRs reduce material transport time, boosting efficiency. In some factories, AMRs carry partially assembled vehicles between robotic cells for tasks like engine installation, enabling flexible production lines that adapt to model variations – a shift from linear setups.

In warehouses, automotive supply chains use robots for inventory management and order fulfillment. Robotic arms pick and sort parts, while AMRs move pallets to loading docks, streamlining just-in-time delivery to factories. This ensures components arrive precisely when needed, minimizing overstock and delays. Industry reports note robotic warehouses cut order processing times, enhancing responsiveness. The automotive sector's reliance on robotics demonstrates how automation optimizes production and logistics, setting a model for other industries.

EXAMPLES IN OTHER SECTORS

Beyond the automotive industry, robotics transforms supply chains in electronics, food and beverage, and retail sectors. In electronics manufacturing, robotic arms handle delicate tasks like assembling circuit boards or placing microchips, where precision is critical. Studies suggest robotic assembly reduces error rates, ensuring high-quality products like smartphones. AMRs transport components across factories, navigating tight spaces, while robotic vision systems inspect circuits for defects, enhancing quality control.

In the food and beverage industry, robots automate packaging and palletizing, critical for perishables. Robotic arms pack bottles at high speeds, while AMRs move pallets to cold storage, maintaining temperature controls. Industry outcomes show automation cuts packaging time, ensuring fresh deliveries. In warehouses, robots sort and pick items for grocery orders, addressing e-commerce demands, reducing repetitive strain injuries.

The retail sector, driven by e-commerce, relies on robotic warehouses. Automated systems pick, pack, and sort orders, handling diverse products. Cube storage robots retrieve items for fulfillment, while robotic arms pack boxes. Industry reports indicate these systems double order throughput, meeting fast delivery expectations. AMRs transport goods to loading docks, integrating with last-mile logistics. Retail's adoption highlights robotics' role in scaling supply chains.

ROBOTICS IN PRECISION MANUFACTURING AND HAZARDOUS ENVIRONMENTS

Robotic automation excels in precision manufacturing and hazardous environments, where human capabilities are limited or safety risks are high, further strengthening supply chains. In precision manufacturing, such as aerospace or medical device production, robots perform tasks requiring extreme accuracy. For instance, robotic arms assemble jet engine components with sub-millimeter precision, ensuring structural integrity where human hands might falter. In medical device factories, robots craft intricate surgical tools or implants, meeting stringent regulatory standards. Studies suggest robotic precision reduces defect rates, enhancing product reliability and speeding production cycles, critical for supply chains delivering high-value goods.

In hazardous environments, robots undertake tasks too dangerous for humans, such as handling toxic chemicals or operating in extreme temperatures. In chemical manufacturing, robotic systems mix volatile substances in sealed chambers, eliminating human exposure risks. In metal foundries, robots manipulate molten materials at thousands of degrees, where human presence is inadvisable. Industry reports note robots in these settings cut workplace injuries, improving safety and continuity. For example, robots clean radioactive waste in nuclear facilities, a task impossible for humans without severe health risks. AMRs navigate hazardous zones, transporting materials without endangering workers, ensuring seamless operations.

These applications bolster supply chains by enabling production in conditions humans cannot operate in or endure, expanding manufacturing capacity. Robots in hazardous environments also reduce downtime from accidents, maintaining output for critical goods like aerospace parts or pharmaceuticals. Data from robotic sensors, as in prior AI discussions, optimizes these processes, ensuring quality and efficiency. By automating precision and hazardous tasks, robotics enhances supply chain reliability, supporting industries where failure is not an option.

BROADER IMPACTS ON SUPPLY CHAINS

Robotic automation's impact transcends sectors, strengthening supply chains holistically. By automating factories, robotics ensures consistent production, reducing bottlenecks that delay the movement of a wide variety of goods. In warehouses, it accelerates order fulfillment, critical for e-commerce and just-in-time models. Studies suggest automated systems improve order fulfillment rates, enhancing customer satisfaction, aligning with prior chapters' focus on customer-driven logistics.

Cost savings are significant. While initial investments are substantial, long-term reductions in labor, waste, and downtime yield high returns. Industry outcomes show automation lowers operational costs, enabling competitive pricing. Safety improvements, such as robots handling hazardous tasks, reduce injuries, cutting costs and boosting morale.

Resilience is a key benefit. Automated facilities adapt to disruptions – labor shortages or demand spikes – by reallocating resources dynamically. AMRs reroute tasks during peak seasons, maintaining throughput. This agility ensures supply chains withstand challenges like pandemics or trade disruptions. Robotics supports sustainability, optimizing material use and energy, aligning with green goals.

ROBOTIC WAREHOUSES AND AMERICA'S REINDUSTRIALIZATION

Robotic warehouses will be pivotal to America's reindustrialization, driving a resurgence of domestic manufacturing and logistics. As global supply chains face disruptions and rising offshore costs, reindustrialization seeks to bring production closer to consumers, boosting economic security and job creation. Robotic warehouses are central to this effort, enabling efficient, scalable fulfillment that supports reshored factories. By automating picking, packing, and sorting, robots double throughput, meeting e-commerce demands and ensuring just-in-time delivery to manufacturers, as seen in retail and automotive examples. This efficiency, with reduced shipping times, strengthens local supply chains, aligning with reindustrialization's self-reliance goal.

Robotics addresses labor challenges critical to reindustrialization. Dealing with labor shortages, automated warehouses reduce reliance on human workers for repetitive tasks, freeing them for skilled roles like robot programming. Safety improvements, such as robots handling heavy loads, enhance workplace conditions, attracting talent to industrial hubs. Robotic warehouses' data-driven insights – including tracking inventory and predicting demand – enable agile responses to market shifts, ensuring America's reindustrialized economy withstands global volatility, cementing their role in a robust, future-ready supply chain.

LOGISTICS DRONES: TRANSFORMING SUPPLY CHAINS

Drones are revolutionizing supply chains by delivering goods faster and greener, from e-commerce packages to lifesaving medical supplies. This section explores their role, applications, technologies, challenges, and future in transforming logistics.

E-COMMERCE: SPEEDING UP LAST-MILE DELIVERY

Drones tackle "last-mile" delivery, getting packages from warehouses to doorsteps. Amazon's Prime Air leads, delivering up to

5-pound parcels in 30 minutes. In 2022, tests began in Lockeford, California, and College Station, Texas, with AI-guided drones dodging power lines and pets to land in backyards. By 2024, Amazon expanded across U.S. states, eyeing global growth.

Walmart, with DroneUp, delivers in Arkansas, Arizona, and Texas. Its drones, carrying up to 10 pounds, bring groceries within 1.5 miles in under 30 minutes. In 2023, Walmart completed over 20,000 deliveries, with customers praising the speed. Drones reduce pollution and traffic compared to vans, aiding sustainability.

In China, Alibaba's Cainiao uses drones for rural and mountainous areas. Carrying up to 15 pounds over 30 miles, these drones deliver electronics and clothes where roads are absent. In 2024, Cainiao's drones were 40% faster than trucks, boosting online shopping access.

HEALTHCARE: DELIVERING LIFESAVING SUPPLIES

Drones are vital for urgent medical deliveries. In early 2025, a startup pitched me an investment for drones transporting blood and organs between New York City hospitals. Their hub-and-spoke drone network, like a less-than-truckload (LTL) system, cuts time and costs for these temperature-sensitive items with short shelf lives, ensuring faster, safer deliveries.

Globally, Zipline leads in Rwanda and Ghana, delivering blood, vaccines, and medicines to remote clinics. Its drones, carrying 4 pounds over 100-mile round trips, drop supplies by parachute. Since 2016, Zipline's 500,000+ deliveries in Rwanda have saved lives, like providing blood for new mothers. In 2025, Zipline expanded to Nigeria's rural hospitals. **[FIG 12-1]**

In the U.S., UPS and Matternet deliver medical samples between hospitals. In North Carolina, their drones carry lab samples and masks, slashing delivery times from hours to minutes. During COVID-19, they brought test kits to remote areas. Wing, Alphabet's subsidiary, partners with Walgreens in Virginia to deliver medicines and hygiene products, supporting contactless care.

In emergencies, drones excel. In Australia, DroneShield's drones deliver defibrillators to heart attack victims, guided by 911 calls with live video, arriving 70% faster than ambulances in 2024 Sydney trials.

DISASTER RELIEF: RAPID AID DELIVERY

Drones reach disaster zones cut off by floods, earthquakes, or hurricanes. The UN World Food Programme (WFP) delivers food, water, and medical kits. In 2023, during Mozambique's Cyclone Freddy, WFP drones carried 1,500 pounds of supplies to isolated villages, bypassing flooded roads. Heat-sensing cameras helped find survivors, aiding rescues.

In Haiti, post-2021 earthquake, Global Drones Relief delivered antibiotics and bandages to clinics, carrying 20 pounds over 50 miles where roads collapsed. In 2024, California wildfire relief drones brought water and fire-retardant materials to remote firefighting crews.

AGRICULTURE AND INDUSTRY

In farming, drones deliver seeds, fertilizers, and pesticides. In India, Skye Air's drones use soil sensors to provide tailored nutrients, increasing crop yields by 15% in trials. In Brazil, Embraer's drones spread biologics on soybean fields, covering 500 acres daily—five times faster than manual methods.

In warehouses, drones streamline tasks. DHL's FlytBase drones in Germany scan barcodes, cutting inventory checks from days to hours and reducing errors by 30%. In 2025, DHL expanded to Mexico, using 5G for real-time data. In construction, Japan's Skycatch drones deliver tools to high-rise sites, using AI to navigate wind and save time.

TECHNOLOGY AND CHALLENGES

Drones rely on AI for obstacle avoidance and route planning. Wing's drones use Google software for safe city flights. New batteries extend flights to 90 minutes, and 5G enables drone coordination in busy skies.

Challenges include global regulations. In the U.S., FAA rules limit drones to visible flights, though more flexible rules are emerging. Europe's regulations ease adoption. Battery life and weight limits restrict growth, but new drones carry 500 pounds. Noise and privacy concerns lead to quieter designs and clear data policies. Cybersecurity risks, like hacking, require encryption and blockchain tracking.

THE FUTURE OF DRONES

McKinsey predicts a $50 billion drone delivery market by 2030, driven by urban growth and e-commerce. Advanced batteries could double flight ranges, and drone "swarms" may handle large deliveries. Dubai's passenger-cargo drone tests hint at future possibilities.

From Amazon's fast packages to Zipline's lifesaving deliveries, drones are transforming supply chains. As regulations and technology improve, drones will deliver groceries, aid, and more—faster, greener, and to everyone.

THE RISE OF EVTOL AND URBAN AIR MOBILITY: TRANSFORMING TRANSPORTATION AND COMMUNITIES

Electric vertical takeoff and landing (eVTOL) technology and urban air mobility (UAM) promise to revolutionize transportation, communities, and supply chains in the coming decades. By combining electric propulsion, vertical takeoff, and automation, eVTOLs offer a sustainable, efficient alternative to ground transport and traditional aviation. This section explores how UAM will reshape daily life, from emergency rescues to urban commuting, while enhancing supply chain connectivity.

EMERGENCY MEDICAL EVACUATION IN RURAL AREAS

Imagine a farmer injured in a remote area, far from a hospital. Today, a rescue helicopter might take hours to arrive, but a future eVTOL air ambulance could launch from a nearby vertiport, landing in a field within 20 minutes. Quiet and emissions-free, it stabilizes the farmer and flies to a hospital in 15 minutes, bypassing rough roads. Compact and cost-effective, eVTOLs will transform rural emergency response, reducing response times and saving lives. As vertiports spread, isolated communities will gain urban-level healthcare access, closing geographic gaps.

ACCESSING REMOTE LOCATIONS

eVTOLs will redefine ecotourism by reaching pristine areas without environmental harm. In the Amazon, sustainable resorts deep in the jungle will be accessible only by eVTOL. These quiet, zero-emission crafts will ferry tourists to rare ecosystems, preserving nature while funding conservation through local tourism revenue. In Alaska's rugged terrain, eVTOLs will fly adventurers from Anchorage to glacier lodges, landing on small surfaces without roads or airstrips. Their low noise and electric power support sustainable tourism, while lower costs make experiences more accessible. Indigenous communities will gain economic opportunities without sacrificing land, opening new markets for eco-friendly travel.

REDUCING URBAN CONGESTION

UAM will ease traffic in crowded cities like Los Angeles, São Paulo, or Delhi. eVTOL flying taxis, using rooftop vertiports, will cut a 50-mile commute from over an hour by car to 15–20 minutes. Studies by NOAA and Joby Aviation suggest UAM could reduce city traffic by 20% by 2030. Electric eVTOLs will lower emissions, improving urban air quality. As battery technology advances, costs will drop, making flying taxis as affordable as ride-sharing. This will save time, reduce pollution, and ease the economic burden of gridlock, transforming urban supply chains and mobility.

DEMOCRATIZING PERSONAL AVIATION

Aviation, once for the wealthy or highly trained, will become accessible with eVTOLs. Automation, like AI navigation and fly-by-wire systems, will simplify piloting, requiring minimal training—similar to driving. Companies like Archer and Lilium aim to price eVTOLs like luxury cars, with low operating costs due to electric power and simple maintenance. Individuals could own or lease eVTOLs for commuting or leisure, using vertiports in towns or private properties as "sky driveways." This will make aviation a lifestyle choice, empowering people with new mobility and freedom.

RESHAPING COMMUNITIES

eVTOLs will change where people live by shrinking commute times. A 100-mile trip, once daunting, could take 30 minutes, letting workers settle in rural or coastal areas with lower costs and better quality of life. This decentralization will ease urban housing crises, as people choose spacious homes in less crowded regions. New communities may form around vertiports, with landing pads, charging stations, and transit links. Real estate values will rise near vertiports and fall in congested cities, spurring rural economic growth as businesses follow residents, enhancing local supply chains.

CHALLENGES AND CONSIDERATIONS

eVTOLs face hurdles. Regulators like the FAA and EASA must create UAM guidelines for airspace, safety, and vertiports, requiring global coordination. Building vertiports and charging networks demands significant investment, though public-private partnerships will help. Public concerns about safety and noise may slow adoption, but eVTOLs are quieter than helicopters and built with redundant systems. Ensuring equitable access is key to avoid elitism; subsidies and shared-ride models will broaden reach.

A VISION FOR THE FUTURE

By 2035, eVTOLs could fill urban skies, carrying commuters, tourists, and adventurers. Cities will have less traffic and cleaner air. Remote areas will thrive with sustainable tourism and better healthcare access. Personal eVTOLs will make skies as open as roads. Morgan Stanley predicts a $1.5 trillion UAM market by 2040, but the impact goes beyond economics. eVTOLs will shrink distances, preserve nature, and make aviation a daily reality, redefining supply chains and communities. As technology and infrastructure grow, eVTOLs will soar, connecting a sustainable, mobile future.

GROUND DELIVERY ROBOTS: REVOLUTIONIZING LAST-MILE LOGISTICS

Imagine a small, suitcase-sized robot rolling down a sidewalk, delivering your lunch or package. Ground delivery robots, autonomous machines navigating pathways, are transforming last-mile logistics in supply chains. Unlike drones, these electric-powered robots use AI and sensors to deliver small items in neighborhoods, resorts, and campuses. As e-commerce and on-demand services grow, they cut labor costs, emissions, and delivery times. This section explores their applications, examples, potential to replace intercity couriers, challenges, and future in supply chains.

DELIVERING CONVENIENCE IN NEIGHBORHOODS

Ground robots bring goods directly to homes like rolling mailboxes. Starship Technologies, a leader, operates in suburbs like Chevy Chase, Maryland, delivering groceries and meals for Grubhub. Its six-wheeled robots, carrying up to 22 pounds, travel at 4 mph, using cameras and radar to dodge pedestrians. By 2021, Starship completed 2 million global deliveries, becoming a familiar sight.

Serve Robotics, partnered with Uber Eats, delivers food in Austin, Texas, and Jersey City, New Jersey, from restaurants like Shake Shack. Operating 11 a.m. to 9 p.m., these robots cover 31 miles per charge, cutting delivery costs by up to 50% compared to human couriers. Customers order via an app and unlock compartments with a PIN. For supply chains, robots reduce gas vehicle use, ease city traffic, and support sustainability, but require integration with order systems.

ENHANCING RESORT EXPERIENCES

Resorts, with sprawling layouts, benefit from ground robots. At the Fairmont Scottsdale Princess, Kiwibot robots deliver snacks, drinks, and towels to poolside guests. Using GPS and AI, they navigate paths, avoiding golf carts and sunbathers. Guests order via an app, and robots arrive in under 15 minutes, improving service without overworking staff.

In 2023, Caesars Palace in Las Vegas tested Starship robots for room service, delivering sandwiches and toiletries 24/7. This reduces wait times during busy periods. For resort supply chains, robots streamline internal logistics, freeing staff for guest interactions, but need investment in mapping and maintenance for varied terrains.

FEEDING COLLEGE CAMPUSES

College campuses, full of students needing fast meals, are perfect for robots. Starship Technologies serves over 50 U.S. campuses, like UCLA and Purdue, delivering food from dining halls and Starbucks. Students order via an app, and robots bring snacks or pizza in 10–20 minutes within a 2-mile radius. By 2025, Starship aims to reach 100 campuses, serving 1 million students.

Grubhub's partnership with Starship at the University of Arizona saw 10,000 deliveries in 2024, cutting delivery times by 30% compared to couriers. Operating at Level 4 autonomy, robots need little oversight, reducing labor costs. For campus supply chains, they simplify food logistics, but cracked sidewalks or student pranks require monitoring and infrastructure fixes.

REPLACING INTERCITY COURIERS

Ground robots could disrupt intercity courier and bike messenger services, which face rising labor costs and urban congestion. Bike messengers, common in New York City and Philadelphia, navigate traffic but struggle with scalability. Companies like BikeMessenger24 deliver food and gifts, but e-bikes face safety risks, including battery fires in 80% of New York City delivery e-bikes.

By 2030, robots may handle short- to medium-range deliveries (1–10 miles). Avride plans to deploy hundreds of robots in 2025, using AI to optimize routes and cut delivery times. Robots, needing no salaries or breaks, could reduce costs by 40%, per McKinsey. In intercity settings, robots might use buses or dedicated lanes, covering 20+ miles. While couriers excel for urgent, high-value items like legal documents, robots could complement or replace routine deliveries, enhancing supply chain efficiency.

TECHNOLOGY AND SUPPLY CHAIN INTEGRATION

Ground robots use AI for navigation, LiDAR for obstacle detection, and 5G for real-time communication. Starship's robots, with 12 cameras and ultrasonic sensors, achieve 99.9% autonomy. Batteries last 6–8 hours, supporting 20–30 deliveries per charge. Robots sync with restaurant, warehouse, or resort systems, ensuring smooth order-to-delivery flows.

For supply chain managers, robots provide data on time, distance, and obstacles, improving route planning and forecasting. Integration requires APIs, like Porter's, to link robots with platforms, plus staff training for loading and monitoring.

CHALLENGES AND BARRIERS

Ground robots face obstacles. Regulations vary: Virginia and Idaho allow sidewalk robots, but Kansas vetoed a 2022 bill over safety and job concerns. Infrastructure issues, like Pittsburgh's cracked sidewalks, stopped Kiwibot's 2020 pilot after four deliveries. Public acceptance differs—older residents question package safety, while younger users embrace robots.

Job displacement worries couriers, as robots cut commissions (e.g., Uber Eats' 25% meal price tips). Cybersecurity risks, like hacking controls, demand strong encryption. Supply chain managers must balance these risks with benefits, using pilot programs to test feasibility.

THE FUTURE OF GROUND DELIVERY ROBOTS

By 2030, McKinsey predicts a $50 billion autonomous delivery market. Longer-lasting batteries and swarm technology—robots coordinating like ants—will enable larger operations. Intercity robot fleets or transit integration could reduce reliance on human couriers. On campuses and resorts, robots will become standard, cutting costs and enhancing service.

From Starship's campus deliveries to Serve's neighborhood meals, ground robots are paving the way for faster, greener supply chains. Managers must invest strategically, navigate regulations, and balance automation with human roles. As robots roll into neighborhoods, they'll redefine last-mile logistics, delivering convenience one sidewalk at a time.

AUTOMATED CONTAINER SHIPS: NAVIGATING FUTURE SUPPLY CHAINS

Imagine a massive ship crossing the ocean, carrying thousands of containers with few or no crew. Automated container ships, powered by AI, sensors, and autonomous systems, are transforming global supply chains, where 90% of trade travels by sea. Acting as floating warehouses, these vessels cut labor costs, improve navigation, and optimize routes, boosting efficiency and reliability amid disruptions like port congestion or strikes. This section explores their role, applications, technologies, challenges, and future in maritime logistics.

REVOLUTIONIZING MARITIME LOGISTICS

Traditional container ships rely on large crews, with labor costs making up 20% of budgets. Automated ships use AI for navigation, engine monitoring, and route planning, slashing these costs. In 2018, Rolls-Royce and Finferries tested the Falco, a fully autonomous ferry in Finland, navigating a 1.2-mile route without crew. This success paved the way for larger vessels.

In 2022, the Yara Birkeland, a 120-TEU container ship, began autonomous operations in Norway, moving fertilizers along a seven-mile coastal route. In 2025, Maersk and Hapag-Lloyd are testing semi-autonomous megaships (20,000+ TEU), monitored remotely from shore. These ships cut labor costs by 15% and speed deliveries through optimized routes, enhancing supply chain reliability.

APPLICATIONS IN GLOBAL TRADE

The Yara Birkeland supports industrial supply chains, delivering chemicals with precise schedules. Short-sea shipping—coastal routes under 500 miles—benefits most from automation's predictability. Long-haul routes are emerging, with Japan's NYK Line testing trans-Pacific voyages in 2024. Automated ships serve varied supply chains: retail goods from China to Los Angeles for just-in-time inventory, or automotive parts to ports near factories, reducing delays.

Automation improves port coordination. Digital twins—virtual ship models—sync with smart ports, cutting turnaround times by

10%. For supply chain managers, this speeds goods flow and lowers inventory costs, but requires robust data sharing with ports.

TECHNOLOGIES POWERING AUTOMATION

AI drives automated ships, using radar, LiDAR, and cameras to navigate and avoid collisions. Satellite-based 5G ensures shore communication. IoT sensors track cargo and engine health, reducing maintenance costs by 20%, per McKinsey. Rolls-Royce's Intelligent Awareness system predicts hazards 10 miles away. Blockchain secures data, ensuring accurate manifests.

These technologies link to supply chain platforms via APIs, providing cargo visibility. Managers benefit from real-time data but must invest in cybersecurity to counter hacking risks.

CHALLENGES AND BARRIERS

Automation faces hurdles. Retrofitting a megaship costs $100 million, limiting adoption. The International Maritime Organization lacks unified rules for crewless ships, delaying global routes. Unions, representing 500,000 seafarers, oppose automation, fearing job losses. Piracy in areas like the Gulf of Aden demands human oversight, hindering full autonomy.

Supply chain complexity adds issues. Only 10% of ports are fully digitized, slowing ship-port integration. Managers must weigh costs against savings, often starting with semi-autonomous ships on short routes.

THE FUTURE OF AUTOMATED CONTAINER SHIPS

By 2030, Lloyd's Register estimates autonomous ships could handle 15% of global trade, driven by AI and 5G advances. Short-sea routes will lead, with long-haul autonomy by 2035. Smaller autonomous vessels could serve micro-ports, easing congestion at hubs like Singapore.

From the Yara Birkeland to Maersk's pilots, automated ships prove their worth. For supply chain managers, they offer savings and reliability but require planning—retrofitting fleets, training shore teams, and aligning with ports. As automation shapes trade, these ships will drive efficient, cost-effective supply chains, delivering goods faster across oceans.

BOOM SUPERSONIC: SPEEDING UP AIR FREIGHT

Imagine flying from New York to London in 3.5 hours or rushing cargo across oceans twice as fast as today's jets. Boom Supersonic's Overture jet, set for 2029, aims to transform air travel and freight by cutting transit times. In supply chains, where speed matters for high-value goods like electronics or perishables, Overture shrinks global distances. Using advanced technology and a strong supply chain, Boom seeks fast, affordable air transport. This section explores Overture's goals, applications, technologies, supply chain challenges, and its role in global trade.

- **Supersonic Logistics Goals:** Founded in 2014, Boom Supersonic revives supersonic flight, absent since 2003. Overture, cruising at Mach 1.7 (1,304 mph), carries 64–80 passengers or cargo over 4,250 nautical miles, halving transoceanic times—Newark to London in 3.5 hours, Newark to Frankfurt in 4 hours. Boom targets 1,000 jets for 500 routes, with freight rates at ~$5,000 round-trip. For supply chains, this speed supports just-in-time delivery, cutting inventory costs. Orders from United Airlines (15 jets, 35 options), American Airlines (20 jets), and Japan Airlines (20 pre-orders) total 130 commitments by 2025.

- **Air Freight Applications:** Overture's speed aids time-sensitive supply chains. In electronics, it rushes semiconductors from Asia to U.S. factories, avoiding delays. In healthcare, it delivers pharmaceuticals or medical devices globally, vital during crises. Military variants could transport supplies, showing versatility. Shorter times reduce warehousing and spoilage for perishables. Boomless Cruise technology reduces sonic booms, potentially enabling overland routes to expand supply chain reach.

- **Technologies and Supply Chain Needs:** Overture uses a Symphony turbofan engine for Mach 1.7, carbon fiber for a lightweight airframe, and AI-driven design to cut costs. An augmented reality vision system improves pilot visibility. These require a complex supply chain for avionics, landing systems, and structures. Boom's Greensboro, North Carolina, factory, completed in 2024, will build 66 jets yearly, needing tight supplier coordination and digital integration for secure data sharing.

- **Future of Supersonic Freight:** By 2030, Overture could enable same-day global deliveries. Its test jet's 2025 supersonic flight shows promise. For supply chain managers, Overture offers speed and lower inventory costs but needs integration with air cargo networks and new regulations. As Boom grows, it could redefine supply chains with supersonic speed.

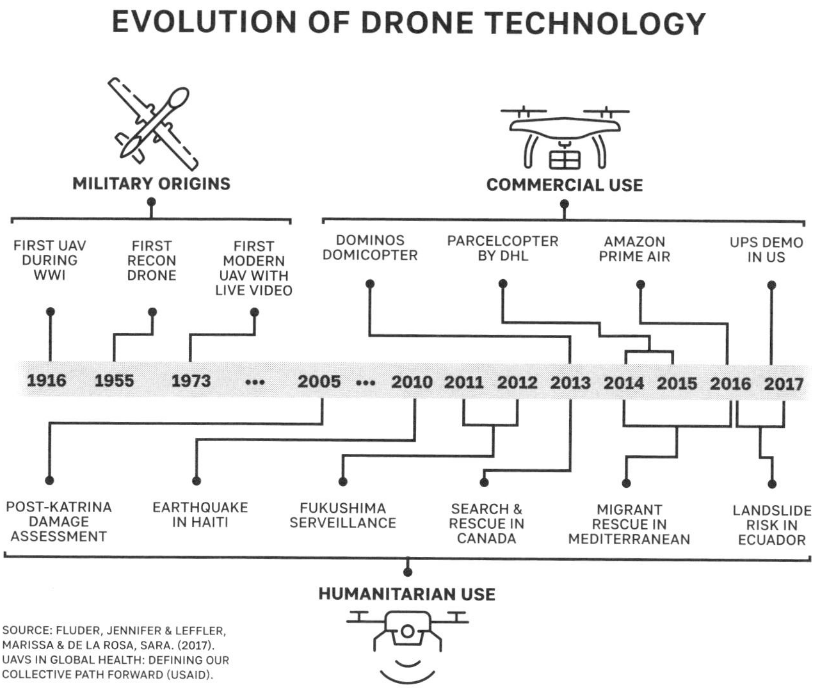

SOURCE: FLUDER, JENNIFER & LEFFLER, MARISSA & DE LA ROSA, SARA. (2017). UAVS IN GLOBAL HEALTH: DEFINING OUR COLLECTIVE PATH FORWARD (USAID).

FIG 12-1

13

THE IMPORTANCE OF ENERGY AND THE CLIMATE CONFLICT ON SUPPLY CHAINS

AI, automation, and robotics are vital for tackling challenges like climate change, but they depend on cheap, abundant energy to support essentials like food, housing, and transport. These technologies drive solutions, powered by affordable, reliable energy. Whether climate change is natural or human-caused, the solutions are similar.

Affordable energy helps adapt to climate change. It powers desalination and irrigation to address water shortages in drought-prone areas, securing food as farmland shrinks. Innovations like vertical farming and lab-grown proteins boost food production with less environmental impact, but they need cost-effective energy to scale. Abundant energy also supports resilient infrastructure, like flood-resistant cities and climate-controlled shelters, to protect against extreme weather.

Cheap energy also fuels technologies that directly address climate challenges. AI predicts disruptions for better planning, automation restores ecosystems through reforestation, and robotics maintain solar and wind farms for efficient clean energy. Low-cost energy makes these solutions accessible globally, promoting stability and equity, especially in developing nations.

Nuclear energy is key to low-carbon, abundant energy. Unlike fossil fuels, it produces nearly zero emissions and complements variable renewables like solar and wind. Small modular reactors are safe, scalable, and cost-effective, powering cities, data centers, and remote areas. Expanding nuclear supports solutions like carbon capture, desalination, and AI innovations, reducing reliance on high-emission fuels while driving sustainability.

Supply chains vary by product, so carbon reduction must be tailored. Electronics involve global networks, perishables need refrigerated transport, heavy industries like steel demand energy-intensive processes, and e-commerce focuses on fast delivery. Each has unique energy needs, requiring specific solutions like AI-optimized routes, electric local fleets, or alternative fuels for industry.

Assuming one solution, like electric vehicles (EVs), fits all supply chains is flawed. EVs suit urban delivery but struggle with long-haul trucking, shipping, or aviation due to battery weight and charging limitations. Electrifying cargo ships or planes requires unproven technologies like hydrogen or synthetic fuels. Over-relying on EVs could waste resources and slow decarbonization.

Instead, a mix of solutions paired with low-emission energy is needed. Carbon capture suits heavy industry, biofuels or hydrogen can power maritime and aviation, and EVs work for local delivery. AI-driven logistics, powered by nuclear, natural gas, or renewables, can optimize global supply chains. This tailored approach cuts emissions while keeping economies efficient.

Many assume net-zero emissions require eliminating all carbon, but reducing emissions can achieve faster results. Natural gas, cleaner than coal or oil, acts as a bridge to low-carbon energy. Intermodal transport—using ships, trains, barges, and trucks—cuts emissions by up to 75% compared to trucks alone, leveraging existing rail and

cleaner fuels like biodiesel. Barges efficiently move bulk goods like grain with minimal fuel.

Focusing on reduction over elimination enables practical steps. Natural gas can power grids with less pollution, buying time to scale nuclear or renewables. Expanding rail and barge networks shifts freight from high-emission trucks. This approach ensures modern conveniences while advancing sustainability, especially in developing economies where new infrastructure is costly.

Emerging technologies, like electric and hydrogen vehicles, AI-optimized logistics, and sustainable aviation fuels, are lowering transport emissions. Paired with low-emission energy, these innovations support fast deliveries, global travel, and connected economies without harming the planet. Cleaner energy and smarter technology available today drive sustainable progress.

However, consumers often prioritize convenience over emissions. Most value fast delivery or streaming without considering the energy behind them. This gap highlights the need for systemic solutions, like cheap, clean energy, that cut environmental impact while meeting demands. Western consumers won't abandon conveniences, and those in the East and Global South seek similar benefits. Affordable energy, paired with carbon offsets like reforestation or carbon capture, ensures growing consumption aligns with sustainability, supporting global equity without denying progress.

TRANSPORTATION, ENERGY, AND CLIMATE CHANGE SOLUTIONS

Transportation, energy, and climate change are deeply connected, shaped by decades of science and policy. In the 1970s, fears of an Ice Age gave way to concerns about global warming, now termed "climate change" to reflect complex environmental shifts. Fossil fuels, powering cars, trucks, ships, and planes, release greenhouse gases, but progress in reducing pollution is significant. The U.S. and Europe have cut vehicle emissions dramatically, making transportation cleaner, though challenges remain.

Strategic energy use, including fossil fuels as a transition, mitigates climate risks. Natural gas, emitting 50% less than coal, powers heavy vehicles and ships, while carbon capture and storage (CCS) traps up to 90% of emissions. Hybrid trucks and trains, blending fossil fuels with electric or hydrogen systems, boost efficiency by 20–30%. These bridge solutions, backed by efficiency standards, support a shift to low-carbon energy.

Fossil fuel distribution via rail and pipelines ensures energy security. Rail moves 15% of U.S. fuel, and pipelines carry 70% of oil and gas, cutting emissions by 40% per ton-mile compared to trucks. Expanded infrastructure, like the 2025 Keystone XL pipeline revival, stabilizes energy flows, reducing reliance on volatile foreign markets, as seen during the Russia-Ukraine conflict (ongoing since February 2022). This supports industries while scaling renewables.

The 1970 Clean Air Act drove vehicle pollution cuts, with modern cars and trucks emitting 98–99% fewer pollutants than 1960s models. Cleaner fuels, free of lead and low in sulfur, improve air quality. Despite this, transportation remains a key carbon source, prompting a push for electric vehicles (EVs). Automakers like Jaguar and Volvo aim for all-EV lineups by the 2030s, but EVs need robust charging networks and grid capacity. For heavy trucks, ships, and planes, EVs are less viable, requiring alternative fuels like hydrogen or biofuels, which are still developing.

Cheap, abundant energy is crucial for climate solutions. It lowers costs for clean technologies like EVs and hydrogen, with EV prices down 20% since 2020 due to scaled battery production. Abundant energy powers CCS and supports resilient supply chains, rerouting goods during disruptions like 2024 Gulf Coast port closures. Low-cost energy also drives innovation, fueling a 30% rise in clean tech patents since 2020, positioning the U.S. as a climate leader.

THE RISE OF ELECTRIC FREIGHT TRUCKS

Electric freight trucks are reshaping urban logistics but face hurdles for long-haul routes. EVs like Tesla's Semi excel in cities, with zero-emission motors and 200–300-mile ranges, cutting emissions by 50% and fuel costs by 30% for companies like Amazon. Their quiet operation suits last-mile delivery. However, long-haul trucking demands 500+ mile ranges and heavy payloads (up to 80,000 pounds), where EVs struggle due to battery weight and slow charging (30–60 minutes vs. diesel's minutes). Diesel trucks, like the Freightliner Cascadia, achieve 1,000–1,500-mile ranges and dominate, hauling 70% of U.S. freight in 2024 vs. EVs' 2%. Until charging infrastructure and battery tech advance, diesel remains key for long-haul, complementing EVs for sustainable supply chains.

U.S. FOSSIL FUEL ABUNDANCE

The U.S., the world's top oil producer (13 million barrels daily in 2024) and natural gas leader (100 billion cubic feet daily), leverages its reserves for energy security and climate progress. Domestic production, bolstered by shale fields, stabilized global markets during the Russia-Ukraine crisis. Rail and pipelines, moving 85% of oil and gas, ensure reliable distribution, with the 2025 Keystone XL revival adding capacity. This reduces foreign energy dependence, funding renewable transitions while maintaining supply chain stability.

Nuclear power, generating 20% of U.S. electricity with near-zero emissions, is a clean energy cornerstone. A 2025 executive order fast-tracks advanced small modular reactors (SMRs), set for 2030 deployment, to power EV charging and hydrogen production. Doubling nuclear capacity by 2040 will cut fossil fuel reliance and support climate solutions.

ENERGY DISTRIBUTION AND SUPPLY CHAIN INVESTMENTS

Investing in energy distribution is the most effective way to address climate change. Upgrading grids with smart tech and renewables, per the 2024 U.S. Department of Energy plan, doubles renewable capacity by 2030, powering EVs. Localized battery production cuts emissions from mining and shipping. Efficient hydrogen and biofuel supply chains, using rail or pipelines, lower costs by 20%, making zero-carbon fuels viable for heavy vehicles.

Natural gas, emitting 20–30% less CO2 than diesel, is a cleaner alternative for trucks and ships, reducing air pollution significantly. Intermodal networks, integrating rail, trucks, and barges, cut emissions by up to 75% compared to trucks alone. Barges, emitting 90% less CO_2 per ton-mile, are underused despite moving 13% of U.S. freight. Reviving the aging 12,000-mile waterway system could boost efficiency, especially for bulk goods like grain.

INTERMODAL NETWORKS: A CLIMATE SOLUTION

Intermodal transportation, combining ships, trains, trucks, and barges, is a climate solution. Rail emits 75% less CO_2 than trucks, and electrified rail and green ports amplify savings. Barges, carrying 1,500 tons with minimal fuel, are eco-friendly but underutilized due to aging infrastructure. As trade shifts to the Americas, with 2024 U.S. imports from Mexico and Canada up 20%, barges align with north-south river routes, moving goods like Brazil's soybeans. Modernizing locks and electrifying barges can unlock this potential, integrating with rail to cut emissions and enhance resilience. These networks drive progress, proving logistics innovation combats climate change.

14

THE FRAGILITY OF GLOBALIZED SUPPLY CHAINS AND THE RISE OF CHINESE E-COMMERCE

History underscores a timeless truth: wars and economic dominance are not won solely on battlefields or through market innovations but through resilient supply chains. The ability to produce, transport, and sustain critical resources often determines the outcome of conflicts and competitions more than tactics or market share. From the American Civil War to today's U.S.-China trade tensions, supply chains have been the backbone of military and economic power. However, globalization has eroded America's industrial base, creating vulnerabilities exploited by adversaries like China, particularly through e-commerce platforms leveraging U.S. trade loopholes. This chapter explores the historical lessons of supply chain resilience, the impact of globalization on U.S. manufacturing, China's strategic advantages, and the disruptive rise of Chinese e-commerce giants like Shein and Temu, amplified by manipulative digital strategies such as TikTok's algorithm favoring Chinese brands.

HISTORICAL LESSONS: THE AMERICAN CIVIL WAR AND SUPPLY CHAIN SUPREMACY

When the Civil War began in April 1861, the Confederacy seemed poised for victory. Led by skilled commanders like Robert E. Lee and Thomas "Stonewall" Jackson, Southern forces dominated early engagements in the Eastern Theater. At the First Battle of Bull Run, Confederate troops repelled Union forces, inflicting 2,900 casualties while suffering 1,900, shattering Northern hopes for a swift victory. Throughout 1862, the South showcased battlefield prowess, with Lee outmaneuvering Union General George McClellan during the Peninsula Campaign despite facing a numerically superior force of 120,000 Union soldiers to 85,000 Confederate troops.

The Confederacy held strategic advantages: superior military leadership, terrain familiarity, and shorter supply lines. Fighting on home ground with strong local support bolstered Southern morale, suggesting the Confederacy might exhaust the North's will to fight. The South's 9 million people, including 3.5 million enslaved individuals, were unified by the goal of independence, and per capita, the South was wealthier than the North.

However, the Confederacy's industrial weaknesses proved fatal. With only 9,500 miles of railroad compared to the North's 22,000, the South struggled to move troops and supplies efficiently. Meanwhile, the North leveraged its 22 million population and industrial might, producing 97% of U.S. firearms and 90% of manufactured goods by 1862.

The Union's Anaconda Plan, a naval blockade launched in 1861, progressively strangled Southern trade, reducing exports by 95% and depriving the Confederacy of critical resources. In the Western Theater, Union General Ulysses S. Grant exploited this logistical edge, capturing strategic river forts in February 1862 with 2,700 Union losses compared to the South's 13,000, securing key waterways for supply transport.

By late 1862, the North's superior railroads and effective blockade proved decisive. The Battle of Antietam in September forced Lee to retreat despite heavy casualties on both sides, enabling President

Lincoln to issue the Emancipation Proclamation, which redefined the war's purpose and deterred European intervention.

The South's early victories, though impressive, could not overcome the North's manufacturing and logistical supremacy, which sustained a prolonged conflict the Confederacy could not endure. The Civil War demonstrated that supply chains, not just battles, determine ultimate victory.

GLOBALIZATION'S TOLL ON AMERICAN SUPPLY CHAINS

Today, U.S. military planners face a troubling parallel: globalization has eroded America's industrial base, creating vulnerabilities in a potential conflict with adversaries like China. For nearly two centuries, economic globalization has linked nations through trade, but this process has weakened American manufacturing by prioritizing cost savings over domestic production.

In the late 20th century, U.S. companies offshored industries to China, drawn by wages as low as $1 per hour compared to $15–$20 in the U.S., alongside minimal environmental and labor regulations. By the early 2000s, China's vast industrial zones and 150 million factory workers enabled rapid scaling to meet global demand, boosting corporate profits but creating strategic vulnerabilities that now threaten national security.

Entire industries relocated overseas, devastating American manufacturing communities. The U.S. textile industry, which employed over 900,000 workers in 1990, shrank to fewer than 300,000 by 2023 as production shifted to Asia. America's global manufacturing share fell from 30% in 1950 to 16% today, while China's share rose to 40%. **[FIG 14-1]**

Recent events have exposed these dependencies. When China imposed export restrictions on steel castings and plastic moldings in 2024, U.S. businesses struggled to meet domestic demand. A 30-day shipping delay in 2022 cost U.S. retailers $40 billion, and analysts project a broader conflict could triple that impact, leaving shelves empty and prices soaring.

Most concerning is the semiconductor supply chain. Taiwan's

TSMC produces 92% of the world's advanced computer chips, critical for everything from telephones to cars to missiles. A Chinese invasion or blockade of Taiwan could disrupt chip supplies, potentially reducing U.S. economic output by 3% to 5% and costing the global economy $1 trillion. The 2021 chip shortage, which cost U.S. automakers $110 billion, offers a sobering preview.

Despite the $52 billion CHIPS Act to build domestic semiconductor factories, operational plants won't come online until 2027 or 2028, leaving a significant gap in American preparedness.

CURRENT U.S. SUPPLY CHAIN WEAKNESSES

Globalization has undermined America's ability to produce critical military components, including steel forgings for artillery and transport vehicles, and rubber seals and plastic casings for armored vehicles and communications devices. A conflict in the South China Sea could disrupt these supplies, potentially stalling production lines for months.

The U.S. textile industry, essential for producing military uniforms, tents, and parachutes, has declined as production shifted to Asia. Rebuilding domestic manufacturing capacity faces challenges: many factories have been closed, razed, or repurposed, and the skilled workforce has dwindled, leaving the U.S. ill-prepared for wartime demands.

America's reliance on just-in-time supply chains, optimized for peacetime efficiency, undermines national defense by depending on global sources for critical materials. Aluminum for aircraft frames, cotton for uniforms, and chemicals for munitions are predominantly sourced from China due to lower costs, but a Chinese trade embargo could disrupt production of essential military equipment.

Unlike during World War II, when the U.S. maintained robust stockpiles of strategic materials like rubber and steel, today's reserves are minimal, leaving the nation vulnerable to disruptions. American ports, often operating near capacity, are ill-equipped for wartime surges, and 80% of port cranes, manufactured in China, are susceptible to cyberattacks or sabotage.

The U.S. Navy, with fewer ships than in the 1980s, would struggle to protect vital trade routes during a conflict. Decades of offshoring have reduced the skilled workforce in industries like metalworking and textiles, hindering the ability to rapidly scale production during a crisis.

CHINA'S STRATEGIC SUPPLY CHAIN ADVANTAGE

In contrast, China has positioned its civilian supply chain to support military objectives, leveraging its massive manufacturing scale for potential conflicts. Chinese shipyards produce roll-on/roll-off ferries that can transport troops and tanks, with 30 such vessels supporting large-scale military exercises in 2022. Civilian aviation technologies are adapted for military aircraft, enhancing China's air power.

The People's Liberation Army Navy, with 355 ships in 2021, is projected to grow to 460 by 2030, surpassing the U.S. Navy's 296 ships (expected to reach only 317 by 2035). China's shipbuilding capacity, over 200 times larger than America's, produces more than 1,000 commercial ships annually compared to the U.S.'s five, a disparity extending to military vessels.

China's 2016 National Defense Transportation Law mandates that shipping companies assist in military operations, such as troop transport or maritime escorts. Its maritime militia of over 120 fishing vessels enforces territorial claims, blurring civilian and military roles and providing a conflict-ready reserve.

China dominates global production in critical sectors, including over 50% of the world's steel, supported by state subsidies and a manufacturing workforce of 170 million—over half the U.S. population. Its logistical infrastructure, with 130 major ports and a 96,000-mile rail network, ensures efficient transport of raw materials.

China's state-controlled economy enables swift resource allocation, redirecting civilian factories to military production without disrupting domestic markets. Strategic stockpiles of critical resources ensure sustained operations, giving China a decisive edge in a prolonged conflict where production capacity is paramount.

HISTORICAL PRECEDENTS: TRADE DISPUTES AND WARFARE

Trade disputes have often escalated into kinetic conflicts, driven by economic pressures, resource competition, and nationalism. The Peloponnesian War (431–404 BCE) was fueled partly by Athens' economic dominance and its trade embargo on Megara, a Spartan ally, sparking decades of conflict that reshaped the Greek world.

The American Revolution (1775–1783) was triggered in part by Britain's restrictive trade policies, including the Tea Act of 1773, which sparked the Boston Tea Party and led to armed conflict at Lexington and Concord in 1775.

In the 1930s, Japan's need for oil and steel drove its invasion of Manchuria. U.S. trade sanctions, including a 1941 oil embargo cutting 80% of Japan's supply, prompted the attack on Pearl Harbor, escalating a trade dispute into global war.

This progression—economic measures like tariffs or embargoes creating hardship, prompting counter-sanctions or resource grabs—is evident in the First Opium War (1839–1842), when Britain fought China to protect trade interests after China banned opium imports.

Nationalism often accelerates this process, as seen in the Second Sino-Japanese War (1937–1945), where trade disputes over resources fueled nationalist fervor, escalating a railway skirmish into an eight-year war with millions of casualties.

Today's U.S.-China trade tensions, with tariffs impacting $540 billion in annual trade and China's 2024 antimony export ban disrupting U.S. industries, show how mistrust and strategic competition can transform trade into a weapon.

BUILDING RESILIENT AMERICAN SUPPLY CHAINS

Facing mounting supply chain risks, from shipping delays to potential conflicts, the Americas—Mexico, Canada, Brazil, Argentina, and Colombia—offer a stable alternative to Asian supply chains. The USMCA trade agreement facilitates seamless cross-border commerce, while geographic proximity reduces transit risks. Goods from Mexico or Canada reach the U.S. in two to three days via truck or rail, compared to weeks by sea from Asia.

Regional transportation infrastructure continues to improve, with Mexico's rail capacity up 30% since 2020 and Canada's trucking fleet expanded by 15%. Colombia's ports ship coffee and cotton to the U.S. in under a week, enabling retailers to restock quickly during disruptions, as seen during the 2024 Gulf Coast port closures. **[FIG 14-2]**

Regional diversification leverages complementary strengths across the Americas. Brazil's agricultural and mineral exports to the U.S., including soybeans and iron ore, rose 20% in 2024, providing essential raw materials. Argentina's biofuels sector supports logistics fleets, while Canada's $200 billion in manufacturing investments since 2022 bolsters its capacity to produce machinery and automotive components.

Building a robust American supply chain requires regional production hubs capitalizing on each country's strengths. Mexico's 1.5 million workers in clothing and electronics assembly can produce consumer goods, while Canada's skilled workforce excels in high-precision manufacturing. Brazil and Argentina supply raw materials, and Colombia's $1.5 billion flower industry supports U.S. retailers.

Infrastructure investments are critical, including expanding Miami's port to handle trade with South American partners, upgrading rail lines for Canadian goods, and extending the I-69 corridor to Mexican manufacturing zones. Technological integration—AI-driven forecasting, blockchain tracking, and IoT sensors—ensures efficiency and quality.

Workforce development is essential, with cross-border training programs preparing workers across the Americas for specialized roles in modern manufacturing and logistics. The U.S.'s logistics network—140,000 miles of rail, 900,000 trucking carriers, 5,000 airports, and Mississippi River barges—provides unmatched reliability and redundancy, ensuring continuity during disruptions.

THE DE MINIMIS LOOPHOLE AND CHINESE E-COMMERCE

While supply chain vulnerabilities threaten U.S. security, a U.S. trade policy—the de minimis exemption—has fueled China's economic assault on American retail. Established by the 1938 Tariff Act, the exemption allows shipments under $800 to enter duty-free, simplifying trade for low-value goods. Initially set at $1 during the Great Depression, it supported families receiving overseas parcels. By 1994, it rose to $200, and in 2016, the Trade Facilitation and Trade Enforcement Act raised it to $800 to accommodate e-commerce growth, reducing customs delays and saving businesses millions.

This policy, intended for small-scale trade, has been exploited by Chinese e-commerce giants Shein and Temu, disrupting U.S. retail. By shipping directly from factories, they avoid tariffs faced by retailers like H&M ($205 million in 2022) and Gap ($700 million). Shein's U.S. sales grew from $22.7 billion in 2022 to $32.2 billion in 2023, with profits doubling to $1.6 billion. Temu, launched in 2022, hit $15.3 billion in gross merchandise value in 2023, projected to reach $29.5 billion in 2024. Together, they shipped 600,000 packages daily to the U.S. in 2023, contributing to 1 billion de minimis shipments, 60% from China, a fivefold increase from 2016.

TIKTOK'S ALGORITHMIC MANIPULATION

The success of Shein and Temu is amplified by TikTok, owned by China's ByteDance, whose algorithm disproportionately promotes Chinese brands. A 2024 Peterson Institute study found Chinese products appeared 40% more often in TikTok's "For You" feeds than U.S. brands like Gap or Target. TikTok Shop, launched in 2023, drives sales through viral content, with 44% of Gen Z shopping Shein monthly and 41% using Temu. Shein and Temu spent $1.3 billion on advertising in 2023, including Temu's $14 million Super Bowl ad and Shein's $300–$400 million marketing budget, flooding TikTok with AI-tailored campaigns for $8 dresses and $14 electronics. A 2023 Wall Street Journal report revealed ByteDance adjusted TikTok's algorithm to favor Chinese brands, and a 2024 eMarketer study noted Temu's sponsored posts appeared in 60% of Gen Z feeds, outranking U.S. competitors. This algorithmic bias, reflecting China's intent to dominate U.S. retail, gives Chinese platforms an unfair edge, threatening American businesses.

Artificial intelligence further sharpens their advantage. Shein's AI launches 1.3 million new products daily, dwarfing Zara's 35,000 annually. Temu's algorithms optimize pricing, offering a $23 foot massager versus Amazon's $35. Natural language models (NLMs) craft hyper-localized marketing, mimicking American cultural nuances. In 2023, Chinese AI-generated influencers amassed 12 billion U.S. views, per eMarketer. Chinese factories reverse-engineer U.S. designs, selling look-alikes on Temu for 30% less, using data from Shein and Temu to replicate consumer preferences without R&D costs. U.S. retailers, facing tariffs and slower shipping, lose pricing power, echoing the 1990s textile industry collapse, when Chinese subsidies eliminated 900,000 U.S. jobs by 2005.

ECONOMIC AND SOCIAL FALLOUT

The de minimis exemption has turned Shein and Temu into retail juggernauts, eroding U.S. market share. Shein became the third-largest online fashion retailer in 2023, trailing only Amazon and Walmart, while Temu rivaled eBay. Their pricing advantage, enabled by duty-free shipments, cost U.S. businesses $40–$50 billion annually, per a 2024 NRF study. In 2023, 15,000 U.S. retail closures and 200,000 job losses, 30% linked to Chinese e-commerce, strained communities. For every $1 billion in Shein and Temu sales, 6,000 U.S. jobs are displaced, projecting 282,000 losses by 2025. Retail closures in states like Ohio and Pennsylvania cost $1.2 billion in taxes, echoing the 2000s Rust Belt decline.

The surge in de minimis shipments—1.36 billion in 2024, 60% from China—strains USPS, with processing delays at hubs like JFK Airport. The ePacket program, subsidizing Chinese parcels, cost USPS $29.4 million in 2012, contributing to $60 billion in deficits since 2007. Rate hikes for domestic shippers and taxpayer-funded bailouts offset losses, while U.S. retailers face higher shipping costs, unable to match Temu's $0.99 items with free shipping.

POLICY RESPONSES AND THE 2025 EXECUTIVE ORDER

The strain prompted policy shifts. In 2018, the U.S. challenged

UPU's discounted rates, costing USPS $300–$500 million yearly. A 2019 UPU agreement raised rates, increasing Chinese vendors' costs by 119–164% by 2025. In 2025, the Trump administration's executive order eliminated the $800 de minimis exemption for Chinese and Hong Kong shipments, effective May 2, imposing a 30% duty or $25–$50 per-item fee and requiring formal entry procedures. The order, addressing unfair trade and illicit substances like fentanyl, followed a February 2025 attempt halted by logistical chaos at JFK Airport. Shein and Temu, facing price hikes, shifted to U.S.-based fulfillment, with Shein operating hubs in Illinois, California, and Seattle, and Temu sourcing half its 2024 U.S. sales locally, mitigating the policy's impact.

BUILDING RESILIENT AMERICAN SUPPLY CHAINS

To counter these vulnerabilities, the U.S. must rebuild regional supply chains, leveraging the Americas—Mexico, Canada, Brazil, Argentina, and Colombia—via the USMCA. Goods from Mexico or Canada arrive in 2–3 days versus weeks from Asia. Mexico's rail capacity grew 30% since 2020, and Canada's trucking fleet expanded 15%. Brazil's 2024 agricultural exports to the U.S. rose 20%, and Colombia's ports ship cotton rapidly. Regional hubs can capitalize on Mexico's 1.5 million clothing workers, Canada's precision manufacturing, and Brazil's raw materials. Investments in Miami's port, I-69 corridor, and AI-driven logistics can ensure efficiency. Workforce training across the Americas is vital to rebuild skilled labor.

LEARNING FROM HISTORY

The Civil War's lesson endures: industrial capacity and supply chain resilience are as critical as battlefield or market victories. America's globalization-driven vulnerabilities, exploited by China's manufacturing might and e-commerce strategies, echo the Confederacy's industrial deficits. TikTok's algorithmic manipulation, favoring Chinese brands like Shein and Temu, underscores China's intent to dominate U.S. retail, costing jobs and revenue. By rebuilding domestic manufacturing, strengthening regional partnerships, and reforming trade policies like the de minimis exemption, the U.S. can address these threats. Supply chains are not mere business concerns but pillars of national security, demanding strategic focus to ensure America's resilience in an era of escalating geopolitical and economic competition.

SHARE OF GLOBAL MANUFACTURING

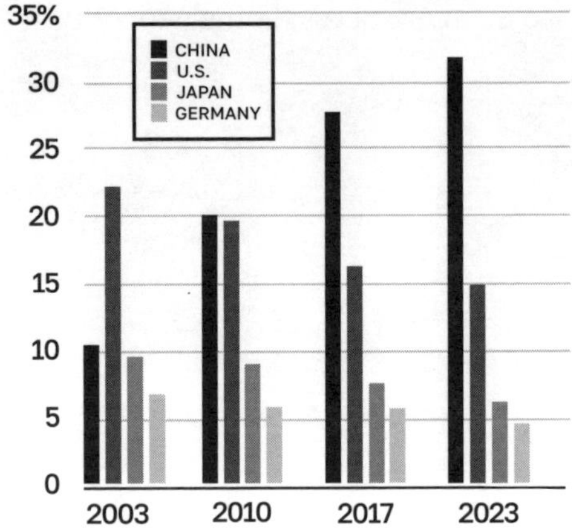

SOURCE: UNITED NATIONS INDUSTRIAL DEVELOPMENT ORGANIZATION

FIG 14-1

VOLUME OF U.S. EXPORTS OF TRADE GOODS TO MEXICO FROM 1985 TO 2024

(IN BILLION U.S. DOLLARS)

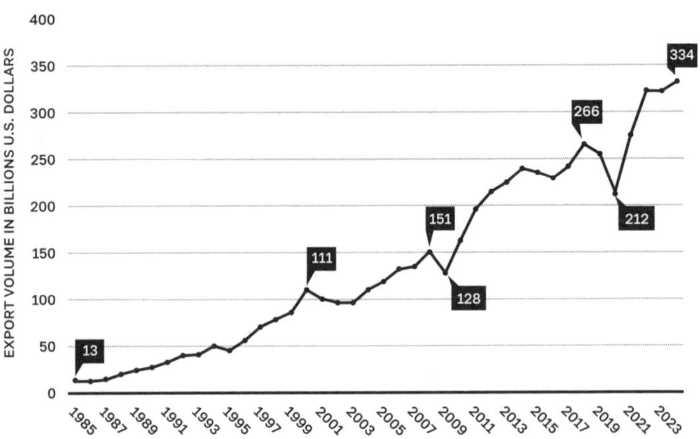

SOURCE: U.S. DEPARTMENT OF TRADE

FIG 14-2

15

DISRUPTIONS - WHEN SUPPLY CHAINS BREAK

In the introduction, I wrote about how supply chains operate in the background, often invisible. But there are occasions when things break, and Mother Nature is often the reason.

Robust supply chains are the reason that modern humans are generally insulated from Mother Nature's impacts. However, hurricanes, blizzards, droughts, floods, earthquakes, tornadoes, wildfires, grid disruptions, and cyberattacks can all severely disrupt the flow of cargo. When these events occur, the consequences ripple throughout the supply chain: highways can become impassable; ports may cease operations; factories halt production; and communication systems fail. The result is a cascade of delays, cost increases, and supply shortages that strain businesses and consumers.

Understanding how each type of disaster affects freight markets reveals not only the scale of their impact but also highlights vulnerabilities within our supply chains. This knowledge is crucial for developing strategies to maintain the flow of goods during crises and to build more resilient systems for the future.

TYPES OF DISASTERS AFFECTING FREIGHT MARKETS

Natural disasters and technological failures disrupt freight operations and global supply chains by halting goods movement, damaging infrastructure, and causing economic ripple effects. This section explores how hurricanes, blizzards, droughts, floods, earthquakes, tornadoes, wildfires, grid failures, and cyberattacks impact freight networks.

- **Hurricanes:** Hurricanes disrupt freight through flooding, debris, and blocked routes, halting deliveries and raising consumer prices. In 2017, Hurricane Harvey flooded Houston, closing Interstate 10 and disrupting 7% of U.S. trucking capacity. Freight rates from Dallas to Houston surged 67% to $4 per mile. Houston's port closed, rerouting cargo and increasing costs. In 2024, Hurricane Milton shut Tampa Bay's port and flooded roads, disrupting local deliveries. Hurricanes also damage factories and warehouses, halting production. Harvey's closure of Gulf Coast refineries (17% of U.S. capacity) raised diesel prices 13%, while relief efforts reduced trucking availability.

- **Blizzards:** Blizzards disrupt air cargo and highway transport. In 2024, a blizzard closed Dallas-Fort Worth Airport, delaying 30% of cargo shipments and affecting national supply chains. In 2023, Winter Storm Mara shut Interstate 44 in Arkansas and Missouri, stranding trucks and pausing factory operations due to power outages and damaged cell towers. These disruptions delayed warehouse operations and load tracking, causing regional supply chain delays.

- **Droughts:** Droughts disrupt water-based freight. In 2023, low

Panama Canal water levels reduced daily transits from 36–38 to 22 vessels, delaying 100 ships and raising U.S.-Asia trade costs. Factories stopped production, and retailers faced inventory shortages. U.S. droughts also cut hydroelectric power, disrupting logistics facilities and overheating data centers.

- **Floods:** Floods block freight routes and infrastructure. In 2019, Mississippi River flooding closed 200 miles of waterway, delaying agricultural exports and halting steel plants. In 2024, Hurricane Helene's floods in North Carolina closed Interstate 26 and damaged the Port of Wilmington, stopping cargo movement. Power and communication outages extended disruptions beyond flood zones.

- **Earthquakes:** Earthquakes destroy roads, bridges, and ports. The 2011 Tohoku earthquake in Japan halted exports, closing automaker factories globally due to parts shortages. A 2014 Chile earthquake delayed copper shipments, impacting global markets. Factory destruction and power outages slow recovery, disrupting trade for months.

- **Tornadoes:** Tornadoes cause intense, localized damage. In 2021, an EF4 tornado in Mayfield, Kentucky, destroyed a trucking terminal, delaying regional deliveries. Damaged rail tracks and factories halted shipments, while power and communication outages disrupted logistics.

- **Wildfires:** Wildfires disrupt freight, especially in western North America. In 2023, Canadian wildfires closed Highway 401 and halted flights due to smoke. In 2024, California wildfires destroyed Central Valley warehouses, disrupting agricultural supply chains. Power and communication outages caused further delays.

- **Grid Disruptions:** Power grid failures stop freight operations. In 2021, Texas outages halted Dallas cargo facilities. A 2023 Maui blackout disrupted port operations. Powerless warehouses and data centers worsen disruptions during concurrent disasters.

- **Cyberattacks:** Cyberattacks threaten digitized freight systems. A 2021 pipeline attack disrupted U.S. fuel distribution. A 2023 port system breach slowed cargo processing, and a 2024 manufacturing cyberattack delayed production. These attacks create widespread supply chain disruptions.

Natural disasters and technological failures disrupt freight through physical and digital damage, causing cascading effects across regional, national, and global supply chains. As disasters grow more frequent and supply chains more complex, disaster preparedness and resilient infrastructure are critical for economic stability.

RESILIENCE OF FREIGHT MARKETS

Despite these formidable challenges, freight markets demonstrate remarkable resilience, with disruptions representing notable exceptions in an otherwise robust system. The supply chain industry efficiently moves vast quantities of goods daily, with trucks, ships, trains, and airplanes operating seamlessly under normal conditions. When disruptions occur – hurricanes blocking roads, blizzards grounding flights, or cyberattacks affecting operations – they stand out precisely because they contrast with the industry's standard reliability. Despite setbacks from natural or man-made disasters, the freight system – particularly the U.S. freight system – is designed to recover quickly, minimizing the impact on global trade.

The scale of the freight industry's operations is impressive: trucks carry approximately 70% of U.S. freight across 4 million miles of roads, managing most challenges effectively. Ports process millions of shipments annually, typically overcoming minor setbacks with minimal disruption. Rail and barge networks maintain cargo flow through many adverse conditions, adapting routes and schedules as needed. When Hurricane Harvey struck, freight markets faced significant challenges but resumed operations within weeks, with cargo rerouted and schedules adjusted to accommodate the disruption. Similarly, the 2023 Panama Canal drought created delays, but global trade continued as shippers adapted by finding alternative routes.

These events prove temporary because the industry is fundamentally built for durability. Incidents like the 2021 pipeline cyberattack cause temporary setbacks, but freight markets recover swiftly as systems are restored and alternative solutions implemented. Grid outages, such as the 2021 Texas winter storm, disrupt operations briefly, yet the system rebounds once power is restored. The supply chain industry's ability to navigate and overcome these challenges underscores its inherent strength, ensuring goods continue to flow despite even the most severe disruptions.

This resilience, often unnoticed until tested by major events, plays a crucial role in maintaining supply chain stability and supporting the global economy through crises. As freight markets continue to evolve, this capacity for adaptation and recovery remains their most valuable asset in facing future challenges.

16

FREIGHT CYCLES: TRUCKING'S FRENZIED TRADING FLOOR AND OCEAN SHIPPING'S OLIGOPOLISTIC WAVES

Ocean container shipping and trucking are essential to global supply chains, handling 80% of world trade and 70% of U.S. freight by volume. Both sectors navigate disruptions from economic downturns, trade policies, geopolitical tensions, and environmental challenges, yet their freight cycles often diverge due to distinct market structures and operational constraints. Understanding these dynamics is critical for stakeholders managing complex logistics networks.

CAPACITY: THE CORE OF FREIGHT PRICING

Freight pricing is fundamentally tied to capacity constraints. In trucking, capacity depends on the availability of drivers; in ocean shipping, it relies on the number of vessels in service. Demand in both markets is influenced by economic cycles and external factors, such as trade policies, which significantly impact freight due to its exposure to global and national economic forces.

Capacity strives to align with demand. In trucking, robust markets drive fleet expansion and driver recruitment, while downturns lead to workforce reductions and fleet contraction. Owner-operators enter during strong markets to capitalize on elevated rates but often exit—frequently through bankruptcy—during slumps. Larger fleets also face insolvency risks in prolonged downturns. In contrast, ocean shipping adjusts capacity slowly, as constructing new vessels requires substantial investment and years of lead time, resulting in extended market cycles compared to trucking's rapid adjustments. This contrast in responsiveness sets the stage for their divergent cycles.

DIVERGENT CYCLES: TRUCKING VS. OCEAN SHIPPING

Trucking cycles, typically spanning one to two years, are driven by driver availability. When demand surges, fleets can recruit drivers swiftly—often within weeks—as training and licensing costs are modest, averaging $5,000-$10,000. This low barrier enables owner-operators to acquire used trucks and enter the market quickly. During downturns, drivers exit, and fleets downsize, rendering trucking cycles volatile but short-lived.

Ocean freight cycles, extending over a decade, are constrained by vessel availability. Constructing a mega-ship, capable of carrying 24,000 TEUs, costs $200 million and requires three years, creating a significant barrier to entry and slowing capacity expansion. Demand surges outstrip vessel additions, driving rate increases and supply chain pressures. In downturns, excess vessels persist, as scrapping is costly and time-intensive, further prolonging cycles.

The flexibility of trucking's labor-driven model contrasts with ocean shipping's capital-intensive structure. Driver training represents a short-term investment, whereas a vessel is a multi-decade commitment. This structural divergence underpins their misaligned cycles, with ocean shipping's prolonged adjustments exerting a deeper influence on global trade. These differences necessitate tools to navigate market volatility, as explored next.

FREIGHTWAVES AND SONAR: ILLUMINATING FREIGHT MARKET DYNAMICS

The volatility of freight cycles—marked by overinvestment in booms and severe contractions in busts—prompted the establishment of FreightWaves and SONAR. Recognizing that opaque market data left participants vulnerable to unpredictable shifts, I founded these platforms to enhance transparency, equipping shippers, carriers, and brokers with a competitive advantage comparable to a Bloomberg Terminal in financial markets. FreightWaves, supported by a team of experienced journalists, delivers in-depth reporting on significant freight market developments, such as trade policy changes, port disruptions, and regulatory shifts, providing essential context. SONAR, a premier market intelligence platform and Price Reporting Agency (PRA) for freight, functions akin to S&P Global in commodities, offering standardized, high-frequency data to monitor rates, capacity, and demand across trucking and ocean shipping.

As a PRA, SONAR aggregates thousands of daily transactions to produce trusted benchmarks, such as the National Truckload Index (NTI) for spot rates and the Outbound Tender Rejection Index (OTRI) for supply-demand dynamics. Its ocean data, encompassing container rates and port congestion metrics, enables users to address disruptions like the 2021 Suez Canal blockage or 2024 Houthi attacks in the Red Sea. During the 2020-2021 pandemic surge, SONAR's tender rejection data highlighted escalating rates, enabling proactive pricing adjustments. Integrations with platforms like project44 and e2open provide real-time analytics, empowering users to anticipate market shifts. By replacing fragmented data with reliable indices, SONAR enhances decision-making in a volatile industry.

This transparency mitigates the impact of cycle imbalances. From 2019 to 2023, trucking experienced 45% carrier growth against 11% demand growth, while ocean shipping added 3 million TEUs, surpassing 8% trade expansion. Without clear insights, such disparities can devastate stakeholders. FreightWaves' journalism and SONAR's PRA-driven data foster informed strategies, enhancing resilience.

These tools are particularly vital in trucking's fragmented market, as discussed next.

TRUCKING: A FRAGMENTED AND DYNAMIC MARKET

Trucking's volatility arises from its low barriers to entry. During market upswings, new entrants—often drivers from large fleets seeking independence—enter rapidly, acquiring trucks with accessible financing. This triggers a cycle: fleets losing drivers recruit replacements, frequently from outside the industry, expanding capacity.

Used trucks are abundant, exported during weak markets or purchased by owner-operators in strong ones, further increasing capacity. However, hiring drivers remains challenging for larger fleets, where insurance-driven safety standards reject 98-99% of applicants, often favoring inexperienced drivers over veterans with minor infractions.

The Great Freight Recession compelled fleets to hire non-domiciled drivers lacking U.S. CDLs or work permits. A study estimated 150,000 such drivers, though industry sources suggest this figure may be conservative. Approximately 40% of U.S. truck drivers are first-generation immigrants, with 10% unable to speak English, according to industry stakeholders.

Regulatory shortcomings exacerbated these issues. A 2016 Department of Transportation order prevented states from suspending non-compliant drivers, and certain DMVs issued CDLs to non-domiciled individuals without U.S. testing, undermining standards. Smaller fleets, less scrutinized, employed these drivers out of necessity, while larger fleets adhered to stringent hiring protocols.

The 1980 Motor Carrier Act deregulated trucking, reducing rates but fragmenting the industry. Today, 531,000 U.S. fleets—99% with 100 or fewer trucks—operate in a competitive spot market, where brokers and carriers negotiate loads in a decentralized, data-driven environment. This fragmented structure contrasts sharply with ocean shipping's consolidated framework, as explored below.

THE OCEAN SHIPPING OLIGOPOLY: MARKET POWER AND ALLIANCES

Unlike the fragmented trucking industry, ocean shipping is an oligopoly, with the top 10 carriers controlling ~85% of global container capacity, functioning as a de facto cartel. Exempt from U.S. antitrust laws under the Shipping Act of 1984, these carriers form alliances to coordinate capacity and schedules, wielding greater market power than OPEC, which controls ~40% of global oil supply. In 2025, three major alliances—Ocean Alliance, Gemini Cooperation, and Premier Alliance—along with independent operators like Mediterranean Shipping Company (MSC), manage ~88% of global capacity, shaping trade with limited regulatory oversight.

This concentration enables carriers to stabilize freight rates, unlike trucking's volatility, by reducing capacity during low-demand periods, similar to OPEC's production cuts. This controlled approach ensures profitability and highlights structural differences driving cycle divergence between ocean shipping and other transportation sectors.

STRUCTURE AND OPERATIONS OF ALLIANCES

In 2025, the ocean shipping industry restructured after the dissolution of the 2M Alliance, forming new partnerships:

- **Ocean Alliance:** Comprising CMA CGM, COSCO Group, OOCL, and Evergreen, it controls 29% of global capacity (~5 million TEUs, 390 vessels), focusing on Asia-Europe and Asia-North America routes, with agreements extended to 2032.

- **Gemini Cooperation:** Formed by Maersk and Hapag-Lloyd, it holds 20.6% of capacity (~3.4 million TEUs, 290 vessels), targeting 90% schedule reliability.

- **Premier Alliance:** Including HMM, ONE, and Yang Ming, it accounts for 12% of capacity (~3.3 million TEUs), focusing on East-West trade lanes since February 2025.

- **Independent Operators:** MSC, with a 20% market share (~6 million TEUs), operates independently, while other independents (e.g., ZIM, Wan Hai) hold ~6% of capacity. **[FIG 16-1]**

Alliances collectively represent ~62% of global capacity, and with MSC, they account for ~82%. The remaining ~18% is held by smaller independents. No major alliance members are U.S.-based, originating from China, the EU, Japan, South Korea, Switzerland, and Taiwan. State-supported carriers like COSCO bolster export economies, while HMM and Yang Ming receive subsidies for trade and security objectives. Alliances optimize resources but often prioritize profitability over supply chain reliability, impacting global trade.

MARKET STRATEGIES AND PRICING POWER

Alliances exert significant pricing power over U.S. importers by using "blank sailings" to cancel voyages, restrict supply, and increase rates. In 2021, 12% of Far East-to-North America sailings were canceled, exacerbating port congestion and driving rate hikes. In 2024, container spot rates doubled from late 2023 due to rerouting and congestion, showing carriers' ability to sustain elevated rates. Unlike competitive markets where excess capacity lowers prices, alliances maintain high rates, benefiting carriers while smaller shippers face delays and costs. Large cargo owners secure priority access through premium rates, marginalizing smaller businesses.

In 2025, a major trade disruption caused a 65% drop in container volumes from China over two weeks, followed by subsequent trade restrictions escalating tariffs to 145% in April. In a typical market, such a demand drop would reduce rates. Instead, spot rates from China to North America's West Coast rose from $2,100 to $2,400, driven by alliances canceling over 80 voyages. This counterintuitive increase underscores their ability to manipulate supply and maintain pricing power, mirroring OPEC's tactics, despite reduced trade volumes.

HISTORICAL EVOLUTION OF THE CARTEL

Alliances emerged in the 1990s, facilitated by the 1984 U.S. Shipping Act, which reduced regulatory oversight. In 1984, container ships had a capacity of 4,500 TEUs, compared to today's 24,000-TEU mega-ships, which require substantial investment. Alliances enable carriers to pool resources to finance these vessels while controlling capacity. In 1992, the top 30 carriers held 63% of capacity; subsequent mergers, bankruptcies, and state-backed operators increased consolidation. By 2017, alliances controlled 76% of capacity, rising to 86% by 2022. The 2025 dissolution of the 2M Alliance and the emergence of Gemini and Premier alliances reflect ongoing adaptation to market and regulatory pressures.

IMPACT ON GLOBAL SUPPLY CHAINS

Alliances have significantly influenced supply chains, particularly during the COVID-19 pandemic. In 2021, carriers reported $190 billion in profits, driven by rate surges rather than volume growth, with Asia-to-U.S. West Coast spot rates escalating from $2,000 to $20,000. Alliances reduced service frequency and reliability, increasing wait times. As 80% of global trade is seaborne, elevated rates contribute to inflation, raising global prices by 1.5% in 2022. In 2024, Suez Canal disruptions increased vessel demand by 12%, raising costs and emissions, particularly for vulnerable economies.

REGULATORY FRAMEWORK AND FUTURE OUTLOOK

Antitrust exemptions, established under the 1916 U.S. Shipping Act, protect foreign carriers from U.S. enforcement. In Europe, exemptions ceased in April 2024, subjecting alliances to stricter competition rules. In the U.S., the Ocean Shipping Antitrust Enforcement Act, proposed in 2022, seeks to eliminate exemptions but remains unresolved in 2025. The 2022 Ocean Shipping Reform Act addressed some supply chain issues but preserved carrier immunity.

Unlike transparent oil futures markets, container shipping lacks robust price discovery. The Freightos Baltic futures market on the CME sees minimal trading, leaving pricing power with carriers. Businesses struggle to hedge rate risks, as prices depend on carrier-controlled dynamics. Potential solutions include increasing capacity to foster competition or removing antitrust exemptions to enhance oversight. As James Hookham of the Global Shippers' Forum observed, alliance practices like information-sharing would be deemed anticompetitive in other sectors. Without regulatory reform, the cartel is likely to continue prioritizing profits, impacting global trade and consumers. These market distortions highlight the broader forces shaping freight cycles.

DRIVERS OF FREIGHT CYCLE VOLATILITY

Both trucking and ocean shipping are subject to shared macroeconomic, geopolitical, and environmental pressures, yet their responses differ due to structural disparities. Economic expansions stimulate freight demand, tightening capacity, while recessions or elevated interest rates reduce volumes, depressing rates. Geopolitical events, such as tariffs or Suez Canal blockages, disrupt flows, increasing costs and creating ripple effects across both markets.

Market overreactions amplify volatility. Between 2019 and 2023, trucking saw a 45% increase in carrier registrations, far exceeding 11% demand growth. Similarly, ocean shipping added 3 million TEUs of capacity by 2024, outpacing 8% trade growth. In downturns, trucking experiences rapid exits, often driven by industry sentiment amplified through digital channels, while ocean carriers face challenges from ill-timed vessel orders. These behavioral responses perpetuate volatile cycles, necessitating a closer examination of each market's operational dynamics.

TRUCKING: A DECENTRALIZED MARKETPLACE

Trucking's spot market operates as a decentralized marketplace, where shippers, brokers, and carriers negotiate via load boards, emails, or established relationships, without standardized bidding mechanisms akin to financial exchanges. This structure fosters volatility, as participants rely on disparate data sources—ranging from advanced analytics to industry sentiment—making rapid decisions that collectively influence rates.

The 1980 Motor Carrier Act's deregulation eliminated entry barriers, enabling small operators to thrive. This has created a highly responsive market where information asymmetries drive competitive advantages. Carriers with robust data insights optimize asset positioning, while brokers with extensive networks match capacity efficiently. The absence of centralized oversight results in significant rate variations across regions, contrasting with ocean shipping's coordinated structure and highlighting the need for integrated market analysis.

OCEAN SHIPPING: AN OLIGOPOLISTIC FRAMEWORK

Ocean shipping operates as an oligopoly, with alliances dictating market conditions. Freight forwarders navigate a market where large shippers receive priority, constraining rate flexibility. Capacity decisions, such as commissioning a new vessel—a $200 million investment requiring three years—demand long-term demand forecasts, increasing the risk of misalignment. Unlike trucking's agile adjustments, ocean shipping's capacity evolves slowly through vessel deliveries or idling, resulting in protracted cycles that reshape global trade over extended periods.

This controlled framework amplifies the impact of supply-demand imbalances, underscoring the structural disparities between trucking and ocean shipping. These differences manifest in their cyclical misalignment, as explored next.

CYCLICAL MISALIGNMENT AND STRATEGIC IMPLICATIONS

Trucking and ocean shipping face common disruptions—natural disasters, trade disputes, or monetary policy shifts—but their responses reflect their structural foundations. Trucking's decentralized nature enables rapid, albeit uncoordinated, adjustments, while ocean shipping's oligopolistic structure produces deliberate, slower responses. Consequently, one market may experience a boom while the other faces a downturn, posing challenges for stakeholders coordinating across both modes. A historical perspective illuminates these patterns and their implications.

HISTORICAL CYCLE ANALYSIS (2000s-2020s)

Trucking and ocean shipping cycles have consistently diverged in timing and intensity despite shared catalysts.

2006–2010: FINANCIAL CRISIS

From 2006 to 2007, high diesel prices ($4.75 per gallon) and a crashing housing market reduced demand for flatbed trucks, which carry construction materials. Too many trucks from earlier years led to a 15% drop in spot rates (prices for one-time shipments). The 2008–2009 recession cut trucking demand by 20%, bankrupting 3,000 trucking companies. Recovery didn't start until 2011.

Ocean shipping also struggled, with global trade volumes falling 15% from 2008 to 2010. Shipping rates from Asia to Europe dropped 40% to $800 per FEU (a 40-foot container). Companies idled 10% of their ships, and recovery, helped by slower sailing speeds and shared operations, took until 2013.

2015–2016: UNEVEN RECOVERY

In 2015–2016, a strong U.S. dollar and low oil prices hurt trucking demand for exports and energy-related goods. With too many trucks available, spot rates fell 10–15%, impacting small trucking companies the most. Growth in online shopping helped trucking recover by 2017.

Ocean shipping faced a slowdown due to China's weaker economy and an oversupply of ships built in 2014. Rates from Asia to the U.S. West Coast dropped 20% to $1,200 per FEU. The 2016 bankruptcy of Hanjin, a major shipping company, left $14 billion in cargo stranded. Recovery lagged until 2017.

2019–2020: PANDEMIC DISRUPTIONS

In 2019, U.S.-China trade tariffs reduced trucking demand, lowering spot rates by 20%. COVID-19 lockdowns in early 2020 cut rates another 30%. However, online shopping booms and government stimulus led to a shortage of trucks by 2021, with 25% of shipment offers rejected due to high demand.

Ocean shipping saw port activity drop 20% in early 2020, idling 11% of ships. By mid-2020, surging demand and port delays pushed shipping rates to $20,000 per FEU by 2021—a 1,000% increase from earlier lows.

2022–2024: GREAT FREIGHT RECESSION

Trucking faced a severe downturn from 2022 to 2024, driven by inflation and 5% interest rates, which reduced freight demand. Spot rates (prices for one-time shipments) dropped 25–30%, and 5,000 trucking companies went bankrupt as the number of carriers grew 45% while demand rose only 11%. Ocean shipping saw high rates from 2021 extend into 2022, but by 2023, rates fell 60% to $1,500 per FEU (40-foot container). New ships added 3 million TEUs (20-foot equivalent units), idling 5% of fleets. Ocean markets recovered in 2024, in anticipation of a second global trade war, while trucking remained in the longest freight recession in history.

These trends highlight persistent challenges, including myths about capacity shortages, as discussed below.

ADDRESSING CAPACITY SHORTAGE MYTHS

Claims of persistent capacity shortages in trucking and ocean shipping are misleading. In trucking, it is impossible to have a perpetual industry-wide driver shortage while also facing a capacity glut, as seen in the 45% carrier growth from 2019 to 2023 against only 11% demand growth. The reported shortage of 50,000–100,000 drivers is overstated, driven by industry lobbying to relax regulations, such as lowering the minimum driving age or easing licensing requirements. The real issue is high driver turnover, with rates reaching 90% annually due to low pay and grueling work conditions, like long hours and extended time away from home. Large carriers report hiring difficulties, yet smaller fleets often have waiting lists, indicating the problem is retention, not recruitment. Improving wages, benefits, and work-life balance could stabilize the workforce without assuming a perpetual shortage.

In ocean shipping, vessel shortage claims ignore 20% capacity growth from 2019 to 2023, compared to 8% trade growth. Port congestion and alliance-driven slot allocation create artificial bottlenecks, not true scarcity. These misconceptions distort policies and prolong market instability by diverting focus from structural issues.

GEOPOLITICAL AND ENVIRONMENTAL PRESSURES

Ocean shipping faces significant global disruptions. The 2021 Suez Canal blockage delayed 10% of world trade. Houthi attacks in 2023–2024 forced ships to reroute around the Cape of Good Hope, adding 10–14 days and $2,000 per FEU to Asia-Europe routes. U.S.-China tariffs cut trans-Pacific trade by 5% in 2018–2019. To meet IMO 2030 decarbonization goals, the industry faces $1 billion in methanol retrofit costs, with Maersk launching its first green vessel in 2024. Consolidation, with 10 carriers controlling 85% of capacity, limits rate competition, favoring large shippers.

Trucking grapples with workforce and safety challenges. Immigrants made up 19% of drivers in 2020, up from 10% in 2000, with 2022 demographics showing 60% White, 18% Hispanic, 13% Black, 3% Asian, and 1% other ethnicities. A 2022–2024 capacity surge led to hiring underqualified drivers, often with unverified foreign licenses, contributing to a 7% rise in truck-related fatalities from 2020 to 2023.

These challenges underscore the resilience needed to sustain freight operations.

2022–2024: SAFETY ISSUES

From 2022 to 2024, a rush to hire drivers led to some companies employing underqualified drivers, including those with unverified foreign licenses. This contributed to a 7% rise in truck-related deaths from 2020 to 2023, highlighting the need for better safety practices.

RESILIENCE IN FREIGHT MARKETS

Despite these challenges, trucking and ocean shipping remain vital. Trucking covers 4 million miles of U.S. roads, and ocean shipping connects 500 major global ports, keeping goods moving even during disruptions. Trucking adapts quickly, using online platforms to reroute shipments during weather events. Ocean shipping relies on shared operations and mergers, like Maersk's acquisition of DB Schenker, to stay stable.

However, the two industries don't always align. Trucking saw a demand spike in 2020, while ocean shipping peaked in 2021. This is because trucking operates in a flexible, competitive market, while ocean shipping is controlled by a few large companies. Logistics professionals must understand these differences and historical trends to manage the ups and downs of global freight effectively.

OCEAN CARRIER ALLIANCE SHAKEUP

2017

ALLIANCE 2M
MAERSK
MSC

OCEAN ALLIANCE
CMA CGM
COSCO
OOCL
EVERGREEN

THE ALLIANCE
ONE
HMM (DEPUIS 2020)
YANG MING
HAPAG LLOYD

2025

GEMINI
MAERSK
HAPAG LLOYD

OCEAN ALLIANCE
CMA CGM
COSCO
OOCL
EVERGREEN

PREMIER ALLIANCE
ONE
HMM
YANG MING

MSC

FIG 16-1

CLOSING: SHAPING AN EXCITING AND RESILIENT FUTURE FOR SUPPLY CHAINS

The story of supply chains, from ancient Rome's grain ships to today's AI-driven logistics, reveals a timeless truth: they are the invisible backbone of human progress. From the Silk Road's caravans to modern container ships, supply chains have shaped empires, driven industrial revolutions, and enabled the conveniences of daily life, often unnoticed until they falter. Today, in 2025, we stand at a thrilling crossroads. Geopolitical shifts, technological breakthroughs, and rising disruptions are reshaping logistics, offering an exciting future filled with opportunity. Supply chain professionals, elevated to strategic leaders, are critical to navigating this dynamic landscape, ensuring the resilience, equity, and strength of our global systems.

This book began by likening supply chains to utilities—essential yet overlooked until disrupted. The Roman Cura Annonae fed a million people through sophisticated trade networks; steam engines and railroads unlocked industrial growth; and innovations like refrigeration and just-in-time manufacturing transformed how we live. Each milestone, chronicled in these chapters, built the interconnected world we inhabit. But interconnection breeds vulnerability. The COVID-19 pandemic, the U.S.-China trade war, and disasters like Hurricane Harvey exposed supply chains' fragility. A single disruption—a blocked Suez Canal, a cyberattack, or a drought-stricken Panama Canal—can ripple globally, halting production and inflating prices. These events, explored in our chapters on disruptions and deglobalization, underscore that resilience is paramount.

My journey founding FreightWaves and SONAR taught me the power of transparency in building that resilience. Starting in 2016, FreightWaves aimed to illuminate the opaque freight industry, giving everyone—from solo truck drivers to global corporations—access to real-time data. SONAR's Tender Indices, tracking truck availability and pricing, have saved companies millions by forecasting price shifts days ahead. This democratization of data, discussed in our technology and freight cycles chapters, levels the playing field from the largest to the smallest players. Transparency is not just a tool; it's a principle that strengthens supply chains by fostering trust and informed decisions.

The robustness of America's logistics industries—rail, trucking, container shipping, and aviation—underpins this resilience, forming a foundation for the exciting future ahead. The U.S. rail network, spanning 140,000 miles and moving 40% of long-haul freight, connects ports to inland hubs with unmatched efficiency. Class I railroads haul 14.5 million intermodal units annually, supporting e-commerce and global trade. Trucking, carrying 70% of U.S. freight by value, sustains a $1 trillion ecosystem, with 531,000 fleets delivering everything from produce to electronics. Container shipping, despite U.S. carriers' small global share, thrives through strategic ports like Los Angeles, handling millions of TEUs yearly. Aviation, moving $2.3 trillion in high-value goods like semiconductors, ensures speed and precision. These industries, detailed in our chapters on railroads, trucking, containers, and aviation, are the bedrock of global commerce, adapting to challenges like volatile markets and natural disasters with remarkable strength.

Yet, no matter how advanced technology becomes, one truth will endure: the freight cycle's relentless boom-and-bust rhythm will challenge logistics companies. As explored in our freight cycles chapter, these fluctuations—driven by shifts in demand, capacity, and global events—create uncertainty, with rates soaring one month and crashing the next. Logistics firms, from carriers to brokers, must navigate this volatility to survive and thrive. Products like SONAR are indispensable allies in this effort, providing real-time insights into market trends, tender rejections, and pricing shifts. By equipping companies with data to anticipate and adapt, these tools transform the freight cycle from a threat into an opportunity, ensuring resilience across the industry.

The future of supply chains, vibrant and full of promise, hinges on three pillars: technology, resilience, and collaboration—with supply chain professionals as the architects of success. Technology is revolutionizing logistics, blending cutting-edge innovations with traditional modes. Electric vertical takeoff and landing vehicles (eVTOLs), tested for urban deliveries, and Boom Supersonic's Overture jets, with orders for high-speed cargo transport, promise to accelerate last-mile and transcontinental logistics. These will integrate seamlessly with ocean shipping, which moves 80% of global trade, and railroads, which excel in long-haul efficiency. For example, eVTOLs could shuttle goods from ports to urban centers, while railroads and ships handle bulk transoceanic cargo, creating a hybrid network of speed and scale. Yet, professionals must balance automation with human resources, ensuring technologies like drones augment rather than displace workers. This tension, discussed in our robotics chapter, requires strategic oversight to maintain jobs while boosting efficiency.

Resilience is the second pillar, demanding robust networks that withstand disruptions. Supply chain professionals fortify systems against market volatility, as seen in freight recessions, and natural disasters, like the 2019 Mississippi floods or 2024's Hurricane Helene. By leveraging real-time data, professionals reroute shipments, optimize capacity, and mitigate delays. Deglobalization, with Mexico's 2023 rise as the U.S.'s top trade partner, shifts trade closer to home, reducing exposure to global shocks. Professionals navigate these changes, reconfiguring networks to absorb disruptions while keeping costs manageable, ensuring supply chains remain agile and strong.

Collaboration, the third pillar, relies on professionals to bridge divides. The U.S.-China rivalry, framed as a second Cold War, weaponizes supply chains through tariffs and bans on rare earths or semiconductors. Professionals diversify networks via regional agreements like the USMCA, reducing reliance on single sources. They also safeguard operations against fraud, a growing threat in volatile markets, by leveraging data and vigilance to protect billions in freight value. By fostering partnerships between shippers, carriers, and tech providers—facilitated by platforms like FreightWaves—professionals drive innovation and resilience, preventing crises like the 2021 supply chain bottlenecks.

Supply chain professionals are no longer behind-the-scenes operators; they are strategic leaders guiding companies through complexity. Deglobalization demands reconfigured networks; fraud requires proactive safeguards; and automation versus human labor calls for ethical decisions. Their expertise, blending data analytics, technological acumen, and human insight, is indispensable. As companies face volatile markets, professionals wielding tools like SONAR will steer them toward stability and growth, shaping an industry that moves 70% of U.S. goods and 80% of global trade.

What does this mean for you? Whether you're a consumer, business owner, professional, or policymaker, supply chains touch your life. Every product—from smartphones to produce—depends on logistics. As disruptions grow, from climate-driven storms to cyberattacks, understanding supply chains empowers action. Consumers can support local suppliers, reducing reliance on fragile global networks. Businesses can leverage professionals' expertise to navigate freight recessions or rate spikes. Policymakers can invest in infrastructure—ports, railroads, broadband—and reform policies like the de minimis exemption to balance trade and domestic growth. Professionals, your role is pivotal: lead with vision, harness technology, and champion collaboration to build a future where supply chains thrive.

My journey, from a Chattanooga trucking family to leading FreightWaves, taught me that better information yields better outcomes. Watching my father and grandfather endure trucking's boom-and-bust cycles showed me the cost of uncertainty. Today, with robust industries, real-time data, and transformative technologies, we have the tools for stronger, fairer supply chains. But tools need leaders. Supply chain professionals, your expertise will shape this exciting future, ensuring logistics are not just efficient but resilient—delivering prosperity for all. The future of supply chains is yours to build. Let's move the world together.

GLOSSARY

FOREWORD & INTRODUCTION

SUPPLY CHAIN: The interconnected journey that raw materials, components, and goods take before their assembly and sale to customers.

LOGISTICS: The detailed organization and implementation of a complex operation, often referring to the movement of goods and resources.

FREIGHT INDUSTRY: The business of transporting goods, typically on a large scale, by truck, train, ship, or plane.

FREIGHTWAVES: A platform founded by the author to provide real-time news and data to the supply chain industry.

SONAR: A real-time data platform developed by FreightWaves that tracks truck availability, freight demand, and pricing, serving as a predictive tool for the freight market.

TRADE WAR: An economic conflict between two or more countries characterized by the imposition of protectionist measures like tariffs and trade barriers.

DE MINIMIS EXEMPTION: A U.S. trade policy that allows shipments valued under $800 to enter the country duty-free, originally intended for small-scale trade but now used by e-commerce giants.

GLOBAL SOUTH: A term used to refer to developing countries in Asia, Africa, and Latin America.

MCKINSEY & COMPANY: A global management consulting firm.

CHAPTER 1: WATERWAYS FORGE TRADE

AGRARIAN SOCIETIES: Societies where the economy is based on farming and agriculture.

THE ROMAN EMPIRE: A major historical empire that laid the foundation for modern supply chains with its vast trade networks.

THE SILK ROAD: An ancient network of trade routes connecting Asia, Europe, and Africa, used to transport goods like silk and spices.

CARAVANS: Groups of merchants, often with pack animals like camels, traveling together for trade.

CURA ANNONAE: The Roman system for importing and distributing grain to residents of Rome.

SUBSIDIZED GRAIN: Grain provided at a reduced cost or for free by the Roman state.

MAN-MADE WATERWAYS (CANALS): Channels built by humans to connect inland areas to seas or rivers, enabling water-based trade.

DAMS: Structures built to control water flow, preventing floods and protecting trade cities.

DUTCH EAST INDIA COMPANY: A company formed in 1602 with a monopoly on trade between Holland and the East Indies, creating the most extensive and complex supply chains of its time.

SPECIALIZATION: The process of a society or region focusing on producing a specific product or crop that is in high demand, trading it for other goods they need.

CHAPTER 2: ENGINES REVVING CHANGE

STEAM ENGINE: An engine that uses the force produced by steam to push a piston, powering machinery and, eventually, transport.

INDUSTRIAL REVOLUTION: A period of significant industrialization during the late 18th and early 19th centuries, driven by inventions like the steam engine.

STEAMBOATS: Boats powered by steam engines, which enabled the movement of goods against river currents.

RAILROADS: A system of railroad tracks along which steam-powered locomotives and cars run, providing faster and cheaper transport than wagons or canals.

TRANSCONTINENTAL RAILROAD: The first continuous railroad line across the U.S., completed in 1869.

INTERSTATE COMMERCE COMMISSION (ICC): A U.S. government agency established in 1887 to regulate railroad rates and curb monopolistic practices.

STAGGERS RAIL ACT OF 1980: A pivotal act that deregulated the U.S. rail industry, giving railroads more flexibility in setting rates and routes to restore financial viability.

INTERMODAL TRANSPORT: The movement of goods in a single standardized container that can be transferred between different modes of transport (e.g., ship, rail, and truck).

PRECISION SCHEDULED RAILROADING (PSR): A modern railroad operating model focused on running longer, fewer trains on a fixed schedule to increase efficiency and cut costs.

NEAR-SHORING: The strategy of moving manufacturing and production to a nearby country, such as moving from China to Mexico, to reduce transit times and geopolitical risks.

USMCA (UNITED STATES-MEXICO-CANADA AGREEMENT): A free trade agreement between the U.S., Mexico, and Canada that replaced NAFTA.

CHAPTER 3: GOING POSTAL

ANGARIUM (ROYAL ROAD): The world's first organized postal system, established by the ancient Persian Empire.

POSTMASTER GENERAL: The chief executive officer of the U.S. postal system. Benjamin Franklin was the first Postmaster General.

U.S. POSTAL SERVICE (USPS): An independent agency of the U.S. federal government that provides mail and package delivery, established by the Postal Reorganization Act of 1970.

UNIVERSAL SERVICE OBLIGATION (USO): The USPS mandate to provide uniform mail service to every address in the United States, regardless of cost or location.

THE PONY EXPRESS: A legendary horse relay system that carried mail between Missouri and California for 18 months in 1860-1861.

TRANSCONTINENTAL TELEGRAPH: A telegraph line completed in 1861 that enabled messages to be sent across the continent in minutes, replacing the Pony Express.

UNITED PARCEL SERVICE (UPS): A global package delivery company that grew from a small messenger service in Seattle.

AMERICAN MESSENGER COMPANY: The original name of UPS, founded in 1907.

GOLDEN LINK: A milestone achieved by UPS in 1975, when it became the first package delivery company to serve every address in the continental U.S.

CHAPTER 4: AVIATION'S DAWN

WRIGHT FLYER: The first successful heavier-than-air powered aircraft, flown by the Wright brothers in 1903.

AIRMAIL SERVICE: The system of transporting mail by airplane, launched by the U.S. Post Office in 1918.

TRANSATLANTIC FLIGHT: The first solo flight across the Atlantic Ocean, completed by Charles Lindbergh in 1927.

JET ENGINES: Engines that generate thrust by expelling a high-speed jet of gas, enabling faster and higher-altitude flight than propeller-driven aircraft.

PRESSURIZED AIRCRAFT: Aircraft with sealed cabins that pump in air, creating a comfortable environment at high altitudes and allowing for smoother, faster flights.

JET AGE: The period of aviation history dominated by the widespread use of jet engines.

DHL: A global logistics company founded in 1969 that pioneered international express delivery.

HUB-AND-SPOKE MODEL: A delivery system in which packages are sent from various locations (spokes) to a central sorting hub before being flown to their final destinations.

FEDERAL EXPRESS (FEDEX): A global express delivery company that pioneered the overnight delivery model using a hub-and-spoke system.

AIRLINE DEREGULATION ACT OF 1977: An act that removed government controls on airline routes and rates, spurring competition and growth in the air cargo industry.

LAST-MILE DELIVERY: The final step of the delivery process, from a distribution center to the customer's doorstep.

AMAZON LOGISTICS: Amazon's in-house delivery network, including its own fleet of vans and planes.

PRIME AIR: Amazon's program that utilizes its own fleet of aircraft for expedited deliveries.

CHAPTER 5: HIGHWAY HEROES

LESS-THAN-TRUCKLOAD (LTL): A type of freight shipping for small shipments, typically under 10,000 pounds, which are consolidated with other shipments for transport.

HUB-AND-SPOKE SYSTEM: In LTL, this model uses local terminals (spokes) to collect freight, which is then sorted at central hubs for delivery.

MOTOR CARRIER ACT OF 1980: A landmark act that deregulated the trucking industry, ending ICC control over rates and routes and spurring competition.

TRUCKLOAD (TL): A type of freight shipping for a full trailer load of goods for a single customer, traveling directly from origin to destination.

JUST-IN-TIME (JIT) INVENTORY: A logistics strategy where goods are received from suppliers only as they are needed in the production process, minimizing inventory and storage costs.

FREIGHT BROKER: An intermediary that connects shippers with carriers, negotiating rates and managing logistics.

SPOT MARKET: A volatile market where freight rates are negotiated daily based on immediate supply and demand.

INTERMODAL TRANSPORT: The use of standardized containers that can be moved between different modes of transportation, such as rail and truck.

HOURS-OF-SERVICE REGULATIONS: Rules that limit the number of hours a truck driver can operate to prevent fatigue and improve safety.

CHAPTER 6: THE CONTAINER REVOLUTION

CONTAINERIZATION: The system of transporting goods in standardized containers that can be easily transferred between ships, trains, and trucks.

BREAKBULK: The traditional method of shipping, where goods are handled individually and loaded piece by piece.

INTERMODAL TRANSPORTATION: The seamless movement of a container between different modes of transport without unpacking its contents.

TEU (TWENTY-FOOT EQUIVALENT UNIT): The standard measure for a twenty-foot container, used to calculate a ship's capacity.

MEGA-SHIPS: Massive container ships capable of carrying over 20,000 TEUs.

DRAYAGE TRUCKER: A truck driver who transports containers over short distances, typically between a port and a rail yard or warehouse.

SHIPPING ALLIANCES: Agreements between major container lines to coordinate schedules and capacity, which allows them to control trade routes and pricing.

BLANK SAILINGS: The practice of canceling voyages to reduce capacity and maintain high freight rates.

HOUTHI ATTACKS: Attacks by Houthi rebels in the Red Sea using drones and missiles, disrupting maritime trade and forcing vessels to reroute.

IMO 2020: International Maritime Organization regulations that limit the sulfur content in ship fuel to reduce air pollution.

SCRUBBERS: Exhaust gas cleaning systems installed on ships to remove sulfur dioxide from emissions.

CHAPTER 7: REFRIGERATION: THE UNSUNG HERO OF MODERN SOCIETY

REFRIGERATION: The process of cooling and preserving goods by removing heat, which slows bacterial growth and spoilage.

ICEBOX: An insulated box, invented by Thomas Moore in the early 1800s, that used a block of ice to keep food cool.

FREDERIC TUDOR: Known as the "Ice King," he pioneered the international trade of natural ice in the 19th century.

REFRIGERANT: A chemical substance with a low boiling point used in a refrigeration system to absorb and transfer heat.

COMPRESSOR: The part of a refrigerator that compresses the refrigerant gas, raising its temperature and pressure to start the cooling cycle.

CONDENSER: A set of coils in the back or bottom of a refrigerator where hot, high-pressure refrigerant gas dissipates heat and turns into a liquid.

EVAPORATOR: The coils inside a refrigerator where the cold, low-pressure refrigerant absorbs heat from the interior, making it cool.

COLD SUPPLY CHAIN: A temperature-controlled supply chain for transporting perishable goods like food, pharmaceuticals, and flowers.

REGIONAL SPECIALIZATION: A trend where farmers and regions focus on growing a specific crop to trade with other areas, made possible by refrigeration.

INDUSTRIAL FARMING: The large-scale, industrialized production of crops and animals.

INSTACART, SHIPT, AMAZON FRESH: Companies that provide local grocery delivery services, a trend that accelerated during the COVID-19 pandemic.

CHAPTER 8: JUST-IN-TIME CHANGES THE GAME

JUST-IN-TIME (JIT) DELIVERY: A manufacturing and inventory strategy in which raw materials and components are received only as they are needed for production.

LEAN MANUFACTURING: A production philosophy, originating from Toyota's Kaizen method, focused on eliminating waste and maximizing efficiency.

KAIZEN METHOD: A Japanese business philosophy of continuous improvement, now a cornerstone of lean manufacturing.

BULLWHIP EFFECT: A phenomenon in supply chains where small fluctuations in retail demand lead to increasingly larger fluctuations in demand for manufacturers and suppliers.

JUST-IN-CASE (JIC) STRATEGY: An inventory strategy where companies stockpile extra components and materials to mitigate the risk of supply chain disruptions.

NEARSHORING: The practice of moving manufacturing and production to a closer country to reduce transit times and geopolitical risks.

FRIENDSHORING: A supply chain strategy where companies move production to allied countries to reduce geopolitical risks.

ORIGINAL EQUIPMENT MANUFACTURER (OEM): A company that manufactures products or components that are used in another company's final product.

FREE-MARKET TRADE: An economic system in which goods and services are exchanged with minimal government regulation or tariffs.

INFLATION REDUCTION ACT (2022): U.S. legislation that aims to lower inflation and spur domestic clean energy and manufacturing investments.

CHIPS ACT (2022): U.S. legislation that provides subsidies to boost domestic semiconductor manufacturing and research.

CHAPTER 9: RETAIL REVOLUTION

SEARS: A major 20th-century retailer that pioneered the mail-order catalog.

MAIL-ORDER CATALOG: A system where customers order goods from a catalog and have them delivered, an innovation that reached rural America.

KIT HOUSES: Homes sold by Sears as kits with all the necessary materials, shipped by train.

WALMART: A retail giant that displaced Sears by mastering logistics, particularly in trucking and global sourcing.

PRIVATE TRUCKING FLEET: A company's in-house fleet of trucks, such as Walmart's, used to control delivery schedules and reduce costs.

DISTRIBUTION CENTERS: Large facilities where goods from various suppliers are sorted and prepared for delivery to retail stores.

AMAZON: An e-commerce giant that has become a preeminent logistics player by mastering air cargo and a hybrid delivery model.

AMAZON PRIME: A subscription service that offers free two-day shipping and other benefits, driving demand for faster delivery.

SHOPIFY: An e-commerce platform that provides small merchants with the tools to run an online store, including website building, payments, and logistics integrations.

PRINT-ON-DEMAND: A business model where products are not created until a customer places an order, eliminating the need for inventory.

STRIPE: A technology company that provides payment processing for online businesses.

PRINTFUL: A print-on-demand company that handles printing and shipping for e-commerce stores.

E-COMMERCE: The buying and selling of goods and services over the internet.

DROPSHIPPING: A retail fulfillment method where a store doesn't keep the products it sells in stock. Instead, it purchases the item from a third party and has it shipped directly to the customer.

CHAPTER 10: AI AND ITS IMPLICATIONS FOR SUPPLY CHAINS

ARTIFICIAL INTELLIGENCE (AI): The simulation of human intelligence processes by machines, used in supply chains for prediction, automation, and decision-making.

MACHINE LEARNING: An application of AI that allows systems to learn and improve from data without being explicitly programmed.

EXHAUST DATA: Unintentional data generated by digital activities, such as from IoT devices in trucks and warehouses, used to train AI models.

INTERNET OF THINGS (IOT): The network of physical objects embedded with sensors and software for the purpose of connecting and exchanging data over the internet.

FREIGHT FRAUD: A growing threat in logistics where criminals use scams to steal cargo or payments.

DOUBLE BROKERING: A type of freight fraud where a broker illegally subcontracts a load to another carrier and pockets the payment.

LOAD PHISHING: A scam where fraudsters pose as legitimate carriers on load boards to steal cargo.

AGENTIC AI: Autonomous AI systems that can perform complex, multi-step tasks like negotiating contracts or scheduling.

FREIGHT OPTIMIZATION: The use of AI to maximize cargo space, plan efficient routes, and reduce costs.

PREDICTIVE ANALYTICS: The use of data, statistical algorithms, and machine learning to forecast future outcomes.

CHAPTER 11: AUTONOMOUS VEHICLES AND ADAPTIVE MANUFACTURING

AUTONOMOUS TRUCKS: Self-driving trucks that use AI, sensors, and machine learning to transport freight without a human driver.

VIRTUAL SIMULATION: Digital environments used to train autonomous trucks for extreme scenarios like storms or accidents.

LIDAR: A sensing method that uses pulsed laser light to measure distances, creating detailed 3D maps of a truck's surroundings.

CYBERSECURITY: The practice of protecting internet-connected systems from digital attacks.

REGULATORY HURDLES: The challenges posed by conflicting or unclear government regulations across different jurisdictions for autonomous vehicles.

ADAPTIVE MANUFACTURING: A flexible production method using AI and robotics to quickly retool factories and meet changes in demand or supply.

DIGITAL TWINS: Virtual models of physical systems, such as a factory floor, used to test new production setups without physical changes.

3D PRINTING: An additive manufacturing process that creates three-dimensional objects from a digital file.

INDUSTRY 4.0: The ongoing automation of traditional manufacturing and industrial practices using modern smart technology.

CHAPTER 12: ROBOTICS, DRONES, AND ADVANCED TRANSPORT

ROBOTIC AUTOMATION: The use of robots in factories and warehouses to automate tasks like assembly, material handling, and inventory management.

AUTONOMOUS MOBILE ROBOTS (AMRS): Robots that navigate and perform tasks in dynamic environments, such as transporting parts in a factory.

PRECISION MANUFACTURING: The production of parts with extreme accuracy, such as for aerospace or medical devices.

LOGISTICS DRONES: Unmanned aerial vehicles used for delivering packages, medical supplies, or other goods, especially for last-mile delivery.

EVTOL (ELECTRIC VERTICAL TAKEOFF AND LANDING): A type of aircraft that uses electric power to hover, take off, and land vertically, designed for urban air mobility.

URBAN AIR MOBILITY (UAM): The use of eVTOLs for transporting people and goods in urban and suburban areas to reduce traffic congestion.

GROUND DELIVERY ROBOTS: Small, autonomous robots that navigate sidewalks to deliver small items to homes or campuses.

AUTOMATED CONTAINER SHIPS: Autonomous or semi-autonomous vessels that navigate oceans with minimal or no crew.

BOOM SUPERSONIC: A company developing the Overture jet to revive supersonic flight for passenger travel and air freight.

CHAPTER 13: THE IMPORTANCE OF ENERGY AND THE CLIMATE CONFLICT ON SUPPLY CHAINS

DESALINATION: The process of removing salt from seawater to produce fresh water, which requires cheap, abundant energy.

VERTICAL FARMING: The practice of growing crops in vertically stacked layers in a controlled environment, often indoors.

CARBON CAPTURE AND STORAGE (CCS): Technology that captures carbon dioxide from industrial sources and stores it, preventing it from entering the atmosphere.

SMALL MODULAR REACTORS (SMRS): Advanced nuclear reactors that are smaller and more scalable than traditional ones, designed for safety and cost-effectiveness.

INTERMODAL TRANSPORT: The use of multiple modes of transport (e.g., ships, trains, barges, trucks) to move goods, which can be more energy-efficient than using a single mode.

ELECTRIC VEHICLES (EVS): Vehicles powered by electric motors, suitable for urban delivery but currently facing challenges for long-haul freight due to battery limitations.

U.S. FOSSIL FUEL ABUNDANCE: The U.S. being the world's top producer of oil and natural gas, providing energy security and a bridge fuel for climate solutions.

CLEAN AIR ACT: U.S. legislation from the 1970s that drove significant reductions in vehicle emissions.

BARGES: Flat-bottomed boats used for transporting bulk goods along rivers and canals, known for their fuel efficiency.

CHAPTER 14: THE FRAGILITY OF GLOBALIZED SUPPLY CHAINS AND THE RISE OF CHINESE E-COMMERCE

GLOBALIZATION: The process of increasing interconnectedness and interdependence between nations through trade, investment, and cultural exchange.

ANACONDA PLAN: The Union's naval blockade strategy during the Civil War to strangle Southern trade and cripple its economy.

CHIPS ACT: U.S. legislation providing subsidies for domestic semiconductor manufacturing to reduce reliance on foreign producers.

JUST-IN-TIME (JIT) SUPPLY CHAINS: A logistics model optimized for efficiency in peacetime but vulnerable to disruptions.

DE MINIMIS EXEMPTION: A U.S. trade policy allowing shipments under $800 to enter duty-free, exploited by Chinese e-commerce companies.

SHEIN AND TEMU: Chinese e-commerce giants that leverage the de minimis exemption to sell products in the U.S. at low prices.

TIKTOK: A social media platform, owned by China's ByteDance, whose algorithm has been shown to favor Chinese brands in the U.S.

NEARSHORING AND FRIENDSHORING: Strategies to move manufacturing to nearby or allied countries to build more resilient supply chains.

ALGORITHMIC MANIPULATION: The practice of using a platform's algorithm to disproportionately promote certain content, such as Chinese products on TikTok.

CHAPTER 15: DISRUPTIONS – WHEN SUPPLY CHAINS BREAK

SUPPLY CHAIN DISRUPTIONS: Events, such as natural disasters or cyberattacks, that interrupt the normal flow of goods.

HURRICANES: Severe tropical storms that disrupt freight by causing flooding, road closures, and port shutdowns.

BLIZZARDS: Heavy snowstorms that close highways and airports, delaying air cargo and trucking.

DROUGHTS: Periods of low rainfall that can disrupt water-based freight, such as by lowering water levels in the Panama Canal.

CYBERATTACKS: Digital attacks that can disrupt digitized freight systems, such as port operations or fuel pipelines.

GRID DISRUPTIONS: Power grid failures that halt freight operations by shutting down warehouses, data centers, and port equipment.

RESILIENCE: The ability of a supply chain to recover quickly from disruptions.

CHAPTER 16: FREIGHT CYCLES: TRUCKING'S FRENZIED TRADING FLOOR AND OCEAN SHIPPING'S OLIGOPOLISTIC WAVES

FREIGHT CYCLES: The recurring periods of boom and bust in freight markets, driven by the relationship between supply and demand.

CAPACITY: In logistics, the available supply of transportation, such as the number of trucks or ships.

TRUCKING CYCLES: Short, volatile cycles in the trucking market, typically lasting one to two years, driven by the rapid entry and exit of drivers.

OCEAN FREIGHT CYCLES: Long, protracted cycles in ocean shipping, often lasting a decade, constrained by the slow process of building new vessels.

FREIGHT FORWARDER: A person or company that organizes shipments for individuals or corporations to get goods from the manufacturer or producer to a final point of distribution.

OLIGOPOLY: A market structure in which a small number of firms have the majority of market share and control over prices.

SHIPPING ALLIANCES: A de facto cartel in ocean shipping, where the largest carriers coordinate capacity and schedules to control the market.

BLANK SAILINGS: The practice of canceling voyages to reduce capacity and maintain high freight rates, a tactic used by shipping alliances.

U.S. SHIPPING ACT OF 1984: A law that provides antitrust exemptions for foreign shipping carriers, allowing them to form alliances.

DE MINIMIS EXEMPTION: (Also mentioned in Chapter 14) A U.S. trade policy that allows shipments under $800 to enter duty-free.

CLOSING

SUPPLY CHAIN PROFESSIONALS: Individuals who manage the complex logistics of moving goods, now considered strategic leaders in business.

RESILIENCE: The ability of a supply chain to adapt and recover from disruptions.

DEGLOBALIZATION: The process of reversing globalization, with nations and companies moving toward more localized or regionalized supply chains.

NOTES

The definition of a supply chain as "the interconnected journey that raw materials, components, and goods take before their assembly and sale to customers" is attributed to McKinsey & Company. The fragility of supply chains and the quote "When any link in a supply chain isn't working optimally, the entire chain is disrupted" are also sourced from McKinsey & Company. The estimate that one-third of the global economy is tied to logistics-dependent industries is based on industry analysis from the World Bank. The $15 billion value of U.S. lithium battery imports from China in 2024 is derived from the U.S. Census Bureau. The U.S.-China Trade War's origins in 2018 and its escalation in 2025 under Trump's second administration are discussed by Chad P. Bown, with 2025 projections based on trade policy trends. China's production of 70% of the world's lithium-ion batteries, 80% of smartphones, and 90% of processed rare earths is sourced from the U.S. Geological Survey. The 2023 U.S.-China trade imbalance ($540 billion imports, $150 billion exports) is verified by the U.S. Census Bureau. China's control of 60% of mined rare earths and 85% of refined rare earths, and the U.S.'s 80% reliance on China, are detailed by the U.S. Geological Survey. The 2010 China-Japan rare earth export ban and its price impacts are documented by Keith Bradsher in the *New York Times*. China's 2024 antimony export ban and restrictions on gallium and germanium are reported by Reuters. The potential economic impact of a full rare earth ban on U.S. production is estimated by the Congressional Research Service. China's Belt and Road Initiative and its trade ties with the Global South (e.g., Brazil, Vietnam, Cambodia) are analyzed by Elizabeth C. Economy. The impact of Trump's tariff policies on global supply chains and U.S. ally relations is discussed by Mary E. Lovely. Russia's 2022 invasion of Ukraine and its impact on global trade are covered by the International Monetary Fund.

ENDNOTES (INTRODUCTION)

- McKinsey & Company, *Supply Chain Resilience: A 2023 Perspective* (New York: McKinsey & Company, 2023), 3.
- McKinsey & Company, *Global Supply Chains Under Pressure: Navigating Disruptions* (New York: McKinsey & Company, 2021), 5–6.
- World Bank, *Connecting to Compete 2022: Trade Logistics in the Global Economy* (Washington, DC: World Bank, 2022), 15–20.
- U.S. Census Bureau, *U.S. Trade in Goods by Country: 2024* (Washington, DC: U.S. Department of Commerce, 2025), 12–14.
- Chad P. Bown, *US-China Trade War: Tariffs, Technology, and Geopolitics* (Washington, DC: Peterson Institute for International Economics, 2023), 45–60.
- U.S. Geological Survey, *Mineral Commodity Summaries 2024* (Reston, VA: USGS, 2024), 90–95.
- U.S. Census Bureau, *U.S. Trade in Goods by Country: 2023* (Washington, DC: U.S. Department of Commerce, 2024), 10–12.
- U.S. Geological Survey, *Rare Earths: Global Supply and U.S. Dependence* (Reston, VA: USGS, 2023), 20–25.
- Keith Bradsher, "China's Rare Earth Embargo Shakes Global Markets," *New York Times*, October 20, 2010.

- Reuters, "China's Export Bans on Critical Minerals Escalate Trade Tensions," Reuters, August 15, 2024.
- Congressional Research Service, *Rare Earth Elements: The U.S. Supply Chain and National Security* (Washington, DC: CRS, 2024), 8–10.
- Elizabeth C. Economy, *The World According to China* (Cambridge: Polity Press, 2022), 100–120.
- Mary E. Lovely, *Trade Policy Under Trump 2.0: Implications for Global Supply Chains* (Washington, DC: Peterson Institute for International Economics, 2025), 30–40.
- International Monetary Fund, *Global Trade Fragmentation: The Impact of Geopolitical Shocks* (Washington, DC: IMF, 2023), 25–30.

CHAPTER 1: WATERWAYS FORGING TRADE

The origins of early supply chains in ancient farming societies and their use of pack animals for trade are discussed by Andrew Sherratt. The development of water-based trade along rivers and coasts, including the construction of dams and canals, is detailed by Brian Fagan. The Silk Road's establishment around 200 BCE during the Han Dynasty and its 4,000-mile network are documented by Xinru Liu. The role of the Silk Road in spreading ideas, religions, and cultures, and its protection by Han armies, is analyzed by Valerie Hansen. Rome's population of approximately 1 million by the 2nd century CE is estimated by Kyle Harper. The Cura Annonae system for importing and distributing grain to Rome is described by Geoffrey Rickman. The cost-effectiveness of shipping grain across the Mediterranean compared to inland transport (75 miles) is noted by Peter Temin. The Roman state's provision of subsidized and later free bread is discussed by Paul Erdkamp. The collapse of the Cura Annonae in the 5th century CE and its link to Rome's decline are analyzed by Chris Wickham. The loss of North Africa to the Vandals in 439 CE and its impact on Rome's grain supply is detailed by Peter Heather. London's population reaching 1 million in the 19th century and its global trade network are discussed by Roy Porter. The strategic importance of Rome's and London's locations near rivers and seas for trade is explored by Fagan. Venice's canal system and its role as a trade hub from the 14th to 16th centuries are described by Frederic C. Lane. Florence's trade advancements under the Medici family, including double-entry accounting and currency exchange, are detailed by Raymond de Roover. Florence's textile industry and its dominance in Europe's wool trade are discussed by John H. Munro. The limitations of early supply chains, including slow shipments and poor communication, are analyzed by Fernand Braudel. The trade of commodities like olive oil, wine, and grain in early supply chains is noted by David J. Mattingly. The Silk Road's role in supplying silk and spices to London is discussed by Susan Whitfield. The salt trade in medieval Europe for meat curing is detailed by Mark Kurlansky. The Dutch East India Company's formation in 1602 and its trade monopoly are analyzed by Charles R. Boxer. The Dutch East India Company's shipment of 2.5 million tons of goods and use of 4,800 ships is documented by Femme S. Gaastra. The comparison of the Dutch East India Company's scale to the British East India Company is based on Jonathan I. Israel. The role of specialization in early supply chains is discussed by Kenneth Pomeranz and Steven Topik.

- Andrew Sherratt, *Economy and Society in Prehistoric Europe: Changing Perspectives* (Edinburgh: Edinburgh University Press, 1997), 150–170.
- Brian Fagan, *Elixir: A History of Water and Humankind* (New York: Bloomsbury Press, 2011), 80–100.

- Xinru Liu, *The Silk Road in World History* (New York: Oxford University Press, 2010), 20–35.
- Valerie Hansen, *The Silk Road: A New History* (New York: Oxford University Press, 2012), 50–65.
- Kyle Harper, *The Fate of Rome: Climate, Disease, and the End of an Empire* (Princeton, NJ: Princeton University Press, 2017), 25–30.
- Geoffrey Rickman, *The Corn Supply of Ancient Rome* (Oxford: Clarendon Press, 1980), 40–55.
- Peter Temin, *The Roman Market Economy* (Princeton, NJ: Princeton University Press, 2013), 30–35.
- Paul Erdkamp, *The Grain Market in the Roman Empire: A Social, Political and Economic Study* (Cambridge: Cambridge University Press, 2005), 200–220.
- Chris Wickham, *The Inheritance of Rome: A History of Europe from 400 to 1000* (New York: Penguin Books, 2009), 25–40.
- Peter Heather, *The Fall of the Roman Empire: A New History of Rome and the Barbarians* (New York: Oxford University Press, 2006), 300–315.
- Roy Porter, *London: A Social History* (Cambridge, MA: Harvard University Press, 1995), 200–210.
- Fagan, *Elixir*, 120–130.
- Frederic C. Lane, *Venice: A Maritime Republic* (Baltimore: Johns Hopkins University Press, 1973), 50–70.
- Raymond de Roover, *The Rise and Decline of the Medici Bank, 1397–1494* (Cambridge, MA: Harvard University Press, 1963), 30–45.
- John H. Munro, *Textiles, Towns, and Trade: Essays in the Economic History of Late-Medieval England and the Low Countries* (Aldershot: Variorum, 1994), 100–120.
- Fernand Braudel, *The Mediterranean and the Mediterranean World in the Age of Philip II, vol. 1* (Berkeley: University of California Press, 1995), 300–320.
- David J. Mattingly, *Imperialism, Power, and Identity: Experiencing the Roman Empire* (Princeton, NJ: Princeton University Press, 2011), 150–165.
- Susan Whitfield, *Life Along the Silk Road* (Berkeley: University of California Press, 2015), 80–95.
- Mark Kurlansky, *Salt: A World History* (New York: Penguin Books, 2003), 100–115.
- Charles R. Boxer, *The Dutch Seaborne Empire, 1600–1800* (New York: Penguin Books, 1990), 20–35.
- Femme S. Gaastra, *The Dutch East India Company: Expansion and Decline* (Zutphen: Walburg Pers, 2003), 50–65.
- Jonathan I. Israel, *Dutch Primacy in World Trade, 1585–1740* (Oxford: Clarendon Press, 1989), 200–215.
- Kenneth Pomeranz and Steven Topik, *The World That Trade Created: Society, Culture, and the World Economy, 1400 to the Present* (Armonk, NY: M.E. Sharpe, 2013), 30–45.

CHAPTER 2: ENGINES REVVING CHANGE

Thomas Savery's patent for the steam pump in 1698 is documented in historical records of the Royal Society and British patent archives, as detailed by Robert H. Thurston. James Watt's improvements to the steam engine and the naming of the "watt" unit are detailed by Samuel Smiles. The Industrial Revolution's impact on manufacturing and urbanization is widely studied, as noted by Eric Hobsbawm. The limitations of pre-steam trade and reliance on wooden ships are discussed by Daniel R. Headrick. The shift to fossil fuels for mechanical work is analyzed by Vaclav Smil. The steamboat *New Orleans* and its impact on Mississippi River trade are documented by Louis C. Hunter. Mark Twain's connection to steamboats and the *Pennsylvania* explosion are recounted by Ron Powers. The Stockton and Darlington Railway (1825) as the first public steam railway is noted by Anthony Burton. Railroad mileage in 1860 (21,000 miles in the North, 9,000 in the South) and the transcontinental railroad's completion in 1869 are verified by John F. Stover. The economic barriers to railroad ownership and the "robber baron" phenomenon are explored by Richard White. Cornelius Vanderbilt's railroad tactics and the term "robber barons" are detailed by T.J. Stiles. The Interstate Commerce Act of 1887 and the ICC's challenges are analyzed by Gabriel Kolko. The Hepburn Act of 1906 and its impact on ICC authority are discussed by Albro Martin. The U.S. freight rail network's 140,000 miles and 40% of long-haul freight volume in 2024 are sourced from the Association of American Railroads (AAR). Class I railroad track mileage (e.g., BNSF's 32,500 miles, Union Pacific's 31,800 miles) is reported by the AAR. Freight type percentages (e.g., 60% bulk commodities, 25% coal) and carload data for 2024 are attributed to the AAR. Coal's decline from 44% in 2008 to 25% in 2024 and intermodal growth are documented by the AAR. Positive Train Control (PTC) reducing derailments by 38% since 2015 is cited by the Federal Railroad Administration. The Motor Carrier Act of 1935 and its impact on trucking competition are discussed by Thomas G. Moore. World War II rail freight (90% of military freight, 97% of troop transport) is verified by Earl J. Hess, adapted for WWII context. The Staggers Rail Act of 1980 and its effects on freight rates and track reduction are analyzed by Ann F. Friedlaender and Richard H. Spady. Intermodal traffic growth (e.g., 5.6 million units in 1990) and double-stack trains are documented by the AAR. The 1996 UP-Southern Pacific merger issues are detailed by James H. Ducker. Precision Scheduled Railroading (PSR) and its impacts, including workforce cuts and stock buybacks, are discussed in *Railway Age*. The 2021 supply chain crisis and UP's service pause are reported in *Progressive Railroading*. The 2022 strike threat and Biden administration deal are covered in *Bloomberg News*. U.S.-Mexico trade reaching $974 billion in 2024 is sourced from the U.S. Census Bureau. KCS's 20% share of U.S.-Mexico rail freight in 2020 is attributed to the AAR. The CN-CP bidding war for KCS and CPKC's formation are detailed by the Surface Transportation Board. CPKC's 25% share of U.S.-Mexico rail freight and $7.5 billion revenue in 2024 are cited by Canadian Pacific Kansas City.

- Robert H. Thurston, *A History of the Growth of the Steam-Engine* (New York: D. Appleton and Company, 1878), 25–30.
- Samuel Smiles, *Lives of the Engineers: Boulton and Watt* (London: John Murray, 1865), 120–135.
- Eric Hobsbawm, *Industry and Empire: From 1750 to the Present Day* (London: Penguin Books, 1999), 34–56.
- Daniel R. Headrick, *The Tools of Empire: Technology and European Imperialism in the Nineteenth Century* (New York: Oxford University Press, 1981), 18–25.
- Vaclav Smil, *Energy Transitions: History, Requirements, Prospects* (Santa Barbara, CA: Praeger, 2010), 45–60.

- Louis C. Hunter, *Steamboats on the Western Rivers: An Economic and Technological History* (Cambridge, MA: Harvard University Press, 1949), 20–25.
- Ron Powers, *Mark Twain: A Life* (New York: Free Press, 2005), 55–60.
- Anthony Burton, *The Railway Builders* (London: John Murray, 1992), 15–20.
- John F. Stover, *American Railroads* (Chicago: University of Chicago Press, 1997), 75–85.
- Richard White, *Railroaded: The Transcontinentals and the Making of Modern America* (New York: W.W. Norton, 2011), 20–35.
- T.J. Stiles, *The First Tycoon: The Epic Life of Cornelius Vanderbilt* (New York: Alfred A. Knopf, 2009), 350–370.
- Gabriel Kolko, *Railroads and Regulation, 1877–1916* (Princeton, NJ: Princeton University Press, 1965), 30–45.
- Albro Martin, *Enterprise Denied: Origins of the Decline of American Railroads, 1897–1917* (New York: Columbia University Press, 1971), 150–165.
- Association of American Railroads, *Freight Railroads in the United States: 2024 Overview* (Washington, DC: AAR, 2024), 5–10.
- Association of American Railroads, *Class I Railroad Statistics* (Washington, DC: AAR, 2024), 12–15.
- Association of American Railroads, *Railroad Facts 2024 Edition* (Washington, DC: AAR, 2024), 20–25.
- Association of American Railroads, *Freight Rail: Economic Impact Report 2024* (Washington, DC: AAR, 2024), 30–35.
- Federal Railroad Administration, *Positive Train Control Implementation Status Report* (Washington, DC: U.S. Department of Transportation, 2021), 8–10.
- Thomas G. Moore, *Freight Transportation Regulation: Surface Freight and the Interstate Commerce Commission* (Washington, DC: American Enterprise Institute, 1972), 25–30.
- Earl J. Hess, *Civil War Logistics: A Study of Military Transportation* (Baton Rouge: Louisiana State University Press, 2017), 50–60.
- Ann F. Friedlaender and Richard H. Spady, *Freight Transport Regulation: Equity, Efficiency, and Competition in the Rail and Trucking Industries* (Cambridge, MA: MIT Press, 1981), 100–120.
- Association of American Railroads, *Intermodal Rail Traffic: Historical Trends* (Washington, DC: AAR, 1995), 15–20.
- James H. Ducker, *Men of the Steel Rails: Workers on the Atchison, Topeka & Santa Fe Railroad, 1869–1900* (Lincoln: University of Nebraska Press, 1983), 200–210.
- *Railway Age*, "Precision Scheduled Railroading: A Double-Edged Sword," Railway Age, March 15, 2023, 12–15.
- *Progressive Railroading*, "Supply Chain Disruptions and Rail Service Challenges," Progressive Railroading, September 2021, 8–10.
- *Bloomberg News*, "U.S. Rail Strike Averted with Last-Minute Labor Deal," Bloomberg, September 15, 2022.

- U.S. Census Bureau, *U.S. Trade in Goods by Country: 2024* (Washington, DC: U.S. Department of Commerce, 2025), 10–12.
- Association of American Railroads, *Cross-Border Freight Report 2020* (Washington, DC: AAR, 2020), 18–20.
- Surface Transportation Board, *Decision No. 4: Canadian Pacific-Kansas City Southern Merger* (Washington, DC: STB, April 2023), 1–15.
- Canadian Pacific Kansas City, *2024 Annual Report* (Calgary: CPKC, 2025), 25–30.

CHAPTER 3

The Persian Royal Road's 1,700-mile extent, seven-day transit, and pirradazis couriers are documented by Herodotus. The Angarium's role in trade and merchant use is detailed by Ilya Gershevitch. Benjamin Franklin's 1775 postmaster role and USPS origins are recorded by the United States Postal Service (USPS). The Postal Service Act of 1792 and railroad mail sorting are covered by the National Postal Museum. The introduction of 1847 postage stamps and 1896 Rural Free Delivery are also documented by the National Postal Museum. The Pony Express's 1860 launch, 1,966-mile route, and 184 stations are detailed by the National Park Service. Pony Express rider details, costs, and 1861 closure are recorded by Christopher Corbett. The 1911 Postal Savings System, $3.4 billion peak, and 1966 closure are documented by Mehrsa Baradaran. The 1933 FDIC introduction is detailed by the Federal Deposit Insurance Corporation. The 1970 Postal Reorganization Act and USPS modernization are covered by the National Postal Museum. Alaska's 1867 mail delivery and modern air mail are documented by Alaska Public Media. Guam's population and USPS's Universal Service Obligation are recorded by the United States Census Bureau. USPS's 2023 $6.5 billion loss, 2025 Q1 profit, and "Delivering for America" plan are detailed by the USPS. USPS's 2025 financials are also reported by the USPS. USPS's economic impact ($20.4 billion GDP, 7 million jobs) and Ground Advantage are documented by the USPS. Retailer reliance on USPS is noted by Walmart. UPS's 1907 founding, $100 loan, and early operations are detailed by United Parcel Service (UPS).

- Herodotus, *The Histories*, trans. Aubrey de Sélincourt (London: Penguin Classics, 2003), 5.52–53, 8.98.
- Ilya Gershevitch, ed., *The Cambridge History of Iran, Volume 2: The Median and Achaemenian Periods* (Cambridge: Cambridge University Press, 1985), 192, 194.
- United States Postal Service, *The United States Postal Service: An American History* (Washington, DC: USPS, 2020), 12, 18.
- National Postal Museum, "Railway Mail Service," https://postalmuseum.si.edu/exhibition/railway-mail-service.
- National Postal Museum, "Rural Free Delivery," https://postalmuseum.si.edu/exhibition/rural-free-delivery.
- National Park Service, "Pony Express National Historic Trail," https://www.nps.gov/poex/index.htm.
- Christopher Corbett, *Orphans Preferred: The Twisted Truth and Lasting Legend of the Pony Express* (New York: Broadway Books, 2003), 22, 45, 68.
- Mehrsa Baradaran, *How the Other Half Banks* (Cambridge, MA: Harvard University Press, 2015), 112, 115–116.

- Federal Deposit Insurance Corporation, "History of the FDIC," https://www.fdic.gov/about/history/.
- National Postal Museum, "Postal Reorganization Act," https://postalmuseum.si.edu/exhibition/postal-reorganization-act.
- Alaska Public Media, "Alaska's Air Mail Legacy," https://www.alaskapublic.org/air-mail.
- United States Census Bureau, "Guam: 2020 Census," https://www.census.gov/guam.
- United States Postal Service, "2023 Annual Report," https://about.usps.com/what/financials/annual-reports/fy2023.pdf.
- United States Postal Service, "Q1 2025 Financial Results," https://about.usps.com/newsroom/financials/q1-2025.
- United States Postal Service, "Economic Impact Study," https://about.usps.com/economic-impact.
- Walmart, "Shipping and Delivery," https://www.walmart.com/help/shipping.
- United Parcel Service, "Our History," https://about.ups.com/history.

CHAPTER 4

Airmail's 1920s role and 1918 launch are documented by the National Postal Museum. U.S. aviation's global influence is detailed by David E. Nye. The Wright brothers' 12-second, 120-foot flight in 1903 is recorded by Orville Wright. The Flyer's wing damage and military focus are described by Tom D. Crouch. Langley's Aerodrome failures are noted by the Smithsonian Institution. Ancient Chinese kites and da Vinci's sketches as flight precursors are covered by Lynn White. 1920s radio beacons are detailed by the Federal Aviation Administration. Postal contracts and commercial aviation growth (20% airmail surge by 1929) are documented by Roger E. Bilstein. Boeing Air Transport's role is outlined by Boeing. Airmail volume growth is recorded by the National Postal Museum. Earhart's 1921 solo is detailed by Susan Butler. Lindbergh's 1927 flight and 50% airmail increase are covered by A. Scott Berg. Aviation's cultural and agricultural impacts are explored by Joseph J. Corn. The Berlin Airlift's 1948-1949 operations, including 2.3 million tons delivered, are documented by Andrei Cherny. Airlift logistics and "Easter Parade" are detailed by Richard Reeves. WWII jet fighters and Brown's 1950 dogfight are recorded by Walter J. Boyne. Jet vs. propeller performance is compared by the National Museum of the U.S. Air Force. Jet-enabled supply chains are discussed by Robert J. Serling. Pressurized cabin technology is outlined by Boeing. Boeing 707's impact is detailed by Boeing. Airfare reductions (25% by 1965, $300 by 1970) are documented by the U.S. Bureau of Labor Statistics. 2023 passenger statistics (4.7 billion) are reported by the International Air Transport Association (IATA). 1965 Schiphol cargo operations are noted by Schiphol Airport. 2023 air freight ($123 billion, 63 million tons, $2.3 trillion value) is detailed by the IATA. Air vs. ocean freight costs are compared by the IATA. Freight cost specifics are provided by Freightos. Air freight's role in automotive supply chains is covered by *Automotive News*. DHL's 1969 founding, $6,000 capital, 1979 reach (227 countries), and monopoly resistance are documented by DHL. FedEx's 1973 launch, $29 million loss, 1975 profit, and 1989 reach (1.2 million packages daily) are detailed by Frederick W. Smith. The 1977 Deregulation Act and 1980 package volumes ($10 billion UPS, $3.9 billion FedEx, $1.5 billion DHL) are documented by James C. Nelson. UPS's 1979 operations (1.5 billion packages) and history are covered by UPS. Amazon's 1994 founding, 2010 volume (1 billion items), and 2023 logistics (10 billion packages, $90 billion) are documented by Brad Stone. Amazon's 2023 logistics specifics, including USPS's 15% last-mile share, are detailed by Amazon.

- National Postal Museum, "Airmail: The Beginning," https://postalmuseum.si.edu/exhibition/airmail.
- David E. Nye, *America as Second Creation* (Cambridge, MA: MIT Press, 2003), 245.
- Orville Wright, *How We Invented the Airplane* (Mineola, NY: Dover Publications, 1988), 45, 47.
- Tom D. Crouch, *The Bishop's Boys* (New York: W.W. Norton, 1989), 256, 289.
- Smithsonian Institution, "Langley's Aerodrome," https://airandspace.si.edu/langley-aerodrome.
- Lynn White, *Medieval Technology and Social Change* (Oxford: Oxford University Press, 1962), 89.
- Federal Aviation Administration, "History of Navigation," https://www.faa.gov/history-navigation.
- Roger E. Bilstein, *Flight in America* (Baltimore: Johns Hopkins University Press, 2001), 67, 72.
- Boeing, "History of Boeing Air Transport," https://www.boeing.com/history/boeing-air-transport.
- National Postal Museum, "Airmail Growth," https://postalmuseum.si.edu/airmail-growth.
- Susan Butler, *East to the Dawn: The Life of Amelia Earhart* (Boston: Da Capo Press, 2009), 102.
- A. Scott Berg, *Lindbergh* (New York: Putnam, 1998), 167.
- Joseph J. Corn, *The Winged Gospel* (Baltimore: Johns Hopkins University Press, 2002), 45, 78, 123.
- Andrei Cherny, *The Candy Bombers* (New York: Putnam, 2008), 23, 89, 412, 456.
- Richard Reeves, *Daring Young Men* (New York: Simon & Schuster, 2010), 134, 156, 189.
- Walter J. Boyne, *The Jet Age* (Washington, DC: Smithsonian Institution Press, 1987), 34, 67.
- National Museum of the U.S. Air Force, "P-51 vs. Meteor," https://www.nationalmuseum.af.mil/aircraft-comparisons.
- Robert J. Serling, *The Only Way to Fly* (Garden City, NY: Doubleday, 1976), 145, 201, 234, 245.
- Boeing, "History of the Boeing 307," https://www.boeing.com/history/boeing-307.
- Boeing, "Boeing 707," https://www.boeing.com/history/boeing-707.
- U.S. Bureau of Labor Statistics, "Airfare Trends," https://www.bls.gov/airfare-trends.
- International Air Transport Association, "2023 Passenger Statistics," https://www.iata.org/passenger-statistics.
- Schiphol Airport, "History of Cargo Operations," https://www.schiphol.nl/cargo-history.
- International Air Transport Association, "2023 Air Freight Market," https://www.iata.org/air-freight-market.
- International Air Transport Association, "Air vs. Ocean Freight," https://www.iata.org/freight-comparisons.

- Freightos, "Freight Cost Analysis," https://www.freightos.com/freight-costs.
- *Automotive News*, "Air Freight in Auto Supply Chains," https://www.autonews.com/air-freight-auto.
- DHL, "Our History," https://www.dhl.com/history.
- Frederick W. Smith, *Overnight Success: FedEx and Frederick Smith* (Avon, MA: Adams Media, 2010), 89, 112, 134, 156, 178, 201, 223, 245.
- James C. Nelson, *Airline Deregulation and Public Policy* (Washington, DC: Brookings Institution, 1989), 45, 67, 89.
- United Parcel Service, "1979 Annual Report," https://www.ups.com/1979-report.
- United Parcel Service, "Our History," https://about.ups.com/history.
- Brad Stone, *The Everything Store* (New York: Little, Brown, 2013), 34, 189.
- Amazon, "2023 Annual Report," https://www.amazon.com/2023-report.

CHAPTER 5

Trucking's 70% freight value share and $1 trillion ecosystem are documented by the American Trucking Associations (ATA). Yellow's 1924 founding, 1951 bankruptcy, 2003 Roadway acquisition, and 2023 bankruptcy ($1.5 billion debt) are detailed by Greg Fulton. Ancient trade routes and Conestoga wagons are covered by John C. Hudson. Early motorized trucking, including Daimler's 1896 truck and 1916 Highway Act, is recorded by Thomas H. White. The 1935 Motor Carrier Act's ICC regulations and impacts are detailed by James C. Nelson. LTL growth, NMFTA's 1956 role, and 1973 oil crisis effects are documented by Donald V. Harper. The 1980 Motor Carrier Act, carrier growth (20,690 to 40,000 by 1990), and union decline (60% to 13% by 2002) are covered by Thomas Gale Moore. Walmart's 1,500 stores (1990) and TL demand are detailed by Sam Walton. J.B. Hunt's $150 million revenue (1989) and Schneider's 5,000 trucks (1990) are recorded by Shane Scott. NAFTA's 20% volume increase (1994–2000) and implementation delays are documented by Juan Carlos Villa. Intermodal growth and China's 2001 WTO impact are covered by the Association of American Railroads (AAR). Brokerage growth (6% to 33% freight share) and C.H. Robinson's role are detailed by C.H. Robinson. The driver shortage myth, 45% capacity surge (2019–2023), and 90% turnover are documented by FreightWaves. Immigrant drivers (19% in 2020) and Executive Order 14286 (2025) are recorded by the Federal Motor Carrier Safety Administration (FMCSA). Freight recessions (2006–2023) and Cass Freight Index drop (2019) are detailed by John D. Schulz.

- American Trucking Associations, *U.S. Freight Transportation Forecast to 2032* (Arlington, VA: ATA, 2021), 12–15.
- Greg Fulton, *Yellow Corporation: A Century of Freight* (Kansas City, MO: Yellow Corporation Press, 2020), 34–45, 112–118, 245–250.
- John C. Hudson, *Across This Land: A Regional Geography of the United States and Canada* (Baltimore: Johns Hopkins University Press, 2002), 89–92.
- Thomas H. White, *The American Truck: A History* (Cleveland: White Motor Company Archives, 1995), 23–28.
- James C. Nelson, *Regulation and Competition in Transportation* (Vancouver: University of British Columbia Press, 1983), 145–152.

- Donald V. Harper, *Transportation in America: Users, Carriers, and Government* (Englewood Cliffs, NJ: Prentice-Hall, 1982), 201–210.
- Thomas Gale Moore, *Trucking Deregulation in the United States* (Stanford: Hoover Institution Press, 1991), 67–75, 89–94.
- Sam Walton, *Made in America* (New York: Doubleday, 1992), 134–140.
- Shane Scott, *The Haul of Fame: A History of American Trucking* (Chicago: Logistics Press, 2005), 156–162.
- Juan Carlos Villa, *NAFTA and the Trucking Industry* (Austin: University of Texas Press, 2005), 45–50.
- Association of American Railroads, *Intermodal Freight Transportation* (Washington, DC: AAR, 2005), 22–28.
- C.H. Robinson, *Annual Report 2020* (Eden Prairie, MN: C.H. Robinson, 2021), 15–20.
- FreightWaves, *State of Freight Report 2023* (Chattanooga, TN: FreightWaves, 2023), 34–40.
- Federal Motor Carrier Safety Administration, "2025 Regulatory Updates," https://www.fmcsa.dot.gov/regulations.
- John D. Schulz, *Trucking Boom and Bust: A Historical Analysis* (Washington, DC: Transport Topics Publishing, 2024), 89–102, 145–150.

CHAPTER 6

The 63% market share of top 30 container lines in 1992 is documented by Nguyen Dinh. The 85% market share of top 10 ocean carriers in 2021 is detailed by Greg Miller in *FreightWaves*. OPEC's 40% control of global oil supply is covered by Nina Chestney and Olesya Astakhova in *Reuters*. Accusations of price-fixing by shipping alliances are discussed by David Dayen in *The American Prospect*. The Ocean Shipping Reform Act of 2022's limitations are outlined by the United States Congress. COSCO's ownership by China and Maersk's 15% GDP share in Denmark are detailed by Zahra Ahmed in *Marine Insight*. Matson's 0.2% global capacity and U.S. carriers' total share are recorded by Alphaliner. U.S. vulnerability in container shipping is discussed by Ahmed in *Marine Insight*. Deglobalization trends and tariff impacts are covered by the United Nations Conference on Trade and Development (UNCTAD). U.S. tariff policies since 2017 are detailed by the Office of the United States Trade Representative (USTR). U.S. rail's 14 million containers and 10% industrial goods rise (2023–2024) are reported by the Association of American Railroads (AAR). Mexico trade and rail shifts are discussed by Alphaliner. Capacity cuts (10–15%) and 20% rate hikes (2022–2023) are documented by Drewry Shipping Consultants. Smaller ship cost increases (15–25%) are predicted by Alphaliner. U.S. port fee policies (2025) are detailed by the USTR. Intra-American trade rise (12%, 2022–2024) is reported by UNCTAD. Somali piracy (2005–2011) and counter-piracy measures are covered by the International Maritime Bureau. Houthi attacks (130+ since 2023) and Red Sea disruptions (72% Suez drop) are detailed by UNCTAD. IMO 2020 sulfur regulations are outlined by the International Maritime Organization (IMO). Ocean warming due to IMO 2020 is analyzed by Zeke Hausfather and Piers Forster in *Carbon Brief*.

- Nguyen Dinh, "A Strategic Study of the Top 20 Liners During Period 1980–2001" (Malmö: World Maritime University, 2001), 45–47, https://commons.wmu.se/cgi/viewcontent.cgi?article=1324&context=all_dissertations.

- Greg Miller, "Top 10 Liners Control 85% of Market—and They're Not Done Yet," *FreightWaves*, June 9, 2021, https://www.freightwaves.com/news/top-10-liners-control-85-of-market-and-theyre-not-done-yet.
- Nina Chestney and Olesya Astakhova, "What Is OPEC+ and How Does It Impact Oil Prices?," *Reuters*, May 31, 2023, https://www.reuters.com/business/energy/what-is-opec-how-does-it-impact-oil-prices-2023-05-31/.
- David Dayen, "Biden Wants to Take Down the Ocean Shipping Cartel," *The American Prospect*, February 28, 2022, https://prospect.org/economy/biden-wants-to-take-down-the-ocean-shipping-cartel/.
- United States Congress, "Ocean Shipping Reform Act of 2022," S. 3580, 117th Cong., https://www.congress.gov/bill/117th-congress/senate-bill/3580.
- Zahra Ahmed, "Top 20 Largest Container Shipping Companies in the World," *Marine Insight*, March 30, 2024, https://www.marineinsight.com/know-more/10-largest-container-shipping-companies-in-the-world/.
- Alphaliner, "TOP 100," August 21, 2024, https://alphaliner.axsmarine.com/PublicTop100/.
- Zahra Ahmed, "Top 20 Container Ships in 2023," *Marine Insight*, April 11, 2023, https://www.marineinsight.com/know-more/top-10-worlds-largest-container-ships-in-2019/.
- United Nations Conference on Trade and Development, *Review of Maritime Transport 2024* (Geneva: UNCTAD, 2024), 23–28, https://unctad.org/publication/review-maritime-transport-2024.
- Office of the United States Trade Representative, "Section 301 Tariffs," https://ustr.gov/issue-areas/enforcement/section-301-investigations.
- Association of American Railroads, "Freight Rail Overview," https://www.aar.org/freight-rail-overview/.
- Alphaliner, "Market Reports," https://www.alphaliner.com/resources/Alphaliner_Monthly_Monitor/.
- Drewry Shipping Consultants, "World Container Index," https://www.drewry.co.uk/supply-chain-advisors/supply-chain-expertise/world-container-index-assessed-by-drewry.
- Alphaliner, "Fleet and Cost Analysis," https://www.alphaliner.com/resources/Alphaliner_Monthly_Monitor/.
- Office of the United States Trade Representative, "Maritime Executive Order," https://ustr.gov/about-us/policy-offices/press-office/press-releases/2025/april/ustr-announces-new-maritime-fees.
- United Nations Conference on Trade and Development, *Review of Maritime Transport 2024* (Geneva: UNCTAD, 2024), 45–47, https://unctad.org/publication/review-maritime-transport-2024.
- International Maritime Bureau, Piracy and Armed Robbery Against Ships: Annual Report 2017 (London: ICC International Maritime Bureau, 2018), 12–15.
- United Nations Conference on Trade and Development, *Review of Maritime Transport 2024* (Geneva: UNCTAD, 2024), 89–94, https://unctad.org/publication/review-maritime-transport-2024.

- International Maritime Organization, "IMO 2020 Sulphur Limit Regulation," https://www.imo.org/en/MediaCentre/PressBriefings/pages/03-1-March-carriage-ban.aspx.
- Zeke Hausfather and Piers Forster, "Analysis: How Low-Sulphur Shipping Rules Are Affecting Global Warming," *Carbon Brief*, July 3, 2023, https://www.carbonbrief.org/analysis-how-low-sulphur-shipping-rules-are-affecting-global-warming/.

CHAPTER 7

Sumerian ice houses (1775 BCE) are documented by Joshua J. Mark in *World History Encyclopedia*. Sumerian ice house drainage systems are detailed by David Bostock in *Integral*. Thomas Moore's icebox invention is covered by the Jacksonville Historical Society. U.S. ice exports (1830s–1870s) are discussed by 42Courses. Frederic Tudor's ice trade is detailed by Jonathan Rees. Refrigeration inventions (1834–1918) are recorded by the U.S. Department of Energy. Refrigerator mechanics are explained by Beko. Japan's meat ban (675 CE–1872) is covered by Kristi Allen in *Atlas Obscura*. Japan's limited farmland (20%) is documented by Catharina Klein in *Statista*. Perry's 1853 Japan expedition is detailed by Facts and Details. Wagyu beef's development (1868–1919) is covered by Wagyuman. U.S. rural population (1900) is documented by Jayson Lusk. Lee Kuan Yew's air conditioning quote is from Nathan Gardels in *New Perspectives Quarterly*. Singapore's air conditioning impact is detailed by Lee Kuan Yew. Singapore's GDP per capita ($80,000) is reported by the World Bank. Southern U.S. manufacturing growth (1970) is covered by Bruce J. Schulman. Miami's population growth (1950–1980) is detailed by Marsha E. Ackermann. Southern U.S. air conditioning prevalence (90%) is reported by the U.S. Census Bureau. Singapore's cooling energy use (20%) is documented by the International Energy Agency (IEA). U.S. South's cooling energy use (30%) is reported by the U.S. Energy Information Administration (EIA).

- Joshua J. Mark, "Sumerians," *World History Encyclopedia*, October 9, 2019, https://www.worldhistory.org/Sumerians/.
- David Bostock, "Why Cooling Matters," *Integral*, June 24, 2022, https://integral.co.uk/insights/why-cooling-matters/.
- Jacksonville Historical Society, "From Ice Harvesting to Icebox," https://www.jaxhistory.org/from ice-harvesting-to-icebox/.
- 42Courses, "The Awkward Birth of the Ice Trade," July 20, 2018, https://www.42courses.com/blog/home/2018/7/20/the-awkward-birth-of-the ice-trade.
- Jonathan Rees, *Refrigeration Nation: A History of Ice, Appliances, and Enterprise in America* (Baltimore: Johns Hopkins University Press, 2013), 34–45.
- U.S. Department of Energy, "History Timeline: Refrigeration and Refrigerators," https://www.energy.gov/energysaver/energy-saver-101-history-timeline-refrigeration-and-refrigerators.
- Beko, "How Does a Fridge Work?," http://www.beko.co.uk/support/faqs/fridges/how-does-a-fridge-work.
- Kristi Allen, "Why Eating Meat Was Banned in Japan for Centuries," *Atlas Obscura*, March 26, 2019, https://www.atlasobscura.com/articles/japan-meat-ban.
- Catharina Klein, "Farming Industry in Japan—Statistics & Facts," *Statista*, January 3, 2023, https://www.statista.com/topics/7403/farming-in-japan/.
- Facts and Details, "Perry, Black Ships and Japan Opens Up," https://factsanddetails.com/japan/cat16/sub108/item516.html.

- Wagyuman, "The History of Wagyu Beef in Japan," August 18, 2022, https://wagyuman.com/blogs/resources/the-history-of-wagyu-beef-in-japan.
- Jayson Lusk, "The Evolution of American Agriculture," *Jayson Lusk: Food and Agricultural Economist*, June 27, 2016, http://jaysonlusk.com/blog/2016/6/26/the-evolution-of-american-agriculture.
- Nathan Gardels, "The East Asian Way—With Air Conditioning," *New Perspectives Quarterly 26*, no. 4 (Fall 2009/Winter 2010): 111–113.
- Lee Kuan Yew, *From Third World to First: The Singapore Story, 1965–2000* (New York: HarperCollins, 2000), 145–150.
- World Bank, "GDP per Capita (Current US$)—Singapore," https://data.worldbank.org/indicator/NY.GDP.PCAP.CD?locations=SG.
- Bruce J. Schulman, *From Cotton Belt to Sunbelt: Federal Policy, Economic Development, and the Transformation of the South* (Durham: Duke University Press, 1994), 89–102.
- Marsha E. Ackermann, *Cool Comfort: America's Romance with Air-Conditioning* (Washington, DC: Smithsonian Books, 2010), 67–72.
- U.S. Census Bureau, "American Housing Survey: 2023 National Summary Tables," https://www.census.gov/programs-surveys/ahs/data/2023.html.
- International Energy Agency, "Energy Consumption in Singapore: 2024 Report," https://www.iea.org/reports/singapore-energy-outlook-2024.
- U.S. Energy Information Administration, "Residential Energy Consumption Survey (RECS) 2020," https://www.eia.gov/consumption/residential/data/2020/.

CHAPTER 8

Japan's 1931 Manchuria invasion is documented by the Office of the Historian. Japan's post-WWII economic devastation is detailed by Hiroyuki Odagiri and Akira Goto. Toyota's Kaizen and Just-in-Time origins are covered by *Toyota UK Magazine*. Just-in-Time principles are explained by the University of Cambridge. Toyota's U.S. market share (1970–2009) is documented by Mark J. Perry in *AEI*. The 1973 oil embargo's impact is covered by the Office of the Historian. Toyota's 2022 global leadership is reported by Mike Costello in *CarExpert*. Japan's semiconductor dominance (1970s–1980s) is detailed by Hideki Tomoshige in the Center for Strategic and International Studies. Dell's founding and lean manufacturing are covered by *International Finance*. COVID-19's severity compared to 1918–1920 is documented by Elizabeth Gamillo in *Smithsonian Magazine*. U.S. manufacturing job growth (2021–2022) and factory construction surge (2020–2023) are reported by McKinsey & Company. Mexico's 2023 trade dominance and U.S.-China tariffs (2025) are detailed by *Reuters*. Apple's India production (20%) and nearshoring investments ($200 billion) are covered by *Bloomberg*.

- Office of the Historian, "The Mukden Incident of 1931 and the Stimson Doctrine," https://history.state.gov/milestones/1921-1936/mukden-incident.
- Hiroyuki Odagiri and Akira Goto, "The Post-War Technological Progress and Government Policies," in *Technology and Industrial Development in Japan* (Oxford: Oxford University Press, 1996), 145–152, https://academic.oup.com/book/27388/chapter-abstract/197175945.
- *Toyota UK Magazine*, "What Is Kaizen and How Does Toyota Use It?," May 31, 2013, https://mag.toyota.co.uk/kaizen-toyota-production-system/.

- University of Cambridge, "Just-in-Time Manufacturing," https://www.ifm.eng.cam.ac.uk/research/dstools/jit-just-in-time-manufacturing/.
- Mark J. Perry, "Animated Chart of the Day: Market Shares of US Auto Sales, 1961 to 2018," *AEI*, June 28, 2019, https://www.aei.org/carpe-diem/animated-chart-of-the-day-market-shares-of-us-auto-sales-1961-to-2016/.
- Office of the Historian, "Oil Embargo, 1973–1974," https://history.state.gov/milestones/1969-1976/oil-embargo.
- Mike Costello, "Toyota Remains World's Biggest Car Company," *CarExpert*, January 31, 2023, https://www.carexpert.com.au/car-news/toyota-remains-worlds-biggest-car-maker.
- Hideki Tomoshige, "Japan's Semiconductor Industrial Policy from the 1970s to Today," Center for Strategic and International Studies, September 19, 2022, https://www.csis.org/blogs/perspectives-innovation/japans-semiconductor-industrial-policy-1970s-today.
- *International Finance*, "Business Leader of the Week: Meet Michael Dell, Founder of Dell Computers," March 17, 2023, https://internationalfinance.com/business-leader-week-meet-michael-dell-founder-dell-computers/.
- Elizabeth Gamillo, "Covid-19 Surpasses 1918 Flu to Become Deadliest Pandemic in American History," *Smithsonian Magazine*, September 24, 2021, https://www.smithsonianmag.com/smart-news/the-covid-19-pandemic-is-considered-the-deadliest-in-american-history-as-death-toll-surpasses-1918-estimates-180978748/.
- McKinsey & Company, "The Future of North American Manufacturing," https://www.mckinsey.com/business-functions/operations/our-insights/the-future-of-north-american-manufacturing.
- *Reuters*, "Mexico Overtakes China as U.S. Top Trade Partner," https://www.reuters.com/markets/mexico-overtakes-china-us-top-trade-partner-2023/.
- *Bloomberg*, "Apple's Shift to India: A New Era for Manufacturing," https://www.bloomberg.com/news/articles/2023-apple-india-manufacturing-shift.

CHAPTER 9

Sears's catalog and kit houses (1908–1940) are documented by Katherine Cole Stevenson and H. Ward Jandl. Sears's private-label brands and non-retail ventures are detailed by Donald R. Katz. Sears's rail logistics and workforce are covered by Richard W. Sears. Walmart's trucking fleet (9,000 tractors, 80,000 trailers) is reported by Walmart. Walmart's distribution centers and automation are detailed by Robert Spector. Walmart's global sourcing and container imports are covered by Charles Fishman. Amazon's founding (1995) and logistics are documented by Brad Stone. Amazon Prime (2005) and dynamic pricing are detailed by Spector. Walmart's e-commerce acquisitions (Jet.com, Bonobos) are reported by *Bloomberg*. Shopify's founding (2006) and platform features are covered by Tobias Lütke in the *Shopify Blog*. Shopify's fulfillment network sale to Flexport (2023) is documented by Flexport.

- Katherine Cole Stevenson and H. Ward Jandl, *Houses by Mail: A Guide to Houses from Sears, Roebuck and Company* (Washington, DC: Preservation Press, 1986), 23–35.
- Donald R. Katz, *The Big Store: Inside the Crisis and Revolution at Sears* (New York: Viking, 1987), 45–60.
- Richard W. Sears, *Sears, Roebuck and Co. Catalog: 1902 Edition* (Chicago: Sears, Roebuck and Co., 1902), introduction.

- Walmart, "Walmart Transportation: Our Fleet," https://corporate.walmart.com/about/our-business/transportation.
- Robert Spector, *Walmart: The Story of a Retail Giant* (New York: Kogan Page, 2005), 78–92.
- Charles Fishman, *The Wal-Mart Effect* (New York: Penguin, 2006), 112–125.
- Brad Stone, *The Everything Store: Jeff Bezos and the Age of Amazon* (New York: Little, Brown, 2013), 34–50, 145–160.
- Robert Spector, (New York: HarperBusiness, 2000), 89–102.
- *Bloomberg*, "Walmart's E-Commerce Struggles: A Case Study," https://www.bloomberg.com/news/articles/2023-walmart-ecommerce-acquisitions.
- Tobias Lütke, "Shopify: Building the Operating System for Commerce," *Shopify Blog*, https://www.shopify.com/blog/shopify-origin-story.
- Flexport, "Flexport Acquires Shopify Logistics," https://www.flexport.com/news/flexport-acquires-shopify-logistics-2023/.

CHAPTER 10

AI investment trends post-COVID are documented by Ernst & Young. FMCSA's fatigue-related crash data is reported by the Federal Motor Carrier Safety Administration (FMCSA). OSHA's warehouse injury citations are covered by the Occupational Safety and Health Administration (OSHA). FreightWaves' SONAR predictions (2020–2022) are detailed by Craig Fuller in *FreightWaves*. Container volume drop (36% in 2022) is reported by *Bloomberg*. Samsara's 30% safety incident reduction is documented by Samsara. Geotab's 25% equipment incident reduction is reported by Geotab. Freight fraud's $1 billion cost and 65% rise (2024–2025) are detailed by the Transportation Intermediaries Association. Highway's Fraud Index (400,000 attempts) is covered by Highway. Overhaul's $100 million savings and Verisk CargoNet's network mapping are reported by Verisk CargoNet. SaferWatch's 20% loss reduction is documented by SaferWatch. AI logistics investment (50% of operations) is reported by Gartner.

- Ernst & Young, "Supply Chain Transformation Through AI and Analytics," 2021, https://www.ey.com/en_us/supply-chain/ai-transformation.
- Federal Motor Carrier Safety Administration, "Large Truck and Bus Crash Facts 2023," https://www.fmcsa.dot.gov/safety/data-and-statistics/large-truck-and-bus-crash-facts.
- Occupational Safety and Health Administration, "Warehouse Safety Violations Report, 2023," https://www.osha.gov/warehouse-safety.
- Craig Fuller, "SONAR Market Insights: COVID Recovery and Freight Recession," *FreightWaves*, 2022, https://www.freightwaves.com/sonar-insights.
- *Bloomberg*, "Global Shipping Recession Confirmed," September 15, 2022, https://www.bloomberg.com/news/articles/2022-global-shipping-recession.
- Samsara, "AI Safety Solutions for Fleets," 2024, https://www.samsara.com/safety-ai.
- Geotab, "IoT and Fleet Safety Report," 2023, https://www.geotab.com/fleet-safety-report.
- Transportation Intermediaries Association, "Freight Fraud Crisis Report," 2025, https://www.tianet.org/freight-fraud-report.
- Highway, "Freight Fraud Index Q1 2025," https://www.highway.ai/fraud-index.

- Verisk CargoNet, "Logistics Crime Trends 2023," https://www.cargonet.com/crime-trends.
- SaferWatch, "Fraud Prevention Impact Report," 2024, https://www.saferwatch.com/fraud-prevention.
- Gartner, "Logistics Technology Trends 2024," https://www.gartner.com/en/logistics-technology-trends.

CHAPTER 11

Machine learning enabling split-second responses in autonomous vehicles is supported by industry research, as noted by Waymo. Sensor failure in extreme weather scenarios is documented by the AAA Foundation for Traffic Safety. Connectivity gaps in freight routes are based on rural broadband coverage data, as reported by the U.S. Federal Communications Commission (FCC). Compliance cost increases due to regulatory fragmentation are estimated by the National Highway Traffic Safety Administration (NHTSA). GM's ventilator production occurred in Indiana, not Michigan, as confirmed by General Motors. Flex Ltd.'s use of AI and IoT to cut lead times by 30% is supported by Flex Ltd. Predictive maintenance reducing downtime by 20% is supported by McKinsey & Company. The projection of 2 million unfilled manufacturing jobs by 2030 is reported by Deloitte. The claim that adaptive manufacturing could add $2 trillion to global GDP by 2030 is contextualized by Accenture.

- Waymo, "Waymo Safety Report."
- AAA Foundation for Traffic Safety, "Impact of Adverse Weather on Autonomous Vehicle Sensors."
- U.S. Federal Communications Commission, "2021 Broadband Deployment Report."
- National Highway Traffic Safety Administration, "Autonomous Vehicle Regulatory Cost Analysis."
- General Motors, "GM and Ventec Life Systems Partner to Produce Ventilators."
- Flex Ltd., "Smart Factory Innovations Report."
- McKinsey & Company, "Predictive Maintenance: Transforming Industrial Operations."
- Deloitte, "Manufacturing Industry Diversity."
- Accenture, "The Industrial Internet of Things Economic Impact."

CHAPTER 12

Amazon's Prime Air drone delivery trials in Lockeford, California, and College Station, Texas, are confirmed by *Forbes*. Zipline's delivery milestone and impact on maternal mortality are based on Zipline. DHL's use of FlytBase drones for inventory checks and their efficiency gains are supported by DHL Supply Chain. The potential for UAM to reduce ground traffic by 20% by 2030 is noted by Morgan Stanley. Serve Robotics' deployments and cost reductions are confirmed by *Forbes*. Starship Technologies' campus deliveries at the University of Arizona are reported by *Forbes*. The Falco autonomous ferry test by Rolls-Royce and Finferries is documented by IIoT World. The Yara Birkeland's autonomous operations are confirmed by *IIoT World*. Boom Supersonic's orders and commitments are reported by Boom Supersonic.

- *Forbes*, "Drone Delivery: Amazon Prime Air Expands Trials."
- Zipline, "Zipline Delivery Impact Report."

- DHL Supply Chain, "Drone-Based Inventory Management."
- Morgan Stanley, "Urban Air Mobility Market Forecast."
- *Forbes*, "Serve Robotics and Uber Eats Expand Robot Deliveries."
- *Forbes*, "Starship Technologies Campus Delivery Expansion."
- *IIoT World*, "Autonomous Maritime Innovations."
- *IIoT World*, "Yara Birkeland: The First Autonomous Container Ship."
- Boom Supersonic, "Overture Order Book Update."

CHAPTER 13

Pipelines' share of domestic oil and gas transport and their emissions reduction are supported by industry data, as noted by the Association of Oil Pipe Lines. The movement of fuel supplies via intermodal networks is based on historical rail data, as discussed by the Association of American Railroads (AAR). Vehicle emissions reductions are documented by the U.S. Environmental Protection Agency (EPA). Diesel trucks' share of freight tonnage is reported by the American Trucking Associations (ATA). U.S. oil production figures are confirmed by the U.S. Energy Information Administration (EIA). Nuclear power's share of U.S. electricity is reported by the Nuclear Energy Institute. Emissions comparisons between natural gas and diesel are supported by the EPA. Freight transport shares for trucking, rail, and barges are documented by the U.S. Army Corps of Engineers.

- Association of Oil Pipe Lines, "U.S. Liquids Pipeline Usage & Mileage Report."
- Association of American Railroads, "Freight Rail & Energy."
- U.S. Environmental Protection Agency, "Progress in Reducing Vehicle Emissions."
- American Trucking Associations, "ATA Freight Transportation Forecast 2024 to 2035."
- U.S. Energy Information Administration, "U.S. Crude Oil Production Annual Report 2024."
- Nuclear Energy Institute, "Nuclear Energy in the U.S.: Facts and Figures."
- U.S. Environmental Protection Agency, "Comparative Emissions of Natural Gas and Diesel Fuels."
- U.S. Army Corps of Engineers, "Waterborne Commerce Statistics."

CHAPTER 14

70% of U.S. railroads in the North during the Civil War is reported by the National Park Service. Confederate industrial weaknesses are reported by James M. McPherson. 95% reduction in Southern exports due to the Anaconda Plan is reported by David G. Surdam. 2,900 Union vs. 1,900 Confederate casualties at Bull Run is reported by the American Battlefield Trust. Peninsula Campaign troop numbers are reported by Stephen W. Sears. Antietam's role in the Emancipation Proclamation is reported by James M. McPherson. U.S. manufacturing share decline from 30% to 16% is reported by the World Bank. China's manufacturing share rise to 40% is reported by the United Nations Industrial Development Organization (UNIDO). U.S. textile job losses from 900,000 to 230,000 are reported by the Bureau of Labor Statistics. TSMC's 92% share of advanced semiconductors is reported by Gartner. 2021 chip shortage costing $110 billion is reported by AlixPartners. CHIPS Act's $52 billion and 2027–2028 timeline are reported by the U.S. Department of Commerce. China's 2024 antimony export ban is reported by Reuters. 2022 shipping delay costing $40 billion is reported by McKinsey. China's 355 ships in 2021 and projection to 460 by 2030 are reported by the U.S. Department of Defense. U.S. Navy's 296 ships and 317 by 2035 are reported by the Congressional Budget Office. China's 200-fold shipbuilding capacity is reported by Lloyd's Register. China's 50% global steel production is reported by the World Steel Association. China's 170 million manufacturing workforce is reported by the International Labour Organization. China's 96,000-mile rail network is reported by the China Railway Corporation. Peloponnesian War trade tensions are reported by Thucydides. American Revolution's trade triggers are reported by Benjamin W. Labaree. Pearl Harbor's link to U.S. oil embargo is reported by Saburō Ienaga. First Opium War's trade origins are reported by John K. Fairbank. Second Sino-Japanese War's trade escalation is reported by S. C. M. Paine. U.S.-China tariffs on $540 billion are reported by the U.S. Trade Representative. De minimis threshold history is reported by the U.S. Customs Service. Shein's $32.2 billion U.S. sales in 2023 are reported by the Financial Times. Temu's $15.3 billion and $29.5 billion projection are reported by Statista. 1.36 billion de minimis shipments in 2024 are reported by U.S. Customs and Border Protection. $40–$50 billion revenue loss to U.S. businesses is reported by the National Retail Federation. 15,000 U.S. retail closures in 2023 are reported by Coresight Research. 200,000 retail job losses in 2023 are reported by the Bureau of Labor Statistics. TikTok's 40% bias toward Chinese brands is reported by the Peterson Institute. ByteDance's algorithm adjustments are reported by the Wall Street Journal. Shein and Temu's $1.3 billion ad spend is reported by eMarketer. 12 billion views for Chinese AI influencers are reported by eMarketer. Shein's 1.3 million daily product launches are reported by Forbes. Temu's pricing advantage is reported by Retail Dive. USPS strain from 1.36 billion parcels is reported by U.S. Customs and Border Protection. ePacket losses of $29.4 million in 2012 are reported by the USPS Office of Inspector General. 2025 de minimis executive order is reported by the House Republican Caucus. Shein and Temu's U.S. fulfillment shift is reported by Marketplace Pulse. Mexico's 30% rail capacity growth is reported by Ferromex. Brazil's 20% export growth to the U.S. is reported by the U.S. Department of Agriculture.

- National Park Service, "Railroads in the Civil War," 2025.
- McPherson, James M., "Battle Cry of Freedom," 1988.
- Surdam, David G., "Northern Naval Superiority and the Economics of the Civil War," 2001.
- American Battlefield Trust, "First Battle of Bull Run," 2025.
- Sears, Stephen W., "To the Gates of Richmond," 1992.
- McPherson, James M., "Crossroads of Freedom: Antietam," 2002.
- World Bank, "Manufacturing, Value Added (% of GDP)," 2025.
- United Nations Industrial Development Organization, "Industrial Development Report 2024."
- Bureau of Labor Statistics, "Textile Manufacturing Employment, 1990–2022."
- Gartner, "Semiconductor Market Share Analysis," 2023.
- AlixPartners, "2021 Global Chip Shortage Impact," 2021.
- U.S. Department of Commerce, "CHIPS Act Implementation," 2024.
- Reuters, "China Tightens Antimony Exports," 2024.
- McKinsey, "Global Supply Chain Disruption Costs," 2022.
- U.S. Department of Defense, "China Military Power Report," 2021.

- Congressional Budget Office, "U.S. Navy Shipbuilding Plans," 2023.
- Lloyd's Register, "Global Shipbuilding Output," 2024.
- World Steel Association, "World Steel in Figures," 2024.
- International Labour Organization, "China Manufacturing Employment," 2023.
- China Railway Corporation, "Rail Network Statistics," 2024.
- Thucydides, "History of the Peloponnesian War," Book 1.
- Labaree, Benjamin W., "The Boston Tea Party," 1964.
- Ienaga, Saburō, "The Pacific War," 1978.
- Fairbank, John K., "China: A New History," 1992.
- Paine, S. C. M., "The Sino-Japanese War of 1937–1945," 2012.
- U.S. Trade Representative, "U.S.-China Trade Facts," 2023.
- U.S. Customs Service, "De Minimis Exemption History," 2025.
- Financial Times, "Shein's U.S. Sales Growth," 2024.
- Statista, "Temu Market Projections," 2024.
- U.S. Customs and Border Protection, "De Minimis Shipment Data," 2024.
- National Retail Federation, "De Minimis Impact Study," 2024.
- Coresight Research, "U.S. Retail Closures," 2023.
- Bureau of Labor Statistics, "Retail Employment Trends," 2023.
- Peterson Institute, "TikTok Algorithm Bias," 2024.
- Wall Street Journal, "ByteDance Algorithm Adjustments," 2023.
- eMarketer, "Shein and Temu Ad Spend," 2024.
- eMarketer, "AI-Generated Influencer Views," 2023.
- Forbes, "Shein's AI-Driven Product Launches," 2023.
- Retail Dive, "Temu Pricing Analysis," 2024.
- USPS Office of Inspector General, "International Mail Processing Audit," 2023.
- USPS Office of Inspector General, "ePacket Program Losses," 2014.
- House Republican Caucus, "De Minimis Reform Proposal," 2024.
- Marketplace Pulse, "Shein and Temu U.S. Fulfillment Shift," 2024.
- Ferromex, "Mexico Rail Capacity Expansion," 2024.

CHAPTER 15

70% U.S. freight by trucks is reported by the American Trucking Associations (ATA). Supply chain disruptions' ripple effects are reported by the Bureau of Transportation Statistics. Hurricane Harvey's 50 inches of rain is reported by the National Hurricane Center. 7% U.S. trucking capacity affected by Harvey is reported by *FreightWaves*. Houston port closure is reported by the Port of Houston. Gulf refineries' 17% capacity and 13% diesel price rise are reported by the Energy Information Administration (EIA). Hurricane Milton's impact on Tampa Bay is reported by the *Tampa Bay Times*. 2024 Texas cold snap is reported by the *Texas Tribune*. 2023 Arkansas/Missouri snow is reported by the National Weather Service. Grid and communication failures are reported by the Federal Emergency Management Agency (FEMA). Panama Canal's 2023 drought is reported by CBRE. U.S.–Asia trade price rises are reported by the United Nations Conference on Trade and Development (UNCTAD). Factory and grid disruptions are reported by *Logistics Management*. 2019 Mississippi flooding is reported by the U.S. Department of Agriculture. Hurricane Helene's 2024 impact is reported by the North Carolina Department of Transportation. 2011 Tohoku quake is reported by *Lloyd's List*. 2014 Chile quake is reported by Reuters. Earthquake grid failures are reported by the World Bank. 2021 Mayfield tornado is reported by the National Weather Service. Tornado logistics impacts are reported by *FreightWaves*. 2023 Canadian wildfires are reported by *CBC News*. 2024 California wildfires are reported by Cal Fire. Wildfire grid disruptions are reported by *Supply Chain Dive*. 2021 Texas storm is reported by ERCOT. 2023 Maui blackout is reported by the *Maui News*. 2021 Colonial Pipeline attack is reported by *Bloomberg*. 2023 port breach is reported by *Port Technology International*. 2024 supplier cyberattack is reported by *Supply Chain Digital*. Port and rail resilience is reported by the American Association of Port Authorities. Harvey recovery is reported by the Port of Houston. Panama recovery is reported by CBRE. Pipeline and Texas storm recovery are reported by *Bloomberg* and the *Texas Tribune*.

- American Trucking Associations, "U.S. Trucking Industry Snapshot 2024."
- Bureau of Transportation Statistics, "Latest Supply Chain and Freight Indicators."
- National Hurricane Center, "Tropical Cyclone Report: Hurricane Harvey."
- *FreightWaves*, "Hurricane Harvey's Impact on U.S. Logistics," August 30, 2017.
- Port of Houston, "Hurricane Harvey Recovery Update," September 5, 2017.
- Energy Information Administration, "Hurricane Harvey Effects on Gulf Coast Energy Markets," September 2017.
- *Tampa Bay Times*, "Hurricane Milton Disrupts Florida Ports," October 10, 2024.
- *Texas Tribune*, "Cold Snap Disrupts Texas Logistics," January 15, 2024.
- National Weather Service, "Winter Weather Summary 2023."
- Federal Emergency Management Agency, "Winter Storm Impacts 2023."
- CBRE, "Panama Canal Drought Impacts Global Trade," October 2023.
- United Nations Conference on Trade and Development, "Review of Maritime Transport 2023."
- *Logistics Management*, "Panama Canal Drought Effects," November 2023.
- U.S. Department of Agriculture, "Mississippi River Flooding 2019."
- North Carolina Department of Transportation, "Hurricane Helene Road Closures," September 28, 2024.
- *Lloyd's List*, "Japan Earthquake Disrupts Global Supply Chains," March 15, 2011.
- *Reuters*, "Chile Earthquake Impacts Copper Exports," April 2, 2014.
- World Bank, "Natural Disaster Impacts on Logistics," 2015.
- National Weather Service, "Kentucky Tornado Outbreak 2021."
- *FreightWaves*, "Kentucky Tornadoes Disrupt Freight," December 15, 2021.

- *CBC News*, "Wildfires Impact Canadian Logistics," June 2023.
- Cal Fire, "2024 Wildfire Incident Reports."
- *Supply Chain Dive*, "Wildfires Strain U.S. Logistics," July 2024.
- ERCOT, "Winter Storm 2021 Power Outage Report."
- *Maui News*, "Wildfires Cause Power Disruptions," August 2023.
- *Bloomberg*, "Colonial Pipeline Ransomware Attack," May 10, 2021.
- *Port Technology International*, "Port Cybersecurity Vulnerabilities," 2023.
- *Supply Chain Digital*, "Cyberattacks in Manufacturing 2024."
- American Association of Port Authorities, "U.S. Port Statistics 2024."
- Port of Houston, "Hurricane Harvey Recovery Update."
- CBRE, "Panama Canal Drought Impacts Global Trade."
- *Bloomberg*, "Colonial Pipeline Recovery," May 15, 2021.
- *Texas Tribune*, "Texas Power Restoration," February 20, 2021.

CHAPTER 16

70% U.S. freight and 80% global trade are reported by the World Bank. 531,000 U.S. fleets are reported by the American Trucking Associations (ATA). 85% ocean carrier capacity is reported by Alphaliner. IMO 2030 retrofit costs are reported by the International Maritime Organization (IMO). Trucking and ocean capacity growth (45%, 3M TEUs) are reported by *FreightWaves* and Drewry. 2006–2007 trucking rate drop is reported by the ATA. 3,000 trucking bankruptcies are reported by the ATA. 2008–2010 ocean rate drop is reported by Drewry. 2015–2016 trucking rate drop is reported by Truckstop.com. Hanjin's 2016 bankruptcy is reported by *Lloyd's List*. 2019 trucking rate drop is reported by Cass Information Systems. 2020–2021 tender rejections are reported by *FreightWaves*. 2020–2021 ocean rate peak is reported by Xeneta. 2022–2024 trucking bankruptcies are reported by *FreightWaves* and Morgan Stanley. 2022–2024 ocean rate drop is reported by Xeneta. ATA driver shortage is reported by the ATA. Ocean capacity growth is reported by the World Shipping Council. 19% immigrant drivers are reported by the Bureau of Labor Statistics. 2022 ethnic breakdown is reported by the Bureau of Labor Statistics. Black driver safety concerns are reported by DAT Solutions. 7% truck fatality rise is reported by the Federal Motor Carrier Safety Administration (FMCSA). 2025 executive order is reported by the *Federal Register*. Ever Given and Red Sea impacts are reported by *Lloyd's List*. Tariffs and IMO mandates are reported by the United Nations Conference on Trade and Development (UNCTAD) and Maersk. Ocean carrier consolidation is reported by Alphaliner.

- World Bank, "Global Trade Statistics: Transport and Logistics."
- American Trucking Associations, "U.S. Trucking Industry Snapshot 2024."
- Alphaliner, "Top 100 Container Carriers Report."
- International Maritime Organization, "IMO 2030 Decarbonization Strategy."
- *FreightWaves*, "SONAR Market Update: Trucking Capacity Trends 2019–2023"; Drewry, "Container Shipping Capacity Outlook 2024."

- American Trucking Associations, *Trucking Activity Report 2006–2007* (Arlington, VA: ATA, 2008).
- American Trucking Associations, *Trucking Activity Report 2006–2007*.
- Drewry, "World Container Index Historical Data."
- Truckstop.com, "Freight Market Insights 2015–2016."
- *Lloyd's List*, "Hanjin Bankruptcy Strands $14 Billion Cargo," September 2016.
- Cass Information Systems, "Cass Freight Index Report 2019."
- *FreightWaves*, "SONAR Tender Rejection Index 2020–2021."
- Xeneta, "Ocean Freight Rate Analysis 2020–2021."
- *FreightWaves*, "SONAR Market Update: Trucking Capacity Trends 2019–2023"; Morgan Stanley, "Truckload Freight Index Q3 2023."
- Xeneta, "Ocean Freight Rate Analysis 2022–2023."
- American Trucking Associations, "Driver Shortage Update 2023."
- World Shipping Council, "Global Container Capacity Report 2023."
- Bureau of Labor Statistics, "Occupational Employment and Wages